THE ULTIMATE SERIAL KILLER COLLECTION

True Crime Stories and Biographies of Ted Bundy, Jeffrey Dahmer, Zodiac Killer, Jack the Ripper, John Wayne Gacy, Richard Ramirez, Edmund Kemper, Manson, & more

By Charles Clark

Table of Contents

Ted Bundy 2
Jeffrey Dahmer 22
The Zodiac Killer 35
Jack the Ripper 48
John Wayne Gacy 59
Ted Kaczynski 72
Charles Manson 85
H.H. Holmes 99
Harold Shipman 109
Aileen Wuornos 118
Elizabeth Bathory 127
Gilles de Rais 137
Ed Gein 145
Alexander Pichushkin 153
John Haigh 160
Richard Speck 167
Richard Ramirez 175
Gary Ridgway 182
Albert Fish 189
David Parker Ray 197
Edmund Kemper 203
Andrei Chikatilo 210
Henry Lee Lucas 217

Ted Bundy

Throughout history, wicked men have lived, some successful, others not. No matter how hard a society might try, completely eradicating crime and hurt is not possible. For many, the thought of how a person can contemplate such evil and follow through with it is hard to comprehend. Even harder to comprehend is the fact that these murderers and rapists were once ordinary children. Somewhere in their life, whether the result of abuse or an injustice, the love for inflicting pain on humanity was created and thus birthed their entrance into a life of crime. One man who was particularly evil was Ted Bundy. During the 1970s, society was terrorized by the antics of Ted Bundy. Murderer, rapist, kidnapper, burglar, and necrophile were among the many words media sources used to describe Ted as they sought to warn the women of America to stay away from this man of pure evil. However, evil would not prevail, and Ted would eventually be caught and executed by the electric chair. Shortly before his death, Ted made a religious profession, the courtesy of Dr. James Dobson reaching out to the man no one in the world wanted to lend care towards. Upon his death, it was found that Ted had murdered over 30 women in crimes stretching across seven states. Ted Bundy's life served no master other than the selfishness within himself. While finding good within the life of Ted Bundy is a difficult task, his life serves as an example that a life of evil will eventually be found out. No amount of running or hiding can mask one from the eventual consequences of inflicting harm on humanity. Through the life of Ted Bundy, humanity can be reminded that a life is best lived in service and love to humanity.

Ted Bundy was born as Theodore Robert Cowell in Burlington,

Vermont to Eleanor Louise Cowell on November 24, 1946. Notably absent from Ted's life was his father. As unfortunate as it was, Ted would never come to know his father. While his birth certificate listed him as the son of an Air Force veteran who was employed as a salesman and named Lloyd Marshall, his mother Louise always held that his biological father was actually a sailor named Jack Worthington. This rumor was later debunked when Louise's sister revealed that Louise had actually been raped by her father and subsequently gave birth to Ted. Though none of these rumors can be proved, historians have found evidence linking Ted's birth to his mother's rape. Regardless, Ted would never meet either of these men in his lifetime. Shortly after he was born, Ted was placed in his grandparents' custody due to the inability of his mother to care for him. So, for Ted's first three years of life, he would reside in a brick home with his grandparents in Philadelphia. During the time in which Ted was born, social standards held those born out of wedlock in judgment, an aspect that Ted's grandparents hope to alleviate by allowing him to stay with them until he was older. Ted's grandparents went so far to protect him from the judgmental stares that they told everyone, even Ted, that they were his true parents and that Ted's biological mother was his sister. This deceitfulness gave way to a very odd home life for Ted during his younger years. However, they could not shield Ted from the truth forever and soon he found out, implicating the entire family in their lie. Ted's revelation of his family's deceit came as a shock to him. After playing with his cousin one day, his cousin referred to Ted as a "bastard" to which Ted questioned the origin of this insult. Ted's cousin proceeded to show him a copy of his birth certificate in which Ted's biological mother was listed as his mother. This revelation led to an even more awkward home life and Ted never forgave his mother for rejecting him as a son. Psychiatrists have pointed to this moment while analyzing Ted's rise to crime as the moment that fed his desire for the acceptance and submission of a woman. However, Ted was still years away from his life of crime.

    Despite hating his mother for her apparent disownment, Ted

loved his grandparents dearly, often stating that his grandfather was his favorite person to talk to. While his grandparents had held their own part in the lies of his childhood, Ted was given a more structured home life from them. However, Ted's love and respect of his grandfather was not healthy due to his grandfather's opinions on race relations and sexism. Often, Ted's grandfather would vocalize his hatred for any other race other than Caucasian and beat Ted's grandmother on many occasions. Ted likely was never told that his grandfather had actually been the one who raped his mother, resulting in his birth. Local authorities also question whether Ted's grandfather was plagued with a demonic possession of sorts, citing that he often talked violently to people who were invisible to everyone but himself. Once, Ted's grandfather even threw his daughter Julia down an entire flight of stairs for simply oversleeping. With a home life fostered in hatred and lack of respect, Ted was given no foundation for any respect towards humanity. Sadly, this verbal and physical abuse was the foundation for his life of evil. Ted began showing alarming signs at just the young age of three. Once, Ted gathered all the knives from the kitchen and surrounded his aunt Julia with the knives while she slept. When she awoke, Ted stood sheepishly by the circle of knives, smiling menacingly. Sadly, Ted was never disciplined for his behavior. Often, Ted's grandfather would laugh at his grandson's alarming antics. Though the family could not see it at the time, they were raising and encouraging a man who would inflict sadness and horrific crimes upon countless families in America.

Shortly after Ted turned four years old, his mother demonstrated her volatility and changed the last name of her small family from Cowell to Nelson. Additionally, Louise moved out of her father's house and moved to Tacoma, Washington where she and Ted lived with her cousin Alan Scott and his wife Jane. Following the family's move, Louise met a cook at the hospital where she worked, a man named Johnny Bundy. The two began seeing each other and shortly thereafter, the two were married. Johnny seemed to try his best at including Ted in the affairs of the family and even adopted Ted as his legal son. However, Ted never allowed Johnny to infiltrate the barrier he had set up towards personal relationships in his life. Ted had been abused enough psychologically and his instincts had been permanently marred. In the years following his mother's marriage to Johnny, Ted would receive four siblings through their marriage. Later, Ted would remark to his girlfriend that he found Johnny to be "a bit off in the head" and "didn't make much money." While Johnny attempted to make a home life for Ted, Ted would continually reject the home life until Johnny ceased his attempts at fathering Ted. For the remainder of Ted's elementary years, he would reside in the city of Tacoma. As Ted began his transition to high school, a marked changed was noticed in his personal habits. Ted became quieter and rarely attended social functions. Though he was known at the high school as being a fun and rowdy boy, his demeanor would change drastically when he went home. Along with becoming more drawn in, Ted became engrossed in pornography and would often scavenge his neighborhood's trash cans for any photographs that included pornographic content. Additionally, Ted revealed that during this time, he became infatuated with crimes that were particularly graphic in nature. His regular reading habits involved books that centered on sexual crimes or contained pictures of mangled or decapitated bodies. In addition to reading pornographic accounts, Ted began drinking during his teenage years, often becoming drunk beyond mobility. Ted also began snooping around neighbor's homes, yearning to catch a glimpse of a woman undressing or other sexual acts. Ted's life began to take on a dark demeanor and he was often quite discontent unless he was able to read his graphic novels or view pornography on a daily basis. While the days of Ted's personal life were dark, the effects of his depressed and ill outlook on life would soon culminate in the harm and death of others.

While Ted's life during high school began to revolve around sex and alcohol, he still enjoyed one less horrifying activity: skiing. Often, Ted would create counterfeit lift tickets for a local ski resort and use equipment he had stolen from his local high school. Ted's fellow students at Woodrow Wilson High School recalled Ted as being a bright lad who was "well known and well liked." However, Ted's recall of his school was far different. "I didn't know what made people want to be friends," recalled Ted. "I didn't know what underlay social interactions." Regardless of his sense of awkwardness, Ted maintained an aura of confidence, an aura that would be shattered by his future crimes. Ted kept a relatively clean police record during his high school years. Arrested twice for suspicion of burglary and auto theft, Ted's high school years were far from perfect. However, his crimes gave no signs of warning to the local authorities and, as is traditional in Washington, his criminal record was expunged upon his 18th birthday. For now, Ted was an ordinary man with no signs of criminal intent.

In 1965, Ted graduated from Woodrow Wilson High School and began college at the University of Puget Sound. However, Ted's purpose was simply to acclimate to college and one year later, he transferred to the University of Washington with the intent of studying Chinese. Ted entered the second relationship of his life during his sophomore year at the University of Washington, the girl a classmate of his who went by several different names in the various accounts of Ted Bundy's college years. While almost all the books contained different names for the female, the most common name recalled was Stephanie Brooks. However, the relationship with Brooks was not enough to keep Ted in college and shortly after the spring semester began in 1968, Ted dropped out of college. While maintaining his relationship with Brooks, Ted worked several jobs in the local area. Additionally, Ted began showing an interest in politics and became a key volunteer for the Nelson Rockefeller presidential campaign. Ted became so instrumental in the campaign that he was actually sent to the 1968 Republican National Convention as the delegate for the Rockefeller campaign. This accomplishment in his life was a stark contrast from the man Ted would eventually become. Despite Ted's apparent interest in professional qualities, Brooks became unhappy with the level of immaturity that he possessed and soon ended their relationship. In later years, Dorothy Lewis, a psychiatrist close to Ted describes this as the "pivotal time in his development" as a criminal. Having been rejected now by two women,

Ted's outlook on life, albeit dark as it was, soon clouded even more, suspending Ted deeper and deeper into depression. Ted became deeply heartbroken from his breakup and ran away from his responsibilities within the Washington area. Making the occasional stop to see family along the way, Ted continued his trek east before settling at Temple University for one semester. During these days of rejection, Ted only furthered this heartbreak by visiting the records office in Philadelphia and finding his birth certificate, a constant reminder that his rejection in life had begun at the earliest stage possible.

After a short stint at Temple University, Ted returned to his life in Washington and struck up a relationship with a new girl, Elizabeth Kloepfer. This relationship, though anything but consistent, would continue throughout Ted's life and even into his short prison sentence preceding his death. Kloepfer was a secretary from Utah who had been recently divorced. For the remainder of his life, Ted and Kloepfer would continually break up and re-start their relationship. Back in Washington, Ted had re-focused his life and was ready to embrace the rigors and responsibilities of a college education. After re-enrolling at the University of Washington, Ted changed his major from Chinese to Psychology, a subject he was oddly proficient in. Ted excelled in his studies and became a favorite student among his teachers due to his hard work and true genius in psychology. During his first year back as a college student, Ted entered employment for Seattle's Suicide Hotline Crisis Center and began his work seated next to Ann Rule. This seating arrangement would prove vital someday as Ann testified on his behalf. In her book written after his incarceration, *The Stranger Beside Me*, Ann retells how "kind, solicitous, and empathetic" Ted was, completely contrary to his eventual public image following his life of crime. In 1972, Ted graduated from his courses at the University of Washington and began his first job out of college as a campaign advisor for Governor Daniel J. Evans. Ted proved particularly pivotal in this race due to his young appearance. With the face of an innocent college student, Ted went undercover as a college student working for Evans' chief opponent, Albert Rosellini. By working for Rosellini, Ted was able to supply Evans' campaign with recorded audio bits of Rosellini's speech, allowing Evans to be working on his rebuttal prior to Rosellini even giving his speech. The ruse worked, and Evans was able to win his campaign. With Evans continuing his tenure as governor, Ted began a new job as an assistant to the Chairman of the Washington State Republican Party. Ted's new employer thought highly of Ted and noted that he was "smart, aggressive, and a believer in the system." Desiring his own career within politics, Ted applied for entrance into the University of Utah to acquire a law degree. Despite performing poorly on the LSAT, Ted achieved entrance and began his days of schooling at the University of Utah.

As a college student seeking a law degree, Ted began to receive various opportunities to acquire valuable leadership for his potential future in politics. During one of these opportunities, his travels took him to California where he was surprised to meet his ex-girlfriend Brooks. At the time, Ted and Kloepfer were still dating but neither Brooks nor Kloepfer were aware that Ted was seeing the respective woman. Brooks was very impressed with the transformation within the lifestyle of Ted, seemingly converting from being a pessimistic, immature man to one concerned about the well-being of others. Brooks and Ted began dating again, leaving Ted with two girlfriends in separate states. Ted continued his schooling and was officially matriculated at UPS Law School in 1973. Throughout this, Brooks continued dating Ted and the two even began discussing marriage. During one meeting with Davis, Ted even introduced Brooks as his fiancée. However, an unknown dispute caused Ted to cease all contact with Brooks in the first month of 1974. For an entire month, Ted refused to answer Brooks' various letters and calls. After a month of no contact, Brooks was finally able to reach Ted, immediately demanding an answer for his refusal to contact her while also imploring him as to why their relationship was ended so suddenly. Without exhibiting any emotion, Ted replied "Stephanie, I have no idea what you mean." With that, Ted hung up without another word and never spoke to Brooks again. Following the phone call, Ted confessed to a friend that he had dated her because "I just wanted to prove to myself that I could have married her." Later, Brooks alleged that Ted had simply dated her for the past months with no intention of actually marrying her, planning the whole fiasco as a means of revenge for her breakup five years prior. However, there was more afoot than simple revenge. Ted had changed since his years of dating Brooks and this time, there would be no going back.

At the time of the breakup between Ted and Brooks, Ted had started skipping his classes at UPS Law. What was once a promising career as a politician and a potential diversion on his road to a life of crime was now simply an afterthought. Only four months later, Ted would completely drop out of school and return to his life of seclusion. Around the same time that Ted quit school, women around the area began mysteriously disappearing. One by one, young women across the area would turn up missing, not to be found until months later after their bodies had disappeared. Sadly, this was no coincidence. Ted Bundy had entered his horrific life of crime, never to return to his life as an innocent civilian.

The life of crime for Ted Bundy has no definitive starting point. Following his incarceration, Ted revealed many crimes to reporters but failed to confirm when his first murder took place, possibly due to his inability to remember the crime. Local authorities hold that Ted's first murder likely took place when he was only 14 years old. As a mere high schooler, Ted kidnapped an 8-year-old girl named Ann Marie Burr before killing her and dumping her body. Though Ted would deny this allegation till his death, evidence exists that places Ted at the scene of the crime. The first kidnapping Ted confessed to took place in Ocean City, New Jersey in 1969 when Ted kidnapped a young girl. However, Ted had no intentions of killing the young girl, leading to his release of her shortly thereafter. The first murder Ted confessed to took place in 1969 after he broke up with Brooks for the first time. Two women in the Atlantic City area were found dead, victims of Ted's insecurity as a man. The first documented murder from Ted took place in 1974 when Ted murdered a hitchhiker for an unknown reason. Partially adding to the inconclusive nature of Ted's murders was his ability to leave as little evidence at the scene of the crime as possible. With Ted leaving little to no evidence at each crime scene, authorities were perplexed as to who they were searching for. All that existed was hearsay regarding a man in a Volkswagen Beetle, nothing more. During his first days as a murderer, Ted's crimes were completely unrelated. The unique nature of each crime led authorities to believe they were looking for a different criminal for each crime. However, Ted began committing his crimes more consistently and to a similar demographic in 1974, leading authorities to begin wondering if the crimes were all related. Soon, the world would get its first glimpse of a man who would assume six aliases, all for the same cause: freedom from his crimes.

On the same day Ted broke up with Brooks, he broke into the basement of Karen Sparks, a fellow student at the University of Washington. Ted began his rampage by beating the woman completely unconscious before sexually assaulting her and beating her even more. Sparks would survive the incident but would be left permanently damaged, physically and mentally. Shortly less than one month later, Ted would break into another young woman's basement, Lunda Ann Healy, and beat her unconscious as well. This time however, Ted chose to dress Healy in casual attire before carrying her to an undisclosed location. Crimes similar to this one began to pile up across the West Coast, leaving police baffled after finding women dead or not finding some women at all. For the first six months of 1974, Ted kidnapped and assaulted at least one female a month, with more unsolved crimes existing within the same region. For the month of March, Ted chose to assault 19-year-old Donna Manson, a college student studying music at the Evergreen State College. Through unknown means, Ted kidnapped Manson before killing her and disposing of her remains, never to be found. For April, Ted kidnapped Susan Elaine Rancourt, a 17-year-old college student enrolled at a college that was located over 100 miles away from where Ted was living at the time. While his acts of murder were becoming routine for him, the murder of Rancourt left him with more than he had wanted: a public image. Shortly after it was found that Rancourt was missing, two of Rancourt's friends approached security and mentioned they had seen a man, impaired by an arm sleeve, request the aid of Rancourt as he attempted to carry his books to his Volkswagen Beetle. However, authorities were only given a small glimpse of the man they were looking for. Unfortunately, there would be many more murders before the authorities even had an idea of who they were looking for.

Due to the systematic and unique nature of the disappearing girls, the local authorities in the Washington area, specifically Seattle and King County, began growing suspicious of the cause of disappearances. Concerns began to mount, and women were warned to increase their safety before going out alone, or even in pairs. Authorities combed the area of the kidnapped women for clues to no avail. When comparing the women who had been abducted, the authorities noted that the similarities were that the women were: Caucasian, young, pretty, and all parted their hair down the middle. Attempting to draw conclusions from such a small area of commonality had authorities frustrated and women scared. The disappearances continued with the abduction of Brenda Carol Ball on June 1 of the same year. Brenda was the oldest of Ted's victims to date at 22, placing her within the apparent age Ted was targeting. Once again, women who observed Ball moments before she disappeared reported seeing a man with brown hair and an arm sleeve talking to Ball prior to her abduction. Only ten days later, Georgann Hawkins was reported missing, her last known location being in an alley next to her sorority house. With the police force already on edge, the force commanded five of their best homicidal detectives to observe every inch of the alley for clues. The men came up empty. With no evidence to go on, the authorities took to the media in an effort to find people who might know something about the disappearances. This method proved to be the most fruitful in garnering evidence as women began coming forward with stories that corroborated the previous witness' accounts. Through the stories, the authorities were able to determine that their suspect was a middle-aged man who had brown hair and drove a tan Volkswagen Beetle. While the authorities were busy determining the appearance of their suspect, Ted was employed by the Department of Emergency Services, an agency that specialized in finding clues about the whereabouts of missing and abducted women. Interaction with this office gave Ted the perfect ear to hear whether the authorities were closing in on him, while also giving him the opportunity to deter investigators away from any pertinent leads they might have. While employed at the agency, Ted became romantically involved with Carole Ann Boone, a divorced woman who was struggling to parent her two sons alone. The two began dating shortly thereafter, thus consummating a relationship that would prove pivotal during the later months of his life of crime. For the time being, the abduction of the six women along with the bludgeoning of Sparks was a consistent topic within the newspapers, both locally and nationally. Women all around America became suspicious of strangers and the female share of hitchhikers decreased significantly. Local authorities were under serious scrutiny as the populous demanded that this rapist and murderer be brought to justice. However, Ted's professionalism in his crimes greatly inhibited them. With little evidence to go on, there was barely enough to form a case on besides the small description the men had of Ted. Additionally, the evidence that the authorities did have was not being revealed to the public with the hope that Ted would grow careless and too self-confident. With the authorities remaining close-lipped about the case, local media outlets began their own investigation, coming to the conclusion that the suspect was targeting his victims at night, near construction sites, and near the time of tests at their respective colleges. Ted's confidence was growing and unfortunately, authorities were still unable to catch the slippery thief.

Ted's growing confidence was evidenced in his next abduction, when he defied all the media's characteristics for his previous abductions by kidnapping two women from an occupied beach in the middle of the day. The occupants of the beach, located in Issaquah, Washington, were unaware that that Ted had even visited, with the only eyewitness reports confirming that a man wearing a sling had been seen at the beach. Finally, after interviewing as many of the witnesses from the beach as possible, the authorities stumbled upon five women who had experienced the most contact with Ted of any of the witnesses. The women noted that a man, saying his name was Ted, had implored the women for help unloading a small boat from his Volkswagen Beetle. The women, unaware that this man fit the description of the serial rapist, followed Ted to his car before noticing that he had no boat in his car. Upon seeing this, the women ran away but continued watching as another woman, unknown to the others, followed Ted to his car. This woman was Janice Anne Ott, a probational officer in the area. The five females saw nothing more after this and returned to their activities on the beach. However, Ted was not finished with just one victim. Four hours after Ott disappeared, Ted assaulted Denise Marie Naslund as she entered the women's bathroom, also at the beach. After dragging the two unconscious women into the woods, Ted forced Ott to watch as he murdered Naslund. Ted would eventually murder Ott as well. While Ted had still been able to complete his devious plan, he had failed to abduct those five females who now held a very clear picture of this man in their head. With their description, the King County Police were able to post a sketch of Ted around the various news outlets while also telling the locals to watch for Ted's car. Ted had finally gone too far; exactly what the local authorities were hoping he would do.

As the sketch of Ted was saturated throughout the King County area before being shown nationally, both Elizabeth Kloepfer, Ted's current girlfriend, and Ann Rule, Ted's cubicle partner at the Suicide Prevention Agency, saw the photo and immediately recognized the man they knew as Ted. Both called the King County Sheriff's Department and identified the man as Ted, but the sheriff's department refused to believe that a man who seemed so professional as a law student would have anything to do with this string of horrible crimes. Though disappointed, both women agreed with the detectives and returned to their respective jobs convinced it was someone who simply looked like Ted. The search for Ott and Naslund was completed on September 6 of the same year when a group of hunters found the remains, now completely decomposed, shortly outside of Issaquah, Washington. This would be the first of the abducted women to be found, but detectives were slightly perplexed. Amidst the remains of Ott and Naslund were a few bones, identified to be a femur and vertebrae. Later, Ted would confirm these were the partial remains of Georgann Hawkins. Only six months after this discovery, a group of students were hiking on Taylor Mountain when they found a mass grave comprised of what appeared to be four people. Detectives would confirm these remains belonged to Healy, Rancourt, Parks, and Ball. Ted was an avid hiker, so it was likely he buried these women after assaulting them in his favorite spot in Washington. Sadly, the remains of Manson, his third known victim, would never be found. While the public had experienced a boost in confidence due to finding the remains of the various women, they were now terrified, knowing the victims of Ted were not survivors.

For one month, there was little known about Ted. His abductions ceased, leaving women to wonder if he had been killed or if he was simply planning some horrific crime. During this time, Ted was busy seeking another degree. This time, he was accepted into the University of Utah Law School. Upon acceptance, Ted relocated to Salt Lake City, Utah. Kloepfer had never told Ted about her reporting him to the police and the two were still dating. Kloepfer would not accompany Ted to Utah, however the two remained dating in good standing. Ted was hardly committed to a single relationship however. At one point, Ted admits to dating "at least a dozen other women" at the same time. As Ted began his studies, he began to notice something different about himself. Whereas he had excelled at the University of Washington under his psychology degree, he was now unable to comprehend the various concepts being introduced each day. Kloepfer reports "He was devastated to find out that the other students had something, some intellectual capacity, that he did not. He found the classes completely incomprehensible. 'It was a great disappointment to me,' he said." Ted was devastated and to cope with his loss, Ted turned to the only actions that left him with fulfillment and desire: assault and murder. The second major series of abductions began one month after his move to Utah. This spree contained crimes unsolved until he confessed to them following his incarceration. The first in the string of assaults committed by Ted occurred on

September 2, 1974 when Ted raped and killed a young woman on a hiking trail in Idaho. Following the assault, Ted proceeded to photograph the woman before dumping her remains in a river. This woman's identity would never be known. Exactly one month later, Ted abducted, raped, and strangled a 16-year-old girl named Nancy Wilcox in Utah. Ted claimed this assault was an attempt to subside his "pathological urges" and that he had not intended to kill Nancy. His original intention was to release her, but according to Ted, he strangled her on accident after she would not stop screaming. After assaulting her, Ted proceeded to bury the remains, which would never be found.

 As Ted continued to use women to subside his urges for security, his next victim was Melissa Anne Smith, a 17-year-old from the Salt Lake City area. Friends had begun to grow worried when Smith had not returned home after leaving a pizza parlor. For nine days after they realized she was gone, the family prayed she was not a victim of this unknown rapist stalking their streets. Their fears were confirmed when she was found, dead and completely nude, on a hiking trail in the mountains of Utah. After performing an autopsy on Smith, doctors determined that she lived for seven days after her assault. However, Ted's "fix" for assaulting women was going unfulfilled and on October 31, Ted assaulted Laura Anne Aime, marking the most assaults Ted had incurred within a month. In the same fashion as her predecessor Smith, Aime was found dead and completely nude on the same trail. The strange fashion of these assaults led authorities to believe their suspect was a necrophile, someone who enjoyed performing sexual acts on dead people. Years later, Ted would confirm that he often returned to the scene of his assault to "touch up the women," many times washing the women's hair and putting makeup on the deceased victims. After a brief respite from assaults, Ted attempted his boldest yet, impersonating a police officer and commanding a woman to accompany him in his car as he recovered her supposedly stolen vehicle. However, this woman was aware of the strange abductions and refused to follow him, noting that his car was not marked and that he did not look like an officer. When Ted attempted handcuffing her, the woman slipped from his grasp and fled the scene. However, as in times before when Ted was unsuccessful with the initial assault, Ted found another woman, 17-year-old Debra Jean Kent, and assaulted her before murdering her. With the assaults seemingly endless, Ted's confidence was at an all-time high. However, his days of freedom were limited and soon, his final spree would come to its end.

Shortly after word of the string of assaults within the Salt Lake City area reached Kloepfer, she began to realize that the coincidences of her lover being in the same vicinity as these separate assaults was more than simply coincidence. Attempting to alert authorities to the likelihood of her boyfriend being the rapist, Kloepfer called the King County Sheriff's Department and reported her findings once again. This time, the authorities were more than willing to accept her opinion and called her in for an interview. Following the interview, the police agreed that Ted fit the description perfectly and was now an official suspect. Once done giving her interview, Kloepfer arranged to fly to Salt Lake City in August. Upon arrival, Kloepfer did not tell Ted of reporting him to the police and Ted did not tell her of his other girlfriends. Following her visit with Ted, Kloepfer called the Salt Lake County Sheriff's Office and relayed her story and accusations against Ted. However, reaching the same road block she had previously reached in Washington, Kloepfer was told that there was no concrete evidence against Ted and no reason to consider him against the other previous offenders in Utah. Additionally, one of the witnesses from an earlier abduction was unable to identify Ted in a photo lineup, deeming him innocent in the eyes of the authorities.

Ted continued his assaults with several more abductions. Carol Campbell was reported missing on January 12, only to be found one month later, fully nude and killed by blunt force trauma. Two months following the assault of Campbell, Ted assaulted and killed Julie Cunningham. This assault proved to be particularly gruesome as Ted later confessed that he travelled to visit her remains three times, making a six-hour trip both ways just to visit and perform sexual acts on the decomposing body. One month later, Denise Lynn Oliverson became another victim she was abducted while riding her bicycle on her way home. Ted abducted Oliverson, drowned her, and took her back to his apartment where he sexually assaulted her. Following his odd habit of sexually assaulting his victims post-death, Ted dumped her body into a local river. Following this assault, Ted was able to maintain his public life and had three of his girlfriends over to visit his house during a one-week span without telling or revealing to any of the women that the bed they were sharing that night would be shared by a different woman the following night. Among those visiting him during this time was Carol Boone, his girlfriend from the DES. One week later, Kloepfer visited Ted and the two began discussing marriage. Just as previous times, Kloepfer did not tell Ted of her suspicions or that she was in contact with the sheriff's department regarding his actions. Though his series of assaults had an extensive record, he was now only one assault away from being caught. While it is unfortunate that Susan Curtis was assaulted and murdered, this was the assault that would finally allow the authorities to catch up with Ted.

In late 1975, Ted padded his respectable public opinion by being baptized at The Church of Jesus Christ of Latter-day Saints. Despite being against most of the teachings of the church, Ted was baptized into membership, declaring his religion as Methodist. On the other side of the country, the King County Sheriff's Department was scrambling to use the data they had acquired productively and efficiently. Because databases were unknown during this phase of the technological expansion, much of the police department's data came from simple paper pools of knowledge. However, a few of the technicians within the sheriff's department wondered if they could use the payroll computer as a database. Inputting all the information into the new database took weeks, but after the technicians had done so, they compared the personal lives, vehicle registration, and crime history with every criminal in the system. Among the 26 that the list narrowed down, Ted was on top and was considered to be the most capable suspect. Additionally, the detectives working on a paper version "Top 100" capable criminals placed Ted Bundy at the top of their suspect list. However, this list served no purpose other than giving the detectives a person to watch. The courts would not be as quick to accept evidence that had been derived from a complicated computer system that could be faulty. While the database was insufficient evidence for an arrest, the authorities were finally watching the correct man and soon Ted would make some costly mistakes.

Almost one month after the detectives had compiled the list, Ted was seen driving through a suburban area at low speeds. When the officer pulled up behind Ted, Ted gunned the engine and accelerated rapidly down the highway. When the officer gave chase, Ted pulled over and obediently gave way to the patrolman's desires. Upon approaching the car, the officer noticed that the front seat had been removed and was awkwardly sitting in the back seat. The officer found this extremely odd and searched the car further. Upon completion of the search, the officer found two ski masks, various tools that could be used to break in somewhere, handcuffs, trash bags, and a number of items that resembled a kit that could be used to strangle someone. Ted was quick to defend his innocence, claiming that the ski masks were in the car because he was a sportsman and that the tools were found at a local thrift shop. Despite Ted's proclamations of innocence, the detective noticed that the man he had just pulled over resembled the man Kloepfer had reported so much earlier. With this information, the detective had enough information to request a search warrant of Ted's apartment and upon completion of the search, found various brochures for the venues where assaults had taken place. However, there was little to no concrete evidence and Ted was unable to be held on such flimsy data. Against their own desires, the authorities released Ted. Later, Ted would reveal that the detectives overlooked a series of photographs that focused on the dismembered bodies of his victims. Of course, these photos were destroyed by Ted shortly after his return home.

Despite being released, Ted was far from out of eye sight of the police department. For 24 hours a day, Ted was kept under surveillance from the Salt Lake City police. Seeking new information, the authorities brought Kloepfer back in for another interview. During this interview, Kloepfer revealed that Ted possessed numerous bags of women's clothing and that she would often wake up after Ted "examined" her with a flashlight under the bed covers. Additionally, Ted had become extremely agitated at the mention of cutting her hair; Kloepfer's hair was parted down the middle. It was also during this time that Kloepfer was introduced to Brooks, the woman Ted had been briefly engaged to before beginning his murderous life. For a while, Ted stayed off the radar but finally, one month after his brief incarceration, Ted made an extremely costly error: he sold his Volkswagen Beetle. Upon learning of the sale of his Beetle, the local authorities rushed to the new owner and purchased it from him for much more than the car was worth; however, this car was invaluable in that it contained evidence. Upon further examination, it was revealed that he car contained hair from the bodies of Caryn Campbell, Smith, and DeRonch. With this evidence, the authorities only needed one more thing: an eyewitness to identify him. This came from DeRonch when the authorities created a lineup consisting of various men, including Ted. DaRonch immediately identified Ted as the man impersonating an officer and the authorities were given enough evidence to arrest Ted. Ted was immediately released on bail, an act of his parents that cost them $15,000. Despite being out on bail, Ted was still under 24/7 supervision. Kloepfer remembers "When Ted and I stepped out on the porch to go somewhere, so many unmarked police cars started up that it sounded like the beginning of the Indy 500." Finally, after seven years of committing the worst of crimes, Ted stood before the judge and was found guilty of both charges, kidnapping and assault. While these charges only stemmed from the two women who were still alive, they were the first in a long line of charges that would lead to the demise of Ted Bundy.

After Ted was sentenced to one to 15 years in the Utah State Prison, he began working towards escaping. On many occasions, the guards would find Ted in an obscure location of the jail with fake identification, fence cutting materials, and flight plans. However,

Ted's greatest chance at escaping came from an unlikely source: the charge of murder in the death of Caryn Campbell. During the first days of the trial, Ted chose to represent himself and due to this, was allowed to walk into the courthouse uninhibited by handcuffs and leg irons. After the first portion of the trial, Ted was excused to go study within the courthouse's library. It was during this time that Ted was successfully able to escape from the library, utilizing a second story window behind a bookcase. After removing the jumpsuit that identified him as a criminal, Ted found street clothes on a local clothes line and walked about the city untouched as authorities rushed to set up roadblocks and begin a massive manhunt for him. The jump from the second story window had left Ted with a sprained ankle so his mobility was severely hampered. After acquiring a gun and various articles of clothing, Ted began making his way back home but got lost after two days. After six days of walking around and a brief stint of stealing a car, Ted was apprehended and returned to jail. For the following six months, Ted planned his next escape, aided by the daily visits his girlfriend Carol Boone paid him. During these visits, Carol often brought materials Ted could escape with. Finally, during the Christmas break of 1977, Ted cut away the ceiling within his cell and escaped through the ceiling of the jail, one cellmate's complaints that the ceiling was moving going unheard. Ted was a free man once again but would soon embark on a long journey that would not end as hoped.

For the next few months, Ted made his way from Ann Arbor, Michigan to Tallahassee, Florida where he assaulted three women in the Chi Omega Sorority house on the campus of Florida State University. The assaults were brutal and grotesque with all three of the women dying. Ted escaped from the scene but left behind his DNA in two hairs and a semen stain on one of the beds. After moving to Lake City, Florida for a brief stint in which he assaulted Kimberly Diane Leach before killing her, Ted met his match when he was pulled over in the city of Pensacola, Florida by Officer David Lee. After Lee attempted to arrest Ted for stealing the car, Ted took off running, only to be apprehended by Lee. As Ted was being led to the car by an officer who had no idea he had just apprehended a criminal residing on the FBI Ten Most Wanted Fugitives, Ted remarked "I wish you had killed me."

Ted's trial was the first nationally televised trial with over 200 reporters on hand from all but two of the continents. After days of hearing witnesses' accounts, the judge found Ted guilty of murder and burglary and sentenced him to death. During Ted's second trial in Orlando, Ted was found guilty of the murder of Kimberly Leach and sentenced to death. Ironically, during one of the hearings, Ted demonstrated his volatile and odd nature by declaring that he and Carole Boone were married, a marriage that was upheld due to a law that marriages declared in a court room were legal. After months of deliberation and trials due to an initial mistrial, Ted Bundy was put to death on January 24, 1989 in the Raiford electric chair at 7:16 A.M. A rapist's life silenced, women were relieved to hear of the death of this villain and men celebrated by setting of fireworks across from the location where Ted was killed. Though Ted had inflicted pain on so many, he now met his maker and was no longer able to hurt anyone, a life wasted by the insecurity of jealousy and rejection.

Jeffrey Dahmer

On May 21, 1960, a baby boy was birthed into the world. An innocent baby boy who would grow to someday deliver unimaginable pain to over twenty families. However, for now this boy was just like any other. As a child, Jeffrey Dahmer was raised in a structured home, his mother working as a teletype machine instructor and his father studying as a chemistry student at Marquette University. At a young age, Jeffrey became starved of his mother's attention. She found the habit of breastfeeding Jeffrey too tiresome to continue, so the majority of Jeffrey's infant years were spent in a crib with a bottle. Family and friends close to the Dahmers also noted that Jeffrey's mother was always looking to be the center of attention, willing to be as loud as needed to get all eyes on her. When Jeffrey began his days of schooling in first grade, his mother became bedridden simply in an effort to achieve more attention from her husband, whose studies had begun to take him away from home. When being bedridden did not alleviate her desire for attention, Jeffrey's mother overdosed on Equanil pills in a futile attempt at suicide. However, this action simply created an addiction to Equanil and scars within her marriage. All throughout this struggle for attention, Jeffrey and his brother were receiving no care and were becoming severely neglected. While Jeffrey was able to maintain his cheerful disposition now, there was a marked difference coming soon.

Jeffrey was always noted as being a normal child with a happy personality. However, when he was three, Jeffrey underwent double hernia surgery, an operation that seemed to stifle the joy he had become known for. Family members remark how timid the boy seemed after his surgery. At the end of his first-grade year, his teacher noted that he had grown timid and was in need of attention from home. However, the teacher was also under the impression that Jeffrey's lack of attention was the result of his mother's condition, as Jeffrey's mother's antics were unbeknownst to the teacher. As a young boy, Jeffrey was known for always being interested in bugs and the preservation of wildlife. Often, Jeffrey would go into the woods, collect various bugs and creatures, and place them in large jars within his room. However, his fascination with wildlife soon turned dark, as he began dissecting these creatures in a violent manner. What started off with bugs soon transgressed into larger animals. Once, Jeffrey even decapitated his friend's dog before nailing the carcass to a tree. After playing with the skull for a while, Jeffrey took it and placed it upon a wooden cross he had driven into the ground behind his parent's house. It was around this time that family members and friends began noticing Jeffrey's love of dead animals. With a specific interest in bones, Jeffrey would ravage the dirt around his house, looking for any bones he could find. In a memoir of his son, Lionel Dahmer recalled that Jeffrey was "oddly thrilled" at the particular sound that rustling bones made. When Jeffrey was six, his father moved the family to Doylestown, Ohio, where Jeffrey's mother gave birth to another son.

Upon the birth of this son, Jeffrey's parents allowed him to name the child. Jeffrey named his little brother David. Around this time, Jeffrey's father graduated from college with his degree in chemistry and took immediate employment as an analytical chemist in Akron, Ohio. With Jeffrey's father employed in Akron, the family decided to move from Doylestown to Bath, Ohio two years later with the hope that the closer proximity to work would allow more family time. Even though Jeffrey was only eight at the time, his love of dead animals had begun to concern his father. This concern was proven prudent at dinner one night when Jeffrey asked his father what the reaction of bleach would be on bones. From that point forward, the preservation of animals began to take a new light in Jeffrey's world. He was now able to preserve more than simply bugs, he was able to preserve the entire bodies of animals. When Jeffrey entered high school, his days of darkness seemingly returned. The only source of happiness that Jeffrey found was through alcohol, an addiction his peers at school grew disgusted with. Jeffrey often wore a green army fatigue jacket to class and did not seem bothered by the lack of friends he had. When asked why he drank hard alcohol and why he did so on school grounds, Jeffrey replied "It's my medicine." Despite having a dark aura about his personality, his teachers regarded Jeffrey as being polite with great potential. Some teachers even referred to Jeffrey as being highly intelligent. During high school, Jeffrey became a skilled tennis player as well as an active member of the high school band. Around this time, Jeffrey began to experience a growing attraction towards members of the same sex. Homosexuality was still regarded as almost a sickness at this time in society, so Jeffrey was careful to not tell of his new attraction to his parents. Though Jeffrey admits to holding a short relationship with another male during high school, the relationship ended quickly, with Jeffrey afraid his peers and parents would find out about his same-gender attraction. However, his fear did not inhibit new sexual fantasies that he was experiencing. During school, Jeffrey would dream of having a male counterpart who fully submitted to his sexual desires. These various dreams began to grow stronger until Jeffrey finally decided it was time to enact a plan. Having seen a male jogger frequent a running path near him, Jeffrey armed himself with a baseball bat and sat in the bushes awaiting his chance to render his victim completely submissive. However, the jogger did not come by that day, leading Jeffrey to scrap the plan.

During this time, Jeffrey's parents were undergoing marital counseling in an attempt to salvage their marriage. These sessions proved futile however and the couple divorced shortly thereafter. Jeffrey had become more engrossed in his alcohol addiction and his grades were now plummeting as a result. Despite his parents enlisting a tutor to help their son in the midst of their divorce, Jeffrey was not to be reasoned with and continued to fail. In 1978, Jeffrey sat in the school's parking lot and drank many cans of beer. When asked by a teacher why he was doing this, Jeffrey replied "I have a lot of problems at home." The teacher let him be and Jeffrey graduated from school one week later. Shortly after this, Jeffrey's parents finalized their divorce and Jeffrey's mother was given permanent custody. Three weeks after his graduation, Jeffrey's mother left to go live in a different home with other family members. Jeffrey's sexual fantasies had returned, and he was ready to consider murder as a means to achieve his sexual desires. His opportunity came one week later, when Jeffrey observed a young man hitchhiking near his house. Jeffrey picked up the man and convinced him to spend the night with him, telling of "all the beer" he had at his house that the two men could enjoy. The young man, Steven Hicks, drank several beers with Jeffrey before announcing he had to leave. At this point, Jeffrey told him he did not want him to leave and proceeded to beat him unconscious with a dumbbell. After Jeffrey rendered Hicks unconscious, he strangled him and proceeded to strip Hicks nude. After masturbating over the dead corpse for several minutes, Jeffrey transported the nude corpse to his crawl space, where he dissected the body into several parts. Using the advice his father had unwittingly given him years earlier about bleaching bones, Jeffrey removed the flesh from the bones of Hicks using an acid solution and then proceeded to pound the bones into a fine dust using a sledgehammer. With the bones pounded into dust and the flesh dissolved in acid, Jeffrey discarded the remains of the flesh into the toilet before spreading the bone dust in a field behind his house. By completely destroying the corpse, Jeffrey was ridding himself of any evidence of the murder while also maintaining his sexual fantasy with the man.

With his sexual fantasies subsided for the moment, Jeffrey continued living alone and heavily drinking alcohol. After a few weeks, Jeffrey's father returned home with his new fiancée. Upon their return, Jeffrey decided to move out and enroll in Ohio State University with a major in business. However, Jeffrey's stay at Ohio State was almost a complete failure. Unable to overcome his incessant alcohol addiction, Jeffrey spent most of his time in his room and did not complete his schoolwork. Halfway through the semester, Jeffrey's father visited him in his dorm and was disappointed to find his son failing every class except shooting. At the end of the semester, Jeffrey's GPA stood at 0.45 out of the typical 4.0 grading scale. Even though Jeffrey's father had paid for an entire year of education for his son, Jeffrey left school after the first semester, never to return. With his collegiate life in shambles, Jeffrey decided a life in the army might be more fitting for him. Jeffrey's father agreed with this pursuit and supported Jeffrey as he went through the application process. Following Jeffrey's acceptance, he became a medical specialist, a position that would give him increased contact with men. Following his discharge from the army, two men came forward accusing Jeffrey of raping them, accounts he would later confess to. However, for the time, Jeffrey was a successful medical specialist with above average skills. Jeffrey was still unable to overcome his alcohol addiction, leading to a decrease in his value to the army. After months of poor performance, the army decided to discharge him, due to his lack of necessity to the army. Because Jeffrey had done no wrong, he was honorably discharged and returned a free man to his life as a civilian.

After his discharge from the army, Jeffrey returned to his father's house, where he helped with odd jobs around the house. Jeffrey's father had remarried, and Jeffrey was quite fond of his new stepmother. Despite Jeffrey's attempt to occupy himself beyond drinking, alcohol remained his Achilles heel and led to a $60 fine for drunk and disorderly conduct. Unable to cope with a son who was so intent on drinking alcohol, Jeffrey's father kicked him out of the house and recommended he go live with his grandmother. With no one else to turn to, Jeffrey moved in with his grandmother. Jeffrey's grandmother has been noted as being the only person in the world who devoted any time or affection towards Jeffrey. For the next two years, Jeffrey would live the life his grandmother sought for him to live. He was accepted as a phlebotomist at the Milwaukee Blood Plasma Center and accompanied his grandmother to most social activities, including church. However, Jeffrey's behavior was due in large part to his ability to work for once. When Jeffrey was laid off after ten months of work, the dark semblance of the man he used to be re-emerged. Suddenly, Jeffrey was no longer thinking of honoring his grandmother; his lusts for the submission of a man had returned.

In August of 1982, shortly after he was released from his position as a phlebotomist, Jeffrey was arrested for indecent exposure, an act he committed in the presence of a group of twenty-five women and children. Jeffrey was given a light conviction and was simply fined $50 and required to recoup the costs of the trial. For the next three years, Jeffrey would live with his grandmother and would remain off the radar of the police and his father. Finally out of money and in need of something to utilize his time, Jeffrey took up a job as a mixer at a local chocolate factory in Milwaukee. With the exception of Saturdays, Jeffrey worked every day from 11 pm to 7 am. While this job filled Jeffrey's days with work and did not allow him time to enjoy his sexual fantasies, a man on the same shift as Jeffrey began to notice him. This man was also homosexual and asked Jeffrey one day if he could perform fellatio on him. Jeffrey refused but the thought of allowing another man to stimulate him as so began to rejuvenate his fantasies that had only recently died down. Armed with more of a curiosity and lust for submission from a man, Jeffrey began making trips to various gay bars and gay bathhouses around Milwaukee. Additionally, Jeffrey robbed a department store of its mannequin and used this as a mean to achieve sexual stimulation. However, Jeffrey's grandmother found the mannequin shortly after he purchased it and commanded him to get rid of it. The bathhouses of Milwaukee became home to Jeffrey's sexual desires, but the lack of submission from his male partners still frustrated him greatly. Additionally, Jeffrey would often complain to himself that his partners were constantly moving during their sexual pleasures, an act that Jeffrey did not appreciate. Jeffrey stifled his partners' ability to move during sex by spiking their drinks with sleeping pills. However, the administration at the bathhouse soon became aware of the ordeal and banned him from the location. Jeffrey was slightly remised by this eliminated opportunity but continued his sexual escapades at a local hotel.

Around this time, Jeffrey found out that an 18-year-old boy had passed away and was being buried the next week. Engrained in his lust for sexual submission, Jeffrey made plans to go unearth the grave and use the corpse for sexual stimulation. However, upon arrival to the cemetery, Jeffrey found the ground too solidified and was unable to dig up the corpse. Jeffrey continued his sexual relations with men and often sported several partners each night. In August of the same year, Jeffrey was fishing alongside the Kinnikinic river when two boys walked up near him. Seeing the boys, Jeffrey proceeded to masturbate in front of the boys and was subsequently arrested for indecent exposure. Despite his initial plea of guilty, Jeffrey proceeded to change his plea to not guilty and claimed he was actually urinating and did not see the young boys there. The judge accepted this response and sentenced Jeffrey to a probation of one year with added counseling. One year following his probation, Jeffrey returned to his sexual deviances, all while still residing with his grandmother. Jeffrey's first victim in this string of assaults was 25-year-old Steven Toumi, a man visiting Wisconsin from Michigan. Jeffrey claims his intention was never to even injure Toumi, just to simply rape him in his sleeping-pill induced coma and then release him. However, Jeffrey rose from his bed to find Toumi flattened below him, his chest a variance of black and blue stripes and blood seeping from his mouth.

Jeffrey then took the deceased Toumi and placed him in his grandmother's basement, where he resided for over a week. Finally, shortly before petrification would have occurred, Jeffrey returned to the body and separated the limbs and head from the body. After this, Jeffrey used a fillet knife to cut the bones away from the flesh before finally dicing the flesh into small pieces. With the flesh pared from the bones, Jeffrey took the bones and pounded them into small pieces before placing all parts of the body, with the exception of the head, into a trash bag and disposing of them in the trashcan. Jeffrey retained the head from Toumi for almost two weeks before attempting to preserve the head through boiling. Jeffrey had hoped he could use the skull in his daily masturbation but the skull began falling apart and Jeffrey was forced to throw it away. The murder of Steven Toumi seemed to ignite a deeper passion within Jeffrey for the submission of an unconscious victim. To gather victims he felt most comfortable with, Jeffrey began lurking around gay bars where he would encounter drunk, homosexual men. After only two months since he murdered Toumi, Jeffrey found his next victim, a 14-year-old named James Doxtator. Jeffrey was able to entice Doxtator to his house, where he promised him $50 if he would allow Jeffrey to take pictures of him unclothed. Once in his grandmother's home, Jeffrey gave Doxtator a drink laced with laxatives before dragging his unconscious body to the cellar and strangling him. Once his victim was dead, Jeffrey destroyed the body much like he had destroyed his previous victim's body, once again retaining the head. Once again, Jeffrey attempted to preserve the skull but was forced to discard it due to its breaking apart. With his sexual fantasies peaking, Jeffrey was eager to engage his next victim. Jeffrey would find this victim at one of his hangouts around a gay bar. The man, 22-year-old Richard Guerro, followed Jeffrey to his grandmother's house where Jeffrey murdered him by strangulation. After engaging in various sexual activities on the corpse, Jeffrey used his signature fashion to destroy the body, routinely retaining the skull for later use only to throw it away two weeks after removal. During his next escapade, Jeffrey was almost caught for bringing another man into the home. Shortly after drugging his victim, Jeffrey's grandmother heard him and called to him "Is that you, Jeff?" Hearing this, Jeffrey was forced to take the victim back outside where he placed him in the care of the County General Hospital for his unconscious condition. Despite escaping the close encounter, Jeffrey was kicked out of his home by his grandmother, who complained of his always bringing other men in and of the strange smells emerging from the basement and garage.

While Jeffrey was disheartened at this occurrence, he welcomed the new privacy and found a nearby apartment that had low rent. Around this time, Jeffrey enticed a 13-year-old boy to his apartment and fondled him. However, Jeffrey was caught for this and arrested on one account of sexual assault. While Jeffrey was convicted of the account, the trial was suspended until May of 1989. For the meantime, Jeffrey returned to his grandmother's house and began planning his next attack. After two months of moving his belongings back into his grandmother's home, Jeffrey assaulted and murdered his next victim, 24-year-old Anthony Sears. Jeffrey had met Sears at a gay bar and enticed the man to return home with him in return for sexual favors. Shortly after returning to his grandmother's home, Jeffrey strangled Sears and destroyed his body as he had done so often before. This time however, Jeffrey retained more than the skull, he also kept the genitals of Sears. For the months following this assault, Jeffrey would keep the genitals of Sears with him wherever he went, a testament to the profound beauty he found in Sears. Almost two months later, Jeffrey entered trial for his sexual assault months earlier. Jeffrey was given a light sentence of one year in the House of Correction with a mandatory registration as a sex offender. Jeffrey was released ten months later on good behavior and immediately found his own apartment, a luxurious apartment in the Oxford Apartments. Jeffrey moved in immediately and brought his collection of preserved body parts with him, including the genitals extracted from Sears. Once settled in his new apartment, Jeffrey set out on the prowl for another victim. Jeffrey's next victim would be 32-year-old Raymond Smith, a prostitute enticed into entering Jeffrey's apartment under the false premise of receiving $50 for having sex with Jeffrey. As done so many times before, Jeffrey gave Smith his drinking potion and watched gleefully as Jeffrey passed into unconsciousness. With Smith unconscious, Jeffrey strangled him with his hands and then proceeded to take pictures of Smith's body in various positions. After taking enough photos, Jeffrey separated the body of Smith and boiled the various components in a kettle in his room. The kettle contained Soilex, a key compound for breaking down materials. With the bones and skin pliable, Jeffrey dumped the remains of Smith, excluding his skull, down the toilet. As a trophy of his accomplishment and experience, Jeffrey spray painted his newest skull and positioned it prominently alongside the genitals of Sears.

Jeffrey's sexual desires had never been stronger, and the desire seemed to grow with each escapade. However, Jeffrey made a costly mistake on the next encounter. During his stage of the attempted assault in which he usually overcame his victims through the sleeping pills, Jeffrey drank the brew that contained the sleeping pills, rendering himself unconscious for over 12 hours. After he woke from the drug-induced sleep, he was incensed to find that the man he had intended assaulting had actually stolen some clothes, his watch, and $300 in cash. Due to the illegal nature of the encounter-turned-burglary, Jeffrey never contacted police regarding the theft of his items. Less than one week later, Jeffrey attempted to retry his skill at overcoming a man by enticing Edward Smith into his apartment. After Smith was dead, Jeffrey tried a new method of preservation: freezing. It was Jeffrey's thought that freezing the body of his victim would dispel all moisture from the body. However, this theory proved to be anything but true and the body contained even more moisture when Jeffrey took it out of the freezer. In a last-chance effort to save the body, Jeffrey placed the body in his oven, a process that yielded worse results when the skull exploded. Jeffrey ended up discarding the entire body, an act he hated, reporting to the local police upon his arrest that he felt "rotten" being unable to save any of the body parts. Jeffrey's string of assaults was given a brief respite as Jeffrey maintained his alcohol addiction. However, after three months, Jeffrey found his next victim, a 22-year-old man named Ernest Miller. Jeffrey was able to entice Miller into his apartment by vowing to pay him $50 if he simply let Jeffrey listen to the beat of his heart. After the two entered Jeffrey's apartment, Jeffrey killed Miller by slicing his carotid artery. Jeffrey proceeded to photograph Miller's corpse completely nude before dissecting the body in his bathtub and removing various sections of flesh to be eaten by him later. This murder established Jeffrey's necrophilia; during the process of dissection, Jeffrey often leaned over to kiss the decapitated head, all while talking to the head as a life form. Jeffrey did not destroy this skeleton, however. This one was bleached before being hung in his closet as "a friend to be talked to."

One month following the assault and murder of Miller, Jeffrey enticed another man to enter his apartment but found himself grow less inclined to rape him. However, he felt he had no choice but to kill him. After strangling the man, Jeffrey simply discarded the body.

While Jeffrey did not retain any of the body parts, he carefully documented the various processes involved in dissecting the body, an attribute that greatly aided authorities in identifying the man later. After his botched assault, Jeffrey ceased his killings for almost five months. During the latter months of this brief respite from killing, Jeffrey's thoughts of suicide greatly increased. Though Jeffrey had always been known to think of various ways he could take his own life, he had never slipped into such a deep depression. With Jeffrey's love of death, it was no surprise that detectives would eventually find out he held long conversations with the skulls of the men he killed.

In 1991, Jeffrey's thoughts of assault began to throb within him again and when Jeffrey saw 17-year-old Curtis Straughter near his house, he connived a way to entice him to his apartment. Offering the teen $50 for nude photographs, Jeffrey invited Straughter into his house and subsequently strangled him. After the strangulation was complete, Jeffrey began the process of dissecting the body, this time making every effort to retain the skin of the young man. While the genitals and portions of muscle retained well, the skin never absorbed the solution and instead began rotting almost instantly. Jeffrey was forced to throw away the skin but retained the genitals atop his shelf at home. Later, Jeffrey passed a man named Errol Lindsey and was consumed with the prospect of overtaking this man. After convincing Lindsey to enter his apartment, Jeffrey rendered Lindsey unconscious before attempting an experiment he had never tried before: injecting hydrochloric acid into the brain. To accomplish this, Jeffrey drilled a hole into the back of Lindsey's head and then dumped the hydrochloric acid into his brain. However, Lindsey awoke halfway through the experiment and complained of his head hurting. With his experiment ruined, Jeffrey strangled Lindsey and dismembered the body before dumping it in the woods behind his house. It was around this time that some of Jeffrey's fellow residents had begun complaining of the smells emanating from his apartment. Additionally, many of these tenants reported hearing chainsaws late into the night. The landlord of the residence repeatedly contacted Jeffrey about these complaints to which Jeffrey reported his freezer had simply broken.

This seemed to appease the landlord and other tenants and the matter was never spoken of again. With Jeffrey being more cautious about the level of sound he created from his killings, he began lurking around, searching for his next victim, whom he found in the form of 14-year-old Konerak Sinthasomphone. After promising to pay the lad $50 for posing nude in photographs, Jeffrey led the child to his house where he rendered the child unconscious using sleeping pills. Jeffrey attempted his injection experiment once more, with his victim waking up once again. However, this time his victim was completely numb of feeling and followed Jeffrey wherever he wanted him to. Jeffrey even led him past the skeleton of past victims, all of which did not phase the young child. Jeffrey did not kill Sinthasomphone but rather observed him and sat back and drank alcohol. After falling asleep, Jeffrey was alarmed to awaken and find his victim missing. After a brief search, Jeffrey found his victim, sitting nude next to a lamppost and under the direct supervision of three women who were calling the police. Jeffrey rushed outside, attempting to call off the police to no avail. Upon the arrival of the police, Jeffrey fabricated a story in which Sinthasomphone was his boyfriend who had simply drank too much alcohol at a party. Despite the pleas of the women to take this man in for questioning, the officers were convinced Jeffrey's story was true and turned the near-unconscious lad over to Jeffrey. Despite one officer's comment about the strange odor of the apartment, no investigation was launched, and Jeffrey was able to continue to experimentation. Back in the apartment, Jeffrey injected a second dose of hydrochloric acid into his victim's brain, an injection that proved fatal this time. Jeffrey was greatly disappointed by this and took an absence from work the next day as he attempted to preserve the body of Sinthasomphone.

During the next two months, Jeffrey would assault four more victims before killing them. Under one of the situations, Jeffrey left a rotting corpse on his bed only to find it infested with maggots when he returned. This did not seem to deter Jeffrey however as he had sex with the corpse before destroying it and retaining the skull and genitals. Despite Jeffrey having kept the police off his trail for most of his life, Jeffrey made one fatal mistake during an attempted murder one year later. On July 22, 1991, Jeffrey encountered Tracy Edwards, a 32-year-old homeless man who was lured to Jeffrey's apartment under the promise of $100 for nude photographs. Upon arrival at Jeffrey's apartment, Tracy Edwards began to grow uneasy by the condition of the apartment. Jeffrey made a futile attempt at handcuffing his wrist to Edwards' wrist, a move that further frightened Edwards. However, through all of this, Edwards remained resolute in the room, fully intending to get his money and leave. Even after Jeffrey began watching the Exorcist III and chanting to himself Edwards failed to run away. Finally, Jeffrey had prepared enough and proceeded to pull a knife out of his pocket and asserted "I'm going to eat your heart." At this, Edwards ran from the house and found the nearest police officer. This officer, Rolf Mueller, returned with Edwards to the apartment where he proceeded to call in backup considering the situation. Upon entering the home, Jeffrey conducted the officers in a tour around the home, where he showcased his preserved genitals, skulls, and even complete skeletons. At this revealing, the officers immediately placed Jeffrey under arrest and called in for backup, revealing one of the worst cases of serial murder in U.S. history.

Upon questioning, Jeffrey confessed to every crime he was asked about, culminating in the known murders of 19 men. Additionally, Jeffrey confessed to assaulting and eating the flesh of many of his victims. On February 15, 1992, Jeffrey was convicted of 15 counts of murder and was given fifteen consecutive life sentences. Two years after his imprisonment began, Jeffrey was found dead in the showers, the victim of another inmate's brutal beating.

The Zodiac Killer

When asked what the greatest fear to mankind is, there would be many answers that abound. From fears regarding financial failure to fears regarding relationships, the fears for every man will differ largely based on the emotional structure of that man. However, the fear of facing an unknown killer is one no one wishes to ever face. Throughout the 1960s and 1970s, a particularly long string of murders went unsolved. With every year that the grisly murders went unsolved, crime technicians thought they were closer to catching the killer, yet these crimes would transcend into present day as they progressed from unsolved to inactive. The man responsible for these crimes remains a mystery to this day, known only by his self-proclaimed alias "The Zodiac." The masterful genius of the Zodiac has perplexed police officers and historians worldwide and the unfortunate reminder of the unsolved murders leaves a void in the workings of justice.

The first documented murder that the Zodiac was responsible for was recorded on December 20, 1968. While there are a number of murders prior to this date that historians believe could have been the works of the Zodiac, the murders lack his name, thus christening 1968 as his consummation as a murderer. The Zodiac Killer's first victims were two high school students, Betty Lou Jensen and David Faraday. David and Betty had just met and were on their way to their first date, which was supposed to be an evening away at the Hogan High School Christmas Concert. However, the couple would never make it there. After briefly talking with a friend and stopping for supper, David and Betty made their way out to Lake Hogan Road where they proceeded to drive down to the end, a common stopping place for lovers. It was around this time that an unknown car pulled in next to the couple and the Zodiac Killer made his entrance. Ordering the couple from their car, the Zodiac Killer proceeded to shoot David, killing him immediately with a shot to the head. Seeing this, Betty proceeded to flee from the scene but would be shot five times after a brief get-away. After checking to ensure his victims were deceased, the Zodiac Killer drove away from the scene. Later that night around 11:00pm, Stella Borges, a nearby neighbor, would find the two bodies and report the crime to the police. For months following the crime, the Solano County Sheriff's Department would investigate the crime but would come up empty on every lead they encountered. No evidence would result from the crime, leaving authorities to wonder whether this was an isolated crime or if there would be more to follow. Unfortunately, the authorities would not have to wait long to find out.

Only six months after the Zodiac Killer made his first attack, he achieved his second attack, one that would leave the investigators surmising they had the beginnings of a serial murderer on their hands. Shortly before the clock reached 12:00 AM on July 4, 1969, two lovers, Michael Mageau and Darlene Ferrin parked their car and watched the moon rise over Lake Herman. Ironically, this location stood only four miles from where the double murder had taken place six months prior. As the lovers continued watching the moon together, a car turned into the gravel lane and abruptly parked behind them. However, the car quickly left, and the couple thought no more of it. The car soon returned however and parked directly behind the couple's car. Without saying a word, the killer walked over to the passenger side of the car and directed a flashlight beam around the interior of the car. After locating Ferrin and Mageau, the killer proceeded to shoot five times into the car. Mageau was shot multiple times, with all the bullets passing through his body and into the body of Ferrin. Initially, the killer began walking away but soon returned when the sounds of Mageau whimpering and moaning reached him. Upon his return to the car, the killer shot both Mageau and Ferrin once more before getting into his car and leaving immediately. With no one in the vicinity of the shooting, Mageau and Ferrin remained unconscious in the car for many hours. In a twisted sense of introducing himself to the world, the Zodiac Killer called the Vallejo Police Station and confessed to committing the crime, giving the authorities the location where they could find the bodies. Additionally, the Zodiac Killer confessed to having murdered Jensen and Faraday six months prior. With the police able to maintain the phone call for several minutes, authorities were able to successfully trace the call to a phone booth located near the police station. When the police arrived at the phone booth however, there was no one there--simply a phone receiver dangling off the hook. When authorities arrived on the scene for the attempted double murder, they were disappointed to find Ferrin dead but encouraged to find Mageau still alive. Despite his extensive wounds, Mageau would make a recovery and would more importantly provide police with their first description of the man. Mageau described the Zodiac Killer as a white male weighing 195-200 pounds and 26-30 years old with light brown curly hair. With the police now possessing a sketch of their man, they felt confident they would catch their perpetrator. Soon, they would receive even more information about their suspect, but this time, it would come from the most unlikely source: the perpetrator himself.

One month after the killing of Ferrin and assault of Mageau, the world was introduced to the Zodiac Killer through three cryptic letters sent to three difference newspapers: *The Vallejo TimesHerald*, the *San Francisco Chronicle*, and the *San Francisco Examiner*. While the initial letters were easy enough to read, the killer also sent along a cryptogram for the use of the police department, promising that when revealed, the cryptogram revealed the identity of the killer. When examined, the style of letters written told of a dark past from someone who was dealing with major insecurity issues. One psychiatrist even noted the letters entailed "…someone you would expect to be brooding and isolated." Armed with the letters, the police were sure they would finally be able to identify this man who had been plaguing their city with fear. However, the cryptograms proved impossible to decode. After many attempts and several promised rewards for someone who could solve the message, the three cryptograms went unsolved and left the police with little option other than to publish the letter with hopes someone might be able to lend a clue. The letter described the crimes that had been committed and claimed responsibility for the previous two murders. Initially, the writer of the letter had demanded that the cryptograms be printed on each of the three papers he had sent them to or else he would be forced to "cruse[sic] around all weekend killing lone people in the night then move on to kill again, until I end up with a dozen people over the weekend." Despite the threat, the police chief of Vallejo did not believe that they were from a credible source and dismissed them as being invalid. For this reason, one third of the cryptogram was only published in one paper, the *Chronicle*. The police chief's gamble paid off and the killer did not go after any more victims in response to his cryptogram not being published. Six days after the original letter was received at the three media outlets, *The San Francisco Examiner* received its second letter from the supposed killer, reading: "Dear Editor, this is the Zodiac speaking." The Zodiac Killer went on to outline his plan along with the reasons he had killed his previous victims. This letter marked the first time the killer referred to himself as the Zodiac Killer, a nickname that the media would use for the rest of his life. In this letter, the killer mentioned that he was surprised the media had not followed his wishes for the cryptogram to be released, adding that his formal identity was included in one of the cryptograms. One day later, a couple located in the lower region of California offered a solution for one of the cryptograms. When deciphered, the cryptogram read "I like killing people because it is so much fun it is more fun than killing wild game in the forest because man is the most dangerous animal of all to kill something gives me the most thrilling experience it is even better than getting your rocks off with a girl the best part of it is that when I die I will be reborn in paradise and those I have killed will become my slaves I will not give you my name because you will try to sloi[sic] down or atop my collecting of slaves for my afterlife ebeorietemethhpiti[sic]." The statement, filled with spelling errors and words that seemed to be simple gibberish, was accepted by the police as the closest and most plausible code that would work for the cryptogram. The couple, Donald and Bettye Harden, asked to remain anonymous for safety reasons but their identity was soon known across California, with the police requesting they work on the remaining two cryptograms. However, their success would run out and they would never be able to decipher the remaining cryptograms.

Almost one month after publishing his second message in the paper, the Zodiac Killer claimed his next set of victims, Bryan Hartnell and Cecilia Shepard. The college couple were enrolled at Pacific Union College and were studying business management and legal office administration respectively. The two had embarked on a weekend getaway to picnic and enjoy each other's company for a while. However, shortly after they had begun their picnic, a man approached the couple and threatened to kill them. This man was 5'11" and appeared to be slightly overweight, perfectly fitting the description the police had been circulating around the area regarding the Zodiac Killer's appearance. The man had a black hooded mask on and was wearing sunglasses to conceal his identity. Additionally, the man had a white bib on his chest that bore the symbol of a cross within a circle. After making small talk and telling the couple a little about his life story, the man asserted he was an inmate at a local jail and had recently escaped. The man claimed to have overpowered the officer that had been assigned to his cell block before stealing a police car and stumbling upon the couple. The man told the couple he would be stealing their car so he could continue his trip to Mexico, a trip that had recently been derailed due to mechanical issues with the police car. Producing two plastic zip ties, the man commanded the woman, Shepard, to restrain the man, Hartnell and tie his hands behind his back. After completing the task, the man checked the hands and grew apprehensive and furious when he found that Shepard had attempted to trick him by leaving Hartnell's hands slightly loose. The man proceeded to tie the hands more tightly before wielding a knife and repeatedly stabbing both people. In the end, Hartnell was stabbed six times and Shepard was stabbed ten times. After completing the murder, the man, now known to be the Zodiac Killer found Hartnell's car and chalked the same cross/circle symbol from his shirt onto the door of the car. After writing the symbol, the killer added the words "Vallejo/12-20-68/7-4-69/Sept 27–69–6:30/by knife."

Roughly three hours after completing his heinous crime, the killer found a payphone at the Napa Car Wash in Napa, California and phoned the Napa County Sheriff's Office. Upon answering the phone call, the secretary was informed by the killer that he wished to report a double murder. The murderer offered no clues as to where the couple was located but did claim responsibility for the crime the police were about to stumble upon. Meanwhile, the couple had been screaming repeatedly for help, to no avail. However, their screams were soon heard by a man and his son who had been hunting nearby. After calling the park rangers, the man and his son tended to the needs of the couple. Sadly, Shepard would die two days later after being in a coma. Hartnell, however would live and tell of his horrifying and tragic experience to the police. Armed with the description of the man and the subsequent phone call, the police readily laid the responsibility for the crime within the growing rap sheet of the Zodiac Killer. One of the police officers from the crime scene investigation, Detective Ken Narlow, would work the case every day until his retirement almost one decade later.

After a brief respite of two weeks in which the Zodiac Killer did not kill anyone, his crimes resurfaced in a bizarre manner of events. On October 11, 1969, a man hailed a cab sometime after 8:00 PM. The man requested to be driven to Washington and Maple Streets in nearby Presido Heights. The driver, Paul Stine, agreed and began driving to the unknown passenger to the destination. However, Stine drove past the street requested by the passenger, whether on purpose or accident never to be known. Seeing this, the passenger, who turned out to be the Zodiac Killer, produced a handgun from his belt and shot Stine in the back of the head once. After killing Stine, the killer stole Stine's wallet, keys, and some spare change from the car. Additionally, the killer used his knife to cut away a portion of Stine's shirt, specifically a section that contained the blood of Stine. Ironically, this entire crime was observed by a group of teenage boys. After seeing the killer wipe the cab clean of Stine's blood, the boys alerted local authorities who began making their way to the scene. On their way there, the police actually passed the Zodiac Killer but did not stop because they had been told to be looking for an African-American man, not a Caucasian man. To this day, no one is sure why the mix-up in descriptions took place. Obviously, there were no suspects when the police arrived on the scene of the murder and the car had been wiped clean of all evidence. However, the four teens who observed the murder were able to give the police a rough sketch of the man they were looking for. Using this sketch, the police were able to circulate thousands of leads, over 2,500, with none producing anything more than frustration. The Zodiac Killer was becoming bolder in his actions, leading authorities to hope he would make a mistake soon, a mistake that would cost him his identity and hopefully exact justice for the lives he had taken thus far.

Three days after having completed his murder, the Zodiac Killer resumed communication with the *Chronicle*, sending in a letter outlining the murders he had completed since he had last communicated with the paper. Among those murders he claimed responsibility for was the murder of Paul Stine with which he proved by sending along the blood-stained portion of the shirt. In addition to outlining his recent murders, the Zodiac Killer also sent along plans and musings he had been holding that focused on murdering schoolchildren from a bus. The Zodiac Killer surmised that he could accomplish this task by shooting out the front tire of the bus and then "picking off the kiddies as they come bouncing out." However, this would never take place and would simply be another one of the Zodiac Killer's empty threats. Six days later, the Zodiac Killer made a phone call to the Oakland Police Department and demanded that either F. Lee Bailey or Melvin Belli, both famous lawyers from the area, be shown as guest stars on the program. Due to Bailey not being available at the time of the show, Belli appeared on the show as a guest. The Zodiac Killer had demanded that all the lines be kept open and after a while, called into the show requesting to meet personally with

Belli in Daly City. Belli agreed but upon the date of the meeting, no one showed up, leaving the Zodiac Killer's identity a mystery. Almost one month later, the Zodiac Killer gave the police their fourth attempt at solving his identity, sending in another cryptogram with the promise that this one contained his identity. A number of solutions were found but police discounted all of these, stating that they were either found using faulty methods or far too easy for the Zodiac Killer to have connived. The Zodiac Killer continued to toy with the police, sending a seven-page letter to the police one day later that outlined a conversation he had held with the police. The Zodiac Killer claims to have been stopped by two policemen three minutes after he had completed his murder of the cab driver Stine. However, the policemen let the Zodiac Killer continue walking, due largely to their command to be looking for an African-American male. The letter was published in the *Chronicle* and infuriated the locals, including the police officers. Years later, Officer Dan Fouke would write his own account of the evening, outlining the faulty description he had been given. The Zodiac rounded out this series of letters by sending a haunting letter to Belli that included a small portion of Stine's bloodied shirt. However, rather than outline his murders or plans to murder, the Zodiac Killer claimed he was ready to cease his killing and sought the aid of Belli. However, he left no contact information, effectively leaving Belli effortless to help him overcome his love and thirst for murder. Sadly, the murders were about to continue with even more tenacity.

In his next attack, the Zodiac Killer would make a surprising mistake in his attempt to murder his next victim. Almost five months had passed since anyone had heard of any movement by the Zodiac, leaving many to wonder whether he had been killed at the hands of his careless lifestyle. However, the hope for seclusion was shattered when the killer made another appearance, this time attempting a kidnapping. However, this attempt would contain bizarre followings that left the killer humiliated. On March 22, 1970, a young mom named Kathleen Johns was returning home to visit her mother, accompanied by her young daughter. On the way to Petaluma from

San Bernardino, Johns noticed a car had begun following her and was honking its horn carelessly. Johns pulled over and awaited the driver of the other car. When the driver appeared at her car, Johns observed that this man appeared to be 5'11" and was heavier than 160 pounds. The man seemed to be genuinely concerned for her safety, noting that her rear tire on the right side of the vehicle was wobbling significantly. Johns thanked the man and implored his help, to which he conceded and lent a helping hand. After using the lug wrench to supposedly tighten the lug nuts on the back tire, the man returned to his car and Johns proceeded to leave the scene, onward to see her mother. However, shortly after leaving, the right rear wheel on her car very nearly came off, rendering her helpless by the side of the road. The stranger had been following close behind and offered to drive Johns and her daughter to a nearby gas station where she could phone her husband. Johns agreed and proceeded to get into the car with her daughter. After a while, Johns noticed that the man had driven past several gas stations, always remarking that he was going to stop at the next one. For over an hour and a half, the man continued to drive various routes around the countryside, never answering Johns when she appealed as to why they were not stopping at any of the gas stations. Finally, unnerved by the entirety of the matter, Johns took the next chance she had to remove herself and her daughter from the car. When the stranger stopped at an intersection, Johns fled from the car and retreated to a nearby field where she flattened herself against the ground with her daughter. The stranger pulled the car to the side of the road and proceeded to search frantically for Johns and her daughter. Thankfully, Johns had the presence of mind to hide in the deepest grass, providing ample cover from the searching gaze of the stranger.

After the stranger searched for a while, he gave up and returned to his car where he fled from the scene. After he left, Johns and her daughter fled to the nearest police station and relayed her story to the police. Of particular interest, Johns was seven months pregnant at the time of the attempted kidnapping, giving new breath to the beauty of her escape. At the police station, Johns was giving her statement to the police chief when her eye caught a glance of a sketch the police had composed of the killer the police believed responsible for the murder of Paul Stine. Upon seeing this picture, Johns recognized this man as the one who had attempted kidnapping herself and her daughter. The police were quite interested in this fact and given the positive identification from Johns, the police were able to determine that the perpetrator was the Zodiac Killer. Additionally, the police were worried that the Zodiac Killer would be unwilling to allow his victim to leave, meaning he would return and attempt to kill Johns at any cost, including the loss of law enforcement lives. With this in mind, the police chief put the entire police station on lockdown and isolated Johns in an unknown location where she sat in total darkness. After a brief search of the surrounding area, the police found Johns' car, completely burned and removed of all seats. While the police were thankful that Johns, her daughter, and her unborn baby were fine, the experience was extremely traumatic for Johns, leaving her fearful for months following the attempted kidnapping.

While the attacks from the Zodiac Killer subsided for the next few months, communication with the killer was still prevalent as he continued to send cyphers to media outlets, the police station, and often his victims. On April 20, the killer sent a letter to the authorities stating "My name is_____" with the blank space being filled with a 13-character cypher. Even though the police dedicated months of time to solving the cypher, no solutions were proved definite and the identity of the killer remained anonymous. In addition to providing a cypher that supposedly contained his identity, the Zodiac Killer also took time to exonerate himself from a recent bombing at the San Francisco Police Station that had killed a sergeant. However, the killer lauded the man who had bombed the police station, stating "there is more glory in killing a cop than a cid[sic] because a cop can shoot back." Additionally, the killer included the ramifications and specifics of a bomb he had prepared that would allegedly "blow up an entire school bus and cill[sic] a ton of cids[sic]." The killer closed out the letter with his famous circle within a cross symbol that was followed by the text "Zodiac=10, SFPD=0," obviously pointing out that the police department had failed at identifying or even inhibiting the Zodiac Killer's antics. Eight days later, the Zodiac Killer followed his recent letter to the police station with a post-card that read "I hope you enjoy yourselves when I have my BLAST." The killer then threatened to carry out his diabolical plan if the newspaper failed to print his recent letter. Additionally, the killer expressed a desire to see people begin sporting "some nice Zodiac butons[sic]." After a brief respite in which no communication between the police department and the Zodiac Killer took place, the Zodiac Killer once again sent a post-card to the *Chronicle*, this time remarking that he had murdered a man recently because he had not seen any people wearing Zodiac buttons. Upon further investigation, the police found that this man was Sergeant Redetich who had been shot while sitting in his car. The police officer was shot once in the head with a .38 caliber handgun and died 15 hours later as a result of his wounds. However, the SPFD continued their investigation and determined that the Zodiac Killer would not even have been in the same vicinity as the murdered sergeant. To this day, the SFPD denies any connection between the murder and the Zodiac Killer. In addition to sending the letter outlining his false murder, the Zodiac Killer also included a Phillips 66 roadmap that detailed the San Francisco Bay area. On the map, the killer had circled a certain area known as Mount Diablo, a popular tourist attraction in the area. Under the circle, the killer outlined how he had planted a bomb in this area and was going to detonate it at a time to be determined later. However, police would have direct access to the location of the bomb if they could successfully decode a cypher the killer had included on the map. As with most of the previous cyphers, the police never solved the cypher and the bomb was never found. However, police were thankful that the communication with the Zodiac Killer was maintained, giving them ample evidence to glean clues from. One month later, the Zodiac Killer mailed another letter to the *Chronicle* and used this letter to claim responsibility for the abduction of Kathleen Johns and her daughter. The *Chronicle* published portions of the letter, including a portion where the Zodiac Killer quoted various lines from the Mikado and customized these lines to include his plan for how he would satisfy himself with his slaves once he reached his fanaticized paradise. This letter was dated with the code "Zodiac Killer=13, SFPD=0." Additionally, the killer added a small hint at the end of the letter stating " P.S. The MT. Diablo code concerns Radians + # inches along the radians." With this telling clue, the police were able to find that if a radian angle was placed directly on top of the Zodiac' s bomb location map, the radian angle produced would point the way to the two locations of the bombs. However, these locations were combed for bombs and clues but left the detectives with nothing but more frustration with the Zodiac Killer.

The Zodiac Killer closed out his letters to the *Chronicle* by sending a 3x5 card to the paper firm and writing the circle-cross symbol in blood on the card. The card contained thirteen holes across the top of it while also containing a message that had been formulated using cutouts of letters from the local paper. The Zodiac Killer maintained communication with the outside world, but this time chose a different source: Paul Avery, a detective who had been assigned to the Zodiac case since its inception. On October 27 of the same year, 1970, the Zodiac Killer composed a message to Paul Avery that read "Peak-a-boo, you are doomed." Given the Zodiac Killer's volatility, the police station took the threat seriously and placed the story on the front page of the *Chronicle*. Additionally, the Zodiac Killer seemed to want more recognition, prompting him to send a letter to Paul Avery that outlined the similarities between his recent murders and a murder that had gone unsolved years ago, the murder of Cheri Jo Bates. Four years prior, Cheri Jo Bates had been studying in the library on the campus of Riverside Community College before leaving to return to her dorm at 9:00 PM. However, neighbors noted that they heard a scream at 10:30 P.M. and Bates would be found the next morning, beaten and stabbed to death. Upon further inspection, the police found that Bates' car had been tampered with, her distributor cap removed from the car. Nearby, police found a Timex watch, but this was quickly discounted as being evidence when the police found that the watch had stopped at 12:24 PM. The police were perplexed by this murder, finding nothing that could act as substantial evidence at the scene of the crime. However, with this evidence years later, police levied the responsibility of this crime with the Zodiac Killer, convinced that a letter showing the similarities was evidence enough. The Zodiac Killer would substantiate this evidence later with another letter that claimed to be responsible for another girl's disappearance, this time the girl being Donna Lass from Sahara. Years later, her body would be found in a makeshift grave at Norden, California but the police would never find substantial evidence beyond the letter of confession to point this murder to the Zodiac Killer.

For three years following the letter confessing to the murder of Donna Lass, the Zodiac Killer went unheard from. With no communication, the police began to wonder once again if he had been killed. However, the Zodiac Killer emerged for one last breath of air on January 29, 1974. Merely sending a letter to the *Chronicle*, the Zodiac Killer gave a short synopsis on *The Exorcist*, a movie he referred to as being "the best satirical comidy[sic] that I have ever seen." After a brief line from The Mikado, the Zodiac Killer closed out his final letter with one last score "Me=37, SFPD=0." After this, the killer was never heard from again. Though numerous attempts have been made to identify him and several thousand suspects were interviewed, there has yet to be a suspect that fits the entire model of suspicion warranted for an arrest. For now, the few detectives still pursuing the identity of the killer are hopeful new DNA identification techniques will reveal the true identity of this man. Despite the disappointment in never finding the killer, the detectives are grateful that the serial killings ceased, thus ending one of the deadliest murder sprees in the history of the United States.

Jack the Ripper

Within the lore of criminal history, there is special attention given to those who have committed serious crimes and have gone unknown their entire life. Whether through mere chance or through intelligent illusiveness, these criminals have taken lives from humanity while also providing humanity with countless stories and legends. One of these legends, Jack the Ripper, has numerous websites, books, and even movies dedicated to the assumptions as to who he was. In fact, the gender of Jack is not even known. While a letter claiming to be "Jack the Ripper" noted his gender as being male, there is no official verification, therefore leading authorities to allow for the remote possibility of Jack being a female. However, the seclusion of men from his crimes seems to link the murderer as being male. The title "Jack the Ripper" came from the same letter leading authorities to refer to the murder as Jack for the rest of their investigation. The crimes led by Jack were none the less gruesome, turning him into a legend that the residents of East London would have been willing to live without; Creating an air of mystery and the precursor to a succession of serial killers that would become well-known to society. Jack the Ripper has culminated into a legend that detectives have been unable to solve.

The foundation for the crime of Jack the Ripper was laid through the compassionate efforts of those in London. The year was 1882 and living conditions in London were deteriorating by the day. With Irish immigrants flooding the London area, thousands of people began arriving only to find a lack of housing. Additionally, a large population of Jews were also immigrating into the London area, providing

England with an immigration crisis. One area that was particularly saturated with immigrants was Whitechapel, a parish located on the Eastern side of London. With the immigrants continuing to flood the area, jobs became scarce and the living conditions deteriorated significantly. Immigrants were resorting to thievery to provide for their families while addictions to alcohol and violent altercations overtook many households. Additionally, the number of single women in the suburbs of London became exorbitant, leading to fierce job competition among women. For those women who were unable to secure a job, prostitution seemed to be the only option, resulting in an estimated 1,200 prostitutes roaming the streets of the Whitechapel area. The amount of prostitution actually worsened the living conditions and social unrest began to rise from the depths of Whitechapel. The police of London were unable to respond to the rising number of calls from the Whitechapel area, further laying the foundation for Jack's future series of heinous acts. The Whitechapel area became known as a racist, violent, anti-Semitic area where any semblance of ordinary life was not found. Unfortunately, the murders and assaults of Jack the Ripper fit so well into this facet of society that his initial attacks were not covered by the local press. However, the press would soon recognize there was a serial killer on the loose in their area and they would begin their media campaigns to no avail.

When pinpointing the exact crimes of Jack, it is extremely difficult to discern the crimes that he was responsible for. There were numerous sexual assaults each night in Whitechapel during this time and murders were not uncommon. However, the grotesque fashion in which Jack assaulted and killed his victims seems to link the murders. During a particularly violent period of time in East London, eleven murders that took place from April 3, 1888 to February 13, 1891 seem to bear the semblance of Jack's handiwork. While there is speculation as to how many of these eleven murders were actually Jack's murders, five of these murders have been confirmed by coroners to have been performed by the same person: the person claiming to be Jack the Ripper. The first murder from this string of murders took place on Osborn Street in Whitechapel when Emma Elizabeth Smith was assaulted and robbed, before succumbing to her wounds and dying the following day. Before her death, Smith identified those responsible for her murder as being two men and a teenage boy. Simply noting that the attack was a group effort, historians are quick to dismiss this as being a crime committed by Jack. However, the letter addressed to the police that would divulge the named "Jack the Ripper" claimed responsibility for this crime, giving historians no choice but to place the responsibility of this crime with Jack.

Three months later, another murder took place that had the characteristics indicative of Jack's handiwork. This time the victim was Martha Tabram, a single woman who worked at a local factory. On the evening of August 7, Tabram was found dead - the victim of 39 stab wounds across every portion of her body. This crime was significantly less extreme than the other crimes committed by Jack, but historians believe this crime may have been one of his earliest crimes. After the murder of Tabram, a series of grotesque murders had followed that became known as the Canonical Five. These murders were particularly gruesome and usually left the victim with missing limbs or the removal of their internal organs. The first victim of the Canonical Five was Mary Ann Nichols, a 21 year old woman. Nichols was found dead on August 31, 1888 at 3:40 AM, assumedly losing her life after a stint as a prostitute. Nichols' body was sliced in several places with slash wounds throughout her abdomen and chest, and the most significant being an incision through her throat, practically decapitating her. Less than one month later, the second victim in this series of crimes had fallen to the attack of Jack, by the name of Annie Chapman. Chapman was found dead on September 8 at 6 AM. Her body was found in a doorway on Hanbury Street on the East side of Whitechapel. Following in the same fashion as the murder of Nichols, Chapman's throat had been sliced open and there was a significant cut along the breadth of her abdomen. After the coroner's inspection, they discovered that Chapman's murderer had removed her uterus. Police were perplexed as to why a murderer would remove the uterus from his victim. After questioning several witnesses who had seen Chapman the evening before, it was established that Chapman had been accompanied by a man bearing the appearance of a homeless man with long, unkempt hair that was dark in nature. Police could not make any connections between the killings of Chapman and Nichols. However, the next victims of Jack would lend themselves to being connected with the previous murders, giving the police more headway on who may be committing these crimes, and the question everyone was asking: why?

The next two victims of the Canonical Five would be killed in short proximity from each other and at roughly the same time of night. The first being Elizabeth Stride, who was a 22-year old prostitute known to frequent the Berner Street area. Her body was discovered on September 30 at 1 AM. When police discovered the body, they found her neck almost completely detached from the result of a knife wound that stretched from one side to the other. Encountering yet another victim of a throat slashing, the police began to grow suspicious that they were dealing with a serial killer and not just isolated murders. This crime did however differ from the previous two in that Jack did not remove any organs from Stride's abdomen. In fact, there were no other incisions other than the incision across her throat. While some historians doubt as to whether or not this murder was actually the doing of Jack, the police reports of the London police give details that support this crime in fact being committed by Jack. When the police questioned those around the area who might have seen Stride the evening before, they were met with nothing but confusion. Some witnesses say she was walking with a man who looked homeless, similar to the man who had killed Chapman. Other witnesses spoke of Stride being accompanied by a handsome looking man who appeared wealthy. With this conflict of stories, police were forced to the realization that the perpetrator responsible for this crime would likely go unidentified. The same morning that Stride was discovered, police came across the body of Catherine Eddowes. Eddowes was discovered in the bushes of Mitre Square in downtown London. Police discovered her body only 45 minutes after discovering Strides, leading to the belief that the murderer had only killed Stride, but seemed more interested in harvesting organs from Eddowes. Upon inspection, police were not surprised to find that Eddowes had died just as the previous three women had: a long and jagged wound severing her throat in two. Additionally, Eddowes' abdomen had been ripped open with a blunt object along with the removal of her kidney and uterus. As police began their task of questioning anyone who might have come in contact with these women before their death, they stumbled upon the testimony of Joseph Lawende. Lawende had walked through the Mitre Square only minutes before the death of Eddowes and had seen her accompanied by a man "of shabby appearance." Corroborating his description, two friends accompanying Lawende gave similar descriptions of the man. With these testimonies, police came to the conclusion that these two deaths were in fact related and began referring to the murders as a double event. Later that night, police were called to a house on Goulston Street in Whitechapel where a local resident had discovered a bloody apron outside of his house. The blood was confirmed to be Eddowes', and police now had a direct link from these murders to the Whitechapel area. Police had noticed writing above where the apron was found, possibly indicting that the murderer had intended for the police to find the apron. Since the writing was so illegible, police were forced to abandon efforts. After washing away the blood from the wall, the police returned to the scene of Eddowes' death, no closer to catching the criminal than they had been before. With the activity increasing by the month, police were concerned that the murderer was growing in confidence, and while the previous murders had been grotesque in nature, they were nothing like the murder the police were about to discover.

On November 9th of 1888, the London police were called to the residence of Mary Jane Kelley, where they found her body completely dismembered on her bed. To date, this murder proved to be the most horrific from Jack and one that would leave the police motivated than ever to finding the criminal responsible. The murder had taken place at 10:45 PM and along with the throat being completely severed, the nature of the disembowelment left police certain this was the action of their mysterious serial killer. This murder seemed to have been fueled by more hatred however, with Jack cutting the throat all the way to the spine and removing all of the organs from the abdomen and dumping them out. Setting an eerie tune to the already mysterious evening, the heart of Mary Jane Kelley was missing from her body. After completing their investigation of the scene of the crime, the police were frustrated to have found no signs or clues that would lend hints as to who the criminal was. Despite not finding any clues, the police were certain of one fact from their investigation: the criminal they were dealing with was a professional and was likely fueled by more than simply anger; this persona had an agenda that was systematically being carried out to completion. The entire Whitechapel area lay crippled in fear as to who would be the next victim of this monster.

When investigating the common nature of these murders, the most compelling aspect that links these murders is how the throats were cut. Coroner reports note that the throats were all cut from left to right and that they were all done by a blade of the same width. While the murders previous to the Canonical Five have been linked to the Canonical Five by contemporary investigators, the London Police firmly believed that the Canonical Five were murdered by one person but were isolated, meaning this murderer did not murder anyone else after the five. This thought was corroborated by Assistant Chief Constable of the Metropolitan Police, Sir Melville Macnaghten who asserted "The Whitechapel murderer had 5 victims [the Canonical Five] —and five victims only." Police surgeon Thomas Bond would also make similar assertions to the head of the London CID, Robert Anderson, noting "The man responsible for the Whitechapel murders has likely ceased his actions and is no longer a threat to London society." While there are countless rumors as to how many murders Jack the Ripper was actually responsible for, belief is that his murder spree spread far beyond the mere Whitechapel murders.

While the local police only credited the Canonical Five to Jack the Ripper, there were numerous murders that followed this murder spree that historians have linked to Jack the Ripper. The first would be Rose Mylett, a victim of strangulation on December 20, 1888. Mylett's body was discovered in the courtyard of Clarke's Yard on High Street, near one of the other murders enacted by Jack. While some believed Mylett had simply hanged herself, others were not convinced this was absent from the work of Jack, leading to the inquest jury's verdict of murder. The second murder victim was Alize McKenzie. McKenzie was found dead on July 17, 1889 with a severed left carotid artery. While police found additional bruises possibly showing a prior to her death, there were no other markings on her body and a lack of the typical dismemberment of the abdominal cavity as was so prevalent with Jack's foregoing victims. This murder proved to hold the most controversy from this series of murders, with pathologists Thomas Bond and George Bagster Phillips holding an aggressive debate as to whether or not this was the work of Jack the Ripper. Although police would never find evidence linking this to Jack, the severed neck has convinced many that there is a connection.

The victim following this crime once again showed comparable wounds of that done by Jack the Ripper. This victim would remain unidentified due to the absence of a head for identification. On September 10, 1889, the mere torso of a woman was found under a bridge on Pinchin Street in Whitechapel. The woman was missing her head, arms, and legs. The crime held every indication of being committed by Jack the Ripper. Police became convinced that Jack had committed this murder elsewhere and had then distributed the various body parts across the city, in an effort to reduce the chances of identification. Without DNA identification practices, during the time, this woman remains unidentified to this day and has become known as The Pinchin Street Torso. Three months later, Francis Cole was murdered under the same bridge where The Pinchin Street Torso was found. Cole's throat had been slashed, leading police to believe this was yet another victim of Jack. While the throat was sliced, the rest of Cole's body remained intact and left police wondering if the murderer had been interrupted and was unable to complete his task of dismembering her and removing key organs. While police were once again unable to link this murder to Jack, they were able to detain a man who had been accompanying Cole earlier in the evening. This man, James Thomas Sadler, fit every description of being Jack the Ripper and police strongly believed they had finally caught the man who had terrorized their city for so long. However, during the trial, the judge felt there was insufficient evidence to detain or even convict Sadler, and he was set free one month later. This move stung the police of London and effectively silenced their cries of victory. For two years, the police had worked diligently to find the man they believed to have caused so much heartbreak across Whitechapel, and the discharge of Sadler made the findings thus far by the police seem useless. In result of the decision by the judge, several law enforcement officials from London quit their jobs in retaliation against the judge who deemed there was insufficient evidence. For now, the man London knew as Jack the Ripper was free to roam the streets in search of his next victim.

After the discharge of Sadler, the police of London began investigating crimes that had been committed prior to the known killings of Jack the Ripper. One of these murders was Annie Millwood who was stabbed in the leg and torso on February 25, 1888. Though Annie would momentarily survive these wounds, she had lost too much blood and passed away hours after being stabbed. Another victim of Jack was Ada Wilson. While Wilson was not murdered and survived her attack, she was stabbed twice in the neck, leading police to believe Jack had attempted to murder her but had been interrupted, thus saving Wilson's life. One mystery that police found that fit the pattern of Jack's killings was the Whitehall Mystery, a killing like that of the Pinchin Street Torso. On October 2, 1888, the police discovered a headless torso in the basement of their police station. Later, an arm from the torso would be found in the river while a leg from the torso would be found near the body. No other body parts would ever be found, but police believe this could have been one of the early works of Jack the Ripper before he began his attacks and killings of the prostitutes of Whitechapel. An additional victim of the same mutilation was found weeks later, when the body parts of Elizabeth Jackson were found across the riverside of Whitechapel. With her body parts being found mostly in the Thames River, the police believe this was the victim of the same person who murdered the Pinchin Street Torso and the body found in the Whitehall Mystery. The youngest victim from this spree of mutilating bodies was John Gill, a seven-year-old who was killed in Bradford on December 29, 1888, placing him in the same time frame and vicinity of Jack's killings. John's legs had been removed from his torso and jagged wounds traced his abdominal cavity. Upon closer inspection, it was found that John's heart and kidneys had also been removed along with missing an ear. When questioning witnesses, police found significant cause to arrest John's work supervisor William Barrett only to lose him from the courts due to lack of evidence, once again.

The last victim that police believe was killed by Jack was Carrie Brown, a 24-year-old playwright from New York City. New York City police believe Jack the Ripper had travelled from London to America to continue his evil killings, with Brown being his first and last victim. Brown was discovered in her room, the victim of strangulation. Brown's body held the telltale mutilation marks that Jack's victims also had, with her abdominal cavity completely ripped apart with a knife. While no internal organs had been stolen, Brown's ovary was found next to her on the bed; police believe this to have been an accident.

Across the ocean in London, a group of citizens had grown tired of living in fear and began taking action they felt the police were not willing to take. Calling themselves the Whitechapel Vigilance Committee, they began patrolling the streets in attempt to both curb the murder rate, while also finding clues that might lead them to the murderer. After the government began offering a reward for information leading to the arrest of Jack the Ripper, citizens began suspecting everyone with their primary target being butchers, slaughterers, and physicians. For six months, this group of citizens investigated every potential suspect in the London area. In the end, the Whitechapel Vigilance Committee had investigated 76 butchers while also investigating every employee from the butchers' shops.

Additionally, the group approached the police surgeon who had investigated all the corpses, asking him for a synopsis of the common traits from the crimes. The police surgeon wrote, "All five murders no doubt were committed by the same hand. In the first four the throats appear to have been cut from left to right. Unfortunately, in the last case owing to the extensive mutilation, it is impossible to say in what direction the fatal cut was made, but arterial blood was found on the wall in splashes close to where the woman's head must have been lying. All the circumstances surrounding the murders lead me to form the opinion that the women must have been lying down when murdered and in every case the throat was cut first." While this report would give light to the style of Jack the Ripper, no leads were derived from the committee and it was disbanded after the murders had subsided for six months.

While the murderer has been called Jack the Ripper by the media since the start of his crimes, the origin of the title can neither be confirmed nor denied. Over time during the crimes, numerous letters poured into the local newspapers, claiming to be responsible for the crimes. Of these letters, three that hold special interest to the police were titled "Dear Boss," "Saucy Jacky," and "From Hell." The first letter, "Dear Boss," was the first time the killer referred to himself as Jack the Ripper, hence the police and media calling the murderer by that name. The second letter, "Saucy Jacky," was sent four days after the "Dear Boss" letter had been received and this letter the murderer had confessed to the murders of Eddowes and Stride. The writer, Jack the Ripper, gave specific details in this letter, confirming the mode of death, time of death, and proximity of the double murder, all details that the police had not made public. The final letter of the trio was sent to George Lusk, the chairman of the Whitechapel Vigilance Committee. This letter came enclosed in a box with the remains of a kidney. The kidney had been cut in half with one half missing. In the letter, the killer claimed to have fried and eaten the other half of the kidney. When examined by a doctor, the kidney in the box was confirmed to have been from the left side; however, this surgeon was unable to determine if the kidney came from one of the victims or not.

It was pointed out that Eddowes had been missing a kidney but without proper testing, the kidney could not be directly linked.

With the East side of London gaining national attention, the other residents of London were convinced that the Whitechapel area needed to be demolished. The decreasing living conditions and high rate of crime was all the city officials needed to be convinced and the Whitechapel area would be demolished shortly thereafter. However, many of the murder sites from the legacy of Jack the Ripper were retained, with city officials aware of the infamous tourist attraction the scenes were quickly becoming. To this day, guided tours visit the remaining murder sites and people are free to create their own opinions of the murderer to rival the innumerable opinions that have been created thus far. Although countless investigations have been launched and millions of people have their own theories as to who and where Jack the Ripper resided, the identity of Jack the Ripper will never be confirmed, and London is left with its greatest legacy.

John Wayne Gacy

Human nature strives for justice. When a person is wronged, their instinctive reaction is to undertake any means necessary to achieve justice and right the wrong. Using the biblical precedent of equal punishment, the levels of justice are not balanced until the punishment paid equals the wrong incurred. For some, this balance of judgement requires imprisonment. For others, a mere fine will suffice. However, there is a select group of people whose wrongs demand the penalty of death – a sad and tragic price to be paid. John Wayne Gacy is an example of a man who lived a life of assault, sodomy, and murder. Though John's actions went unknown for years, his past was sooner or later uncovered and the world saw the monster that had so long hid under the mask of a clown and businessman. The life of John Wayne Gacy serves as an example to mankind that justice can be served for those with a life of crime, a life that left society broken and encompassed with fear.

John Wayne Gacy was born on March 17, 1942 to John and Marion Gacy in Chicago, Illinois. From an early age, it became evident to John Wayne that he was not loved by his father. Despite his mother's attempts to shield her son from violence and abuse, John Sr. spared no violence from his son when in an angry rage. In a memoir published shortly before John Wayne's death, he revealed that his earliest memory of his father was being smacked repeatedly with a leather belt when he was just four years old. The cause of the punishment rested in the actions of John who had accidentally mixed up a series of car engine parts his father had been working on. Furthermore, John Wayne was also verbally abused by his father who would continually refer to him as being less valuable and less of a human than his sisters. Constantly, John Wayne was called "dumb" and "stupid" by his father, giving him no semblance of a caring home where he was valued. As he got older, the belittling and abuse continued, once resulting in him suffering a blow to the head from a broomstick – a blow that drove him into unconsciousness and caused seizures for months after. This was the lifestyle that John endured for the entirety of his childhood at home. While the actions of his life later hold no room for excuse or causation, his years as a child left him with no example of how a man was to act, given the absence of a loving father figure. Though he claims he experienced no hatred for his father, John Wayne certainly did not have a good reason to love his father.

John Wayne had his first sexual experience when he was seven years old when he and his friend fondled a younger girl. After his father heard of his actions, he punished him by striking him repeatedly with a razor strip. That year, John Wayne was sexually assaulted for the first time, the perpetrator being a contractor who knew the Gacy family quite well. Though John knew the situation was wrong and was tempted to call the police or tell his father, he lived under the fear of his father holding him responsible for the situation, thus never told anyone what had happened. In school, John had a small friend group in high school that mostly consisted of the children who known to be excessively rowdy and unruly. While John maintained friendships with these children, he was identified by teachers as a positive influence on the other children well-liked by his teachers. Often, he would be trusted with taking care of select activities and tasks for teachers. His teachers began to notice John Wayne being unusually short on breath and brought the concern to his mother's attention; John was taken to the hospital for testing where he was diagnosed with a heart condition. The doctor instructed John to cease from any sports or exerting physical activities. This caused John to gain a significant amount of weight leading to him being subsequently made fun of regularly. John Wayne faced further health troubles in fourth grade when he began passing out unexpectedly without reason. After a series of seizures hospitalized him for three weeks, it was found that his blackouts had been the result of a burst appendix and was taken in for emergency surgery to remove it. During these months of seclusion from school, John's grades began to decline and his father threatened to take him out of school completely if he did not raise his scores. Part of the wrath from John's father stemmed from his assumption that John was faking his illness. Though John was clearly ill, doctors were never able to officially diagnose his condition, unable to prove his condition to his father.

John Wayne's life took on new purpose when he turned 18 and began his involvement with the local politics. After attending various meetings, John became the assistant precinct captain for the Democratic candidate who was located in his neighborhood. This did not sit well with his father however, who thought he was being fickle and often called him a "patsy" when he heard of his son's political involvement. Later in his life, John would explain that he made the decision to be politically involved simply in an attempt to receive acceptance from someone in his life. John's father made an unexpected gesture of kindness while John was growing in his political career—he bought John a car. John was dumbfounded at his father's kindness until his father revealed that his kind gesture was just another formality; John was forced to repay his father for the car in monthly payments. When John and his father would have arguments he would take the keys away as punishment. Playing along, John Wayne made a second set of car keys that he hid from his father. However, it wasn't long until John's father soon found out and began taking key components of the car's operation away. After his father placed the car parts back in his car, John ran away from home, taking the car and driving all night to Las Vegas. In Las Vegas, John began work as an ambulance servicer before switching jobs and working at Palm Mortuary as an attendant. During his tenure as an attendant for the Palm Mortuary, John began to experience odd feelings of attraction to some of the corpses. Because John slept at the morgue, he was given access to the corpses, and during one night, he climbed into the coffin of a deceased male and began fondling and caressing the corpse. After a short while, John came to the realization of what he was doing and jumped out of the coffin in a fit of shock and embarrassment. This incidence troubled John and he decided to return home to Chicago immediately. Even though John had never completed his high school education, he was able to enroll in the Northwestern Business College and began seeking a degree in management. After graduating in 1963, John began working as a trainee in the Nunn-Bush Shoe Company where he was transferred to Springfield, Illinois and became a salesman. He succeeded within his job and was rewarded with a promotion as manager. While employed at the department store, John began dating Marlynn Myers, and later in 1964 the two had married. Marlynn came from a business-oriented family; with her father purchasing three Kentucky Fried Chicken restaurants shortly after the couple was married. With his new son-in-law a promising management intern, John's father-in-law placed him in control of the Waterloo Iowa branches of Kentucky Fried Chicken and gave John his old house in Waterloo.

John's political affiliation had led him to join the politically-centric organization known as the Jaycees. This group was a body of people who sought to change the leadership of their cities through political activism. John became very active in the organization and accepted by the Jaycee members. Rising in leadership, John was made Key Man in April 1964, being noted as being the most influential Jaycee at the time. While the Jaycees were fiercely political, there were numerous rebellions formulated from the group. The group provided John with more homosexual activity as well, with many homosexuals belonging to the group. Shortly before his move to Waterloo, John was named vice-president of the group and continued to show his dominance.

In Waterloo, John began leading the three Kentucky Fried Chicken restaurants to success and was compensated quite nicely for his efforts, being paid $115,274 annually. A new chapter of Jaycees began to rise in Waterloo and John once again became actively involved.

Despite his rigorous schedule of working 12-14 hours each day, John attended the chapter's daily meetings and was always willing to help out when needed. This chapter of Jaycees soon began to follow John just as much as his previous chapter had, though many of them noted he was quite braggadocios. Only one year after joining, John was named vice-vice-president and was on his way to achieving the highest position available within the chapter. John spiced up his meetings by bringing complimentary chicken and was often called "Colonel" for his actions. In 1966, John was proud to watch his wife bring his first child, a son, into the world. Michael Gacy was born in February and he was everything John had wanted. John would often recall these moments as being the most perfect moments he had experienced in his life. Only one year later, John and his wife Marlynn gave birth to another child, a daughter this time, named Christine. They then received an unexpected visit from John's father and mother where his father took time to apologize for his horrible actions throughout John's childhood. In the apology, his father noted, "Son, I was wrong about you. You have made me so proud and I wish I could change the things I said and did to you." Despite the perceived sincerity in his father's voice, John could not bring himself to forgive his father for how he had blamed and criticized John when he was young.

The Jaycee's were known for their political activism, but additional attributes that were not as comely also accompanied the name; Pornography, prostitution, and wife swapping were among the grosser of the actions most Jaycees were involved in. Despite later noting that he had struggled with homosexual tendencies, John was a regular user of prostitutes and was known to cheat on his wife often. One year after joining the Jaycees of Waterloo, John created a nightclub in his basement where he allowed Jaycees to roam and do as they please. This nightclub soon transitioned into a full-fledged nightclub that employed local teens. It was noted during this time that John relatively ignored his female employees and only conversed with the male employees. John was known to have made sexual offers to his male employees, all of whom turned him down. John swore that he was simply testing their loyalty to the restaurant. However, the truth was that John was experiencing strong sexual urges towards his male co-workers and was pursuing his homosexual instincts. In August of the same year, John coupled his life as a homosexual with his life as a criminal, committing the first of many sexual assaults. The first victim was Donald Voorhees, a fifteen year old who was the son of one of John's closest friend in the Jaycees. In committing the act, John told Voorhees that he had a phenomenal pornographic film collection that he would be willing to share with him if he came to his house. Once at John's house, John served Voorhees large amounts of alcohol and then forced Voorhees to perform oral sex on him.

Throughout the next few months, John's homosexual urges would compel him to assault many more boys while also causing him to sacrifice many of his own things simply for the thrill of oral sex. In one scenario, John connived one of his male employees to have sex with John's wife, telling him that he wanted the youth to experience the same thrills he had during sex with his wife. After the boy accepted John's offer, John then forced the boy to perform oral sex on him, and if he refused, he would tell the boy's father of "his treasonous deed." Another method John used in his thirst for the homosexual experience involved convincing his neighbor's sons that he was a doctor investigating the homosexual experience. Telling the neighbors he needed to experience oral sex with a man in order to complete his experiment, John paid each of the boys $50 for their "contribution" to his experiment, when in reality, they were simply appeasing his addiction. One year after being assaulted, Voorhees went to his father and told him of the time John had sexually assaulted him. Voorhees' father was enraged at these actions and had John arrested immediately. John was charged with oral sodomy, a charge he subsequently denied. Per his request, John took a polygraph test and passed, though police officers did perceive that he was quite nervous throughout the test. John declared that Voorhees Sr. was making up this entire ruse in an effort to remove John from the Jaycees, increasing his chances of the position atop the Jaycees. Despite his maintaining that he was innocent, investigators believed otherwise and John was charged with sodomy on August 30, 1968. Following his charge, John was given a psychiatric evaluation that outlined his ability to have an alibi for almost every situation he was accused of. However, the alibis would soon run out leaving John with the grim realization that he was facing a long stay in jail.

Shortly after being charged with oral sodomy, John fashioned a plan to remove the key witness, Donald Voorhees, from trial. John convinced Russell Schroeder, a close friend of Voorhees, to persuade Voorhees to not testify at the trial. Schroeder agreed to help with the promise of $300 and convinced Voorhees to follow him to a secluded portion of a park. Once out of sight, Schroeder sprayed Voorhees in the face with a can of mace before repeatedly punching and kicking him. Shortly before Voorhees was near unconsciousness, Schroeder commanded him not to testify at the trial if he wanted to stay alive. Schroeder walked away and Voorhees ran back to his house where he told his father of the occurrences. Voorhees' father called the police and Russell Schroeder was immediately arrested where he spoke of John's request for him to assault Voorhees. John was charged with obstruction to justice and impeding a witness and was ordered to undergo specific psychiatric testing. During this time, doctors came to realize that John was suffering from an antisocial personality disorder but was sane enough to undergo the trial. John's days behind bars were about to begin.

John's attorney was convinced there was no way he could win against the strong testimony of several witnesses. Therefore, John pled guilty to the one count of oral sodomy but pled not guilty to the other charges that stemmed from various youth around the Waterloo area. Despite pleading guilty, John tried to convince the court that he was coerced into the sexual relation by Voorhees. The jury failed to empathize with his story and John was convicted of sodomy, sent to spend the next ten years in the Anamosa State Penitentiary. John's wife was beside herself with the conviction and filed for divorce the following day. While John was scheduled to be in prison for the next ten years, Marlynn was filing for the home, property, alimony payments, and sole custody of their two children. The courts sided with his wife and John would go the rest of his life without seeing his children or wife again.

While an inmate at the prison, John's influence began to ripple throughout the prison and he developed himself a following. Prisoners began to look up to John and the staff recognized him as being obedient and willing to go the extra mile, just like his teachers in school. In regards to this, John was given a leadership role in the prison, being made head cook with employees under his supervision. Additionally, the inmates of the prison had begun a Jaycee chapter and with John joining the chapter, their membership increased from 50 to over 650 members in just the few months he was incarcerated. Throughout the first year of his tenure, John continued to grow in rank and popularity throughout the prison. One endearing factor was his ability to convince the administration of the police station that a pay raise was necessary. A few months after his petition to raise the wages, each prisoner was granted a raise in their pay, an action credited to the persistence and reputation of John. One year after entering the prison, John asked for an early release, citing his good behavior as a substantial reason for early release; the prison did not accept his proposal. However, the Board of Parole for the state of Iowa did give John hope that if he completed a select number of high school courses, he might be eligible for early release. After completing 16 high school courses, John was awarded his diploma in 1969. Only one month later, John learned that his father had succumbed to cirrhosis of the liver and had passed away. When told the news, John collapsed to the floor and began sobbing hysterically. Despite this show of affection towards his father, the prison administration still denied three subsequent requests from John to attend his father's funeral.

The following year, John was rewarded for his good behavior with parole and twelve-month probation. However, John was only released on the warrant that he had to live with his mother and forced to remain in the house after 10 PM every night. John had been fired from his job at Kentucky Fried Chicken and could not afford to live in his house, leaving him with no option other than staying with his mother. In plans to right his life again, John obtained a job as a short-order cook and was soon experiencing his homosexual urges again. Back in the public's eye, John was a new man – more business-minded and maintaining a guise of professionalism, the wrongs of his past were pushed aside, and people were eager to accept him once again, namely those in his Jaycee chapter. Unfortunately, John's reprieve from the law lasted a short while however, with a young man claiming John sexually assaulted him while at a bus stop in Chicago. John Wayne was given the benefit of the doubt when the young man who claimed he was assaulted did not show up for his court date. Even though John may not have committed this act, he did break violate his parole when he did not reveal the situation to his parole officer. Lucky for John, the parole board would never hear of either offense and John's probation period ended a few months later. John Wayne was relieved to know his criminal record would be sealed and in the past. Little did he know that his future was far more horrifying than his past was.

After coercing his mother into purchasing a house for him, John moved into a house located in the Northwood Park Township, shortly outside of Cook County. John's mother moved into the house with him. Eventually, John began dating another woman, Carole Hoff. John knew Carole from high school and had even dated her while in school. After dating for a short while, John and Carole became engaged and Carole moved in with John and his mother. Nevertheless, John's sexual fantasies with men continued to haunt him. One week before John and Carole were to be wed, John was arrested and taken in for questioning regarding an accusation that stated John had forced yet another young man to perform oral sex on him. John was free of these charges when it was found that the young man was attempting to collect money from John in an offer to drop the charges. With the charges dropped, John and Carole married and John moved out of his mother's house into Carole's house. Returning to his businessman ways, John established the company PDM Contractors. Sadly, this business would be where many of John's sexual fantasies turned into murders. PDM Contractors became very successful, and by 1978 the company was grossing $200,000 a year. Ultimately, John admitted to Carole that he had become sexually active with men and was uninterested in having sex with her any more. By 1976, John was regularly dating several other men, a habit Carole found most distasteful. With the very premise of marriage destroyed, Carole divorced John in March and the two would never see each other again.

John's demeanor changed following the divorce. As it appeared, the only factor holding him back from his life of crime had been his wife, and without her, he felt as if he had nothing. In January of 1972, John committed his first known murder; stabbing Timothy McCoy numerous times after letting the boy spend the evening with him. The murder had been accidental but John recounts undergoing a thrill as he stabbed the youth. "That's when I realized that death was the ultimate thrill," collectively reveals John's consumption as his life as a murderer. Two years later, John would kill a man who would never be identified. The man was found in the barbecue pit of John's backyard but was so decomposed that identification was futile. John's sexual activity with males began to increase, a habit he began referring to as "cruising." From 1976 to 1978, John killed almost 90% of his 33 victims. The first victim during these years would be 18-year-old Darrell Sampson, a student at Senn High School. John coerced Darrell into entering his car where John rendered him unconscious with a strangulation device before killing him. Shortly after, John killed Randall Reffett, another boy from the same school as Darrell. Both boys were buried under the crawlspace of John's home, the final resting place for most of his victims. Only two hours after killing Reffett, John abducted and murdered Samuel Stapleton, also burying him in his crawlspace. For John, the thrill of murder was unsurpassable, going beyond the thrill of sex with countless males.

One month after his triple killing, John killed Michael Bonnin, a 17-year-old from nearby Lakeview. Just ten days later, John also killed a 16-year-old from Uptown named William Carroll. These two males were buried in a shallow grave behind John's house. Between June and July, John would kill four males who would never be identified but would be buried on top of each other also behind John's house. In July of 1976, John entered a sexual relationship with one of his workers, David Cram. David was 18-years-old and regularly drank with John. During a night of drinking, John handcuffed David's hands and told him he was going to rape him. David was able to escape from the handcuffs quickly and ran out of the house. Later, David returned to gather his belongings and left John's house for good. However, his bedroom would not be vacated for long, as another one of John's employees, Michael Rossi would soon move in.

In the next two months, John killed another two men who would never be identified. These males were buried atop the bodies of the other murder victims John had buried earlier in 1976. Ten days following, John abducted two friends, Kenneth Parker and Michael Marino before killing them both. A few hours later, John strangled and killed one of his employees, William Bundy, before burying all three victims in his crawl space. The control John had over his victims in the murders seemed to provide John with a new source of fulfillment. John's first victim in 1976 was a 17-year-old named Gregory Gozdik. On his way home after dropping his girlfriend off for the evening, Gregory was suddenly attacked and killed by John. Before the attack, Gozdik had informed his parents that John was having him dig under the crawl space in his house so that he could install a drainage pattern. The Gozdik family insisted John be investigated following Gregory's murder, but police refused to open any investigation given John's reputation in the community and lack of evidence.

One month following John's killing of Gozdik, John killed 19 year old John Szyc whom he buried directly atop Gozdik in his crawl space. Additionally, John added to his mounting murder charge with the murder of an unidentified man police think to have been aged at 25. This murder would be followed by the murder of another young lad whom police would also struggle identifying. These bodies were found buried in John's crawl space but would never be identified or connected with any other murder. In April of 1977, John murdered his next victim, a young man from Crystal Lake named Matthew Bowman. When burying Matthew, John left the strangulation device attached to his neck, a mistake police would use to incriminate him when they uncovered the numerous bodies. Police grew more suspicious of John when the car belonging to John Szyc was found being used by Michael Rossi, who was still living with John. However, the police tabled the matter when John informed them Szyc had sold him the car shortly before leaving for Las Vegas. In the next month, John would kill six more men, all under the age of 21. The first of these men would be Robert Gilroy. This youth was found in John's crawlspace and was the apparent victim of strangulation. The second victim was John Mowery, a former US Marine who had held no previous connection to John. Russell Nelson, a 21-year-old, the third murder victim during this time was found dead near the bodies of the previous two victims. The fourth victim was Robert Winch, a 16-year-old from Kalamazoo, Michigan. This boy was suffocated before being disposed of in the crawl space with the others. Tommy Boling would be the fifth victim. He had just become the father of a baby girl shortly before being killed by John. The final victim from this string of six would be David Talsma, another U.S. Marine who was possibly lured into the home of John by the influence of John Mowery before he was murdered.

John's next victim was not assassinated as quickly as his previous victims, being tortured for several hours before being killed. The victim, Robert Donnelly, once even begged John to "get it over with." "I'm getting around to it," was John's insensitive response. Lastly, William Kindred would be the last victim John would stow under in his crawl space; The next set of victims would all be dumped into the Des Plaines River. The first victim to be dumped into the river was Tim O'Rourke who John killed in June of 1978. The next two victims, Frank Landingin and James Mazzara, would both be the last victims of John, as he was about to make a crucial mistake. Following these murders, John abducted Jeffrey Ringall and raped him before dumping him, alive. Though Jeffrey had been under severe trauma, he was able to identify John's car to the police and John was arrested on charges of sodomy. A subsequent search of John's home revealed the numerous bodies and John was charged with 33 counts of murder. Following a missing person's case, the police were able to supply ample evidence to the courts and John confessed to the murders following a short stint of house arrest. Finally, on December 22, 1978, John confessed to the murders of 33 men and was placed in jail. After a lengthy trial, John was found guilty of the murders and committed to execution on June 2, 1980. Through efforts to save his life, John's execution was substantially delayed, until May 9, 1994 when John Wayne Gacy Jr. was killed by lethal injection at the Statesville Correctional Center. The infamous life of horror and tragedy had come to an end and justice was restored to the families of his victims.

Ted Kaczynski

Throughout history, countless men have carried their cross and pledged their life to changing the status quo or challenging the rising belief. Many have died for this while many have lived to see the changes brought into place. Regardless of their destiny, the common ground all these men share is that they fought for what they believed in. While many would think of men such as Thomas Jefferson or Nathan Hale when considering those who have died for their beliefs, other men have died for their causes, though these causes were the opposite of these patriarchs; the plans of these men held a devious nature and were consumed with the selfish greed of having a world the way they wanted it. Among these men was Ted Kaczynski, a man of Polish descent who used violence and murder as a means of unveiling his discontentment in the world with those closest to him. When looking at the differences between the patriarchs and Ted, the market difference is that while the patriarchs acted out of a necessity for the betterment of mankind, Ted acted out of pure selfishness in his perceived injustice in America. The life of Ted Kaczynski offers an example to mankind of what happens when society becomes centered on the issues of personal opinion instead of the greater good for society. Through servanthood and true compassion, the world can avoid the trap Ted fell into, a trap that ultimately led to the death of many while changing countless lives for the worse.

Ted Kaczynski was born to Theodore Kaczynski and Wanda Theresa on May 22, 1942, in a suburb outside of growing Chicago, Illinois. Ted had shown all the signs of being a normal child until in 1942 when he experienced a particularly ravaging outbreak of hives at only nine months old. With this condition, Ted was not allowed to have contact with anyone for the next two months. After this, Ted appeared to show no reaction to seeing anyone in his life, a trait doctors blame on him not able to be held for the many months he was isolated with hives. Despite showing no reaction to lack of human interaction, Ted did have a sympathetic side, often showing animals affection and care. Additionally, Ted disliked seeing animals behind fences or in any way inhibited from living freely. This trait was also attributed to his extended stay in the hospital as a young child.

Ted began his childhood just as any child would, entering first grade when he was eight years. Ted's first four years of schooling were spent at Sherman Elementary School, nestled in the heart of the growing populous of Chicago. The teachers at this school regarded Ted as being a child with normal desires but accelerated learning skills and comprehension. After Ted turned ten, his family moved away from Chicago and into the smaller city of Evergreen Park, Illinois. In Evergreen Park, Ted was enrolled in the school district of Evergreen Park Central School where his teachers once again noted his learning ability. His learning had amplified so much that his teachers requested that he skip sixth grade, a decision corroborated by the board of education once they saw his robust learning capacity. At the young age of 11, Ted took an IQ test and scored a 167. Investigators would later look at this and point at his unbelievable intelligence, no doubt the foundation for his future bomb-manufacturing skills. While living in Evergreen Park, Ted maintained good relationships with those who lived around him, leading to their describing him as a "civic-minded child." Additionally, the neighbors of Ted and his family often recalled that Ted's parents were willing to do anything for their children and sought to make their childhood as full as it could be. While Ted's skipping a grade was beneficial to his quest for graduating young, it did lead to him being ostracized as a young child. The children in 7th grade noted his younger age and never included him in their plans, often bullying him and making him perform mundane tasks. While the teachers saw that Ted continued to grow in his intelligence, they did also note that Ted appeared to be sinking deeper into a sort of depression, always keeping to himself and refusing to socialize with other people. Ted's mother also observed his sullen expressions and briefly considered admitting him to a school that aided autistic children. However, the instructor was an unruly individual who seemed too rude for Ted's mother to admit him.

Ted's life took a dramatic turn in 1990 when his father was found dead in the family home, the victim of a self-inflicted gunshot wound. Ted's father had been battling terminal cancer for a long time and rather than allow his family to watch him slip into the ill-effects of life-long cancer, Ted's father decided to end his life prematurely. Ted was devastated by his father's death and vowed to begin living a healthier lifestyle to ward off any chance of getting cancer. During his father's last days on earth, Ted had noticed that his father was increasingly interested in spending time with the family, a sad reminder to Ted that life on this earth was short. Family and friends note that following his father's death, Ted became a new man. No longer interested in the comedic side of life, Ted began to take his education to the next level. He began playing instruments while also leading several clubs on campus. However, even through all this exposure to different facets of society, Ted continued to keep to himself, friends stating that, "He was never really seen as a person, as an individual personality. He was always regarded as a walking brain, so to speak." Additionally, one of Ted's classmates remembered him as being "the smartest kid in the class...just quiet and shy until you got to know him. Once he knew you, he could talk and talk." Ted continued to learn and excel far beyond his classmates, skipping the eleventh grade entirely. Upon his graduation at the age of 15, Ted applied for and was accepted to Harvard. Friends close to the situation recognized that Ted did not want to attend Harvard at such a young age. "They packed him up and sent him to Harvard before he was ready," the friend remembered. "He didn't even have a driver's license." While this would not be any excuse for his future actions, Ted's admittance to Harvard at such a young age appeared to mature him before he was ready, an action that would be irrevocable.

Once at Harvard, Ted moved into his student housing on Prescott

Street, which was housing notorious for being designed solely for the young students at the school. Ted would remain at this house for three years, though during this time, his focus was completely on academics without leading a social life. Often, Ted's suite-mates recalled him running through the social quarters of their living arrangements and retreating to his room for the evening. After three years, Ted graduated from Harvard and was awarded a Bachelor of Arts while achieving a 3.12 GPA. Ted's days at Harvard were not days of joy, however. In accordance with Ted's drive to do as much and be a part of as much as possible, Ted allowed himself to be subjected to a study in which he was "purposely brutalized by a psychological experiment." The experiment entailed Ted composing several essays which contained the very crux of what he believed. These essays were then handed to a professor who would read them and challenge every point of the essay. Often, the contributors of the essays were belittled and told how worthless their opinions were. This experiment took the entirety of Ted's stay at the college and left him helpless and humiliated. At the conclusion of the study, Ted had spent almost 200 hours being harassed and manipulated by attorneys across the breadth of the study. While not as evident at the time, this harassment was directly linked to the hostility he would one day exhibit towards mankind. The study was never made public, but many people have asserted that this study was actually operated by the CIA and was designed to see how much the human mind could be manipulated. While this was never proven, Murray was in direct contact with the government leaving little room for doubt. Philosopher Jon Moreno believes that while the experiment did not alleviate pressure being experienced by Ted, the experiment could not be the sole cause for the rampage Ted would lead later in his life.

After graduating with his bachelors, Ted went on to work for the University of Michigan where he was employed as a teacher and was able to simultaneously achieve his master's and doctoral degrees in the field of mathematics. Ted had previously applied at the University of California and the University of California, Berkeley and had been accepted for the master's programs but there was no teaching position available. Ted was not thrilled about his opportunity to teach at the University of Michigan but was constrained by a lack of financial income and was therefore obligated to accept the deal. For his teaching position, Ted was compensated $2,310 a year. While at the University of Michigan, Ted was able to extensively study complex analysis while narrowing in on geometric function theory. Ted's hard work and foundation in ethics had not been affected by the strenuous activities of his experiment, thus impressing his peers and professors extensively. Peter Duren, one of his teachers, explained that "He was an unusual person. He was not like the other graduate students. He was much more focused about his work. He had a drive to discover mathematical truth." Another classmate noted, "It is not enough to say he was smart." While Ted was achieving high marks both in his classes and with his teachers socioculturally, he was grossly unimpressed with the "low standard" of education he was receiving. When congratulated for his success in achieving 5 B's and 12 A's through the course of his 18 classes at the University of Michigan, Ted chastised the school stating, "My memories of the University of Michigan are NOT pleasant. The fact that I not only passed my courses but got quite a few As shows how wretchedly low the standards were at Michigan." While discontent, Ted continued to achieve great respect from his peers and teachers, with many considering him to be among the smartest students on the campus.

Ted wrote a dissertation in 1967 as part of the requirements for his completion of a doctoral degree, a dissertation he entitled "Boundary Functions." The dissertation was a tremendous work and was awarded the Sumner B. Myers Prize for its prestige and flawlessness. One member on the board of education at the University of Michigan noted that is was among the greatest dissertations that he had ever read. Maxwell Rhoades, one of the men who was tasked with approving the dissertation, proclaimed, "I would guess that maybe 10 or 12 men in the country understood or appreciated it." To award him for his tremendous work, Ted was granted a position as assistant professor at the University of California, Berkeley. Ted, at the age of 25 had already achieved his doctoral and was the youngest assistant professor ever at the University of California, Berkeley. The board of directors at the university knew of the tremendous genius they were housing and was interested in maintaining his employment as long as they could. Although Ted was a genius, he was extremely inadequate in teaching his students, often dismissing questions he considered "simple" while refusing to answer any other questions saying that students should do as he did and teach themselves. Finally, after a particularly rough bout of student evaluations, Ted abruptly resigned from his teaching position and left the University California, Berkeley on June 30, 1969. J.W. Addison, the chairman of the mathematics department, declared that Ted's resignation was "sudden and unexpected." Ted had been known among numerous mathematics departments worldwide, with the vice chairman of the University of California, Berkeley, asserting that Ted "...could have advanced up the ranks and been a senior member of the faculty today." Ted had made numerous developments within the mathematics field and though his departure was premature, left the mathematics field for the better with his presence.

Ted's life seemed to plummet after his departure from the university. During his last days at the university, Ted had become obsessed with the possibility of living a life that could withstand a worldwide foot shortage. To achieve this, Ted began making plans to live in the wilderness and "live off the land." Ted's resignation gave him his first chance at this, with his departure granting him the freedom he had so long wished for. To make better plans for this preparation, Ted moved to his parent's house in Lombard, Illinois. Two years later, he was ready for the transition and began moving into a small cabin he had spent months building in Lincoln, Montana. This cabin was primitive in nature, housing no running water or electricity and thus offering Ted the life of simplicity and fortitude he had been longing for. To make money for these first few months, Ted performed odd jobs around the Lincoln area while also getting a monthly stipend from his parents. During his first months, Ted busied himself with learning the surrounding area of his cabin. An apt learner, Ted self-taught himself various survival skills that included hunting and tracking animals without the use of modern weaponry, being able to correctly assess plants that were edible and plants that were not, while also being able to start a fire using only a few sticks. To travel throughout the area, Ted stole a bicycle from the nearest town and used it to transport himself to and from the city. To Ted's advantage, the area he was located in was not un-accustomed to the behavior exhibited by Ted. Often, people lived such lifestyles leaving Ted relatively unnoticed by the locals. However, Ted's intent to live a primitive lifestyle took a hit when he came to the realization that a life of living autonomously was impossible due to the numerous deforestation efforts being carried out by the local government. The local government had become infatuated with the numerous sources of income, should they allow new efforts for real estate to be carried out. With his original plan ruined, Ted began his efforts at sabotaging the local efforts at real estate.

As Ted began his sabotage, his life as a local terrorist had begun. Ted began paying nighttime visits to the various real estate developments near his cabin and destroying portions of them. He began reading various books on sociology and political philosophy. Ted's view on nature had always been a position of conservation, and during his life in the cabin, he fell more in love with the nature that surrounded him. For Ted, nature was his family and seeing the elements of nature destroyed was as difficult as watching a loved family member pass away. Ted retells the story of one time when he found his beloved nature destroyed and altered: "It's kind of rolling country, not flat, and when you get to the edge of it you find these ravines that cut very steeply in to cliff-like drop-offs and there was even a waterfall there. It was about a two days' hike from my cabin. That was the best spot until the summer of 1983," recalls Ted. "That summer there were too many people around my cabin, so I decided I needed some peace. I went back to the plateau and when I got there I found they had put a road right through the middle of it ... You just can't imagine how upset I was. It was from that point on I decided that, rather than trying to acquire further wilderness skills, I would work on getting back at the system. Revenge." Ted's drive for revenge had begun with the perceived injustice of development and his campaign against those development companies until they ceased.

In Ted's eyes, the humans near his house were focusing on developing their city through the "path of least resistance." Meaning that these people could develop their land through more complex routines that would leave the nature unharmed, but instead chose to destroy nature and develop their companies there because they were unwilling to work harder. Ted also mentioned that his frustration had worsened due to his fear of losing the property. In relation to his frustration, Ted explained, "To create a situation where people get uncomfortable enough that they're going to rebel. So, the question is, how do you increase those tensions?" In Ted's mindset, he was the one who had been instigated and that he now must follow with his own retaliation, through whatever means necessary, to show mankind his anger at their carelessness. While various methods were considered in an effort to get his point across, Ted went with a method that would get his message across very clearly, and painfully. Ted chose the violent route and decided his only method would be to inflict pain on mankind. Thus, in 1978, Ted began his seventeen-yearlong bombing spree that would leave many injured and some dead.

To begin his spree of violence that he hoped would channel his message, Ted created a bomb and mailed it to Buckley Crist, one of the prominent engineering teachers at the Northwestern University. Seeking to misguide Crist into opening the box in which he had laid the bomb, Ted sent the box as a "return to sender" box, hoping Crist would assume he had mailed a package that was undeliverable. However, When Crist was notified of the package bearing his return address at the university's post office, he was immediately alarmed, certain he had sent no such package at any time to anyone. Campus security was called immediately and upon discovery, proceeded to open the package which exploded, causing burns and shrapnel injuries to Officer Terry Marker, the security guard who opened the package. As the police began their investigation of the bomb, they noticed the primitive way it had been constructed. While other pipe bombs of the time were quite sophisticated in their makeup, this bomb had been fashioned of common elements and was not professional in its appearance. The bomb consisted of a simple pipe bomb that was connected with wooden plugs. Upon closer inspection, the police found that the bomb could have been substantially greater had Ted used a threaded pipe fitting on the end of the pipe rather than the wooden plugs he had fashioned himself. The wooden plugs compromised more quickly than fitted pipes would have, destroying the chances for a major blast from the pipe bomb. None-the-less, Terry Marker was injured in the explosion and police were wondering if they had a mischievous prankster on their hands or if they were seeing the beginning of a serial bomber. As police continued their inspection, they found that Ted fashioned the trigger through simple geometry, with rubber bands holding the nail taught before drawing the nail over six match heads quickly, thus igniting the flame which would subsequently ignite the powder. As police continued to surmise the character of the individual responsible for this action, they concluded that they were the witnesses of a very smart man who was using primitive means as a way to disguise who he truly was.

After his first bombing, Ted left his wooded cabin to return to Chicago where he resided with his parents once again. While in Chicago, Ted and his brother joined their father at work in a foam rubber factory. With his brother as his supervisor, Ted was free to work as hard or as little as he wanted without risk of being fired. However, Ted's brother drew the line when Ted was found to be writing degrading poems about one of his supervisor on the walls of the establishment. It would later be discovered that Ted and this supervisor, a woman, had been romantically involved for a short period before she left him, citing his unpredictable nature as a red flag. When asked about this apparent stint of dating Ted, the female recalled that Ted did indeed work for her and was "intelligent yet quiet," but refused to admit that she and Ted had dated. After being fired, Ted left Chicago and returned to his remote cabin once again with anger and frustration boiling from his emotions. Back in the woods with his cabin, Ted was met with the urbanization of the land he had so long known. Where groves and forests once stood, now stood buildings and residential areas. Ted's anger was ignited even further, and he began creating another bomb that he hoped would vent his frustration. The bomb was modeled loosely after his original bomb but would be detonated by a timing mechanism this time rather than a trigger. Ted stowed the bomb in the storage area of an American Airlines flight that was leaving Chicago on its way to Washington D.C. With his bomb safely aboard the plane, Ted returned to his parents' home once again to await the news of his mass destruction. However, that news would thankfully never come. Ted had made an apparent mistake causing the timing mechanism to fail. The bomb would never explode but smoke would begin emanating from the bomb, causing the pilots to enact an emergency landing. Upon landing, the bomb was discovered by the police and taken to the station for examination. At the station, the police were able to detonate the bomb and realized how powerful of a bomb they had removed. "Had this bomb succeeded, it would have obliterated the plane" were the exact words of one of the detectives who examined the bomb. While the first bomb had been investigated solely by local and state police, the aircraft bomb was enough to attract the attention of the FBI who became actively involved after hearing of the damage this bomb might have incurred. While Ted's bomb had been a failure, this attack did render the assassin one new feature: his own nickname. Following the event, the police and media began referring to Ted as the UNABOMBER, short for University and Aircraft Bomber.

One of the features of Ted's bombs that made them specifically unique was the trail of false clues that Ted would leave inside every bomb. Ted, a meticulous man, left virtually no accidental clues in his bombs, but did leave a myriad of purposeful clues that were designed to throw the authors off the trail. In his first bomb, Ted attempted to throw authorities off his trail by stamping his pipe bomb "FC." Within the aircraft bomb, Ted stapled a note that read "Wu—it works! I told you it would—RV." Such clues were picked up by authorities and deemed as true clues but would never lead to anything significant, other than Ted becoming quite amused as authorities played into his hand and chased the clues innocently. For the time being, Ted was playing the authorities and was leading the entire investigation himself.

Between 1978 and 1982, Ted sent a total of seven bombs to various locations around the nation. In total, five of the bombs actually detonated but none of the bombs were considered serious, with the most severe injuries only being minor cuts and bruises from the shrapnel. The majority of these locations were universities and colleges where Ted found most of the destruction to be coming from. In 1985, Ted detonated his first bomb that authorities considered of lethal power. John Hauser was a graduate student within the United States Air Force and was currently on active duty when the mysterious box arrived at his office. Rather than call the bomb squad or security, Hauser proceeded to open the box that had been sent to him from Ted. The bomb detonated upon opening and destroyed most of Hauser's hand, causing loss of vision in one eye and the complete loss of four fingers. As the authorities continued their investigation, they found that the bomb had been made similar to the other bombs that they considered the work of the UNABOMBER. Shortly after Hauser was wounded, Ted detonated his first deadly bomb. Hugh Scrutton, owner and operator of his own computer store, was investigating a suspicious package left in his parking lot when it exploded and killed him. Ted, once a vandal in the cause of liberty, was now a murderer and the most wanted man in the United States.

For two years, the bombings ceased but came back with a vengeance when Gary Wright was seriously injured after a bomb bearing the appearance of a piece of lumber was detonated after Wright attempted moving it. Authorities awaited another bombing, but for six years, nothing happened. Some surmised that the UNABOMBER was dead. However, just as authorities were growing convinced that their vigilance had paid off, Ted appeared again, this time detonating two bombs within two days at separate universities. The first was at Yale University where David Galernter was severely injured but survived. The second occurred two days later when

Charles Epstein at the University of California in San Francisco lost three fingers when the bomb exploded from within the package he was opening. Authorities were dejected and quite discouraged after the succession of these two bombings. What had appeared to be finished was suddenly re-ignited and with no further clues.

For the years 1994-1995, Ted focused on sending lethal bombs to two high figure individuals who he considered personal enemies of his success. The first was Thomas J. Mosser of the organization Burson-Marsteller. Ted had targeted this man because he apparently aided Exxon in their Exxon-Valdez catastrophe. The second individual was Gilbert Brent Murray, who was the current president of the California Forestry Association, the association largely responsible for the loss of Ted's beloved woods. With both of these men killed immediately upon detonation of the bombs, authorities were growing worried of the future bombings this UNABOMBER would incite. Ted's confidence was growing but this same confidence would lead to his demise one day.

After his third deadly killing, Ted mailed a copy of a personal essay he had written titled, "Industrial Society and its Future," to many major media outlets. These essays were accompanied by the promise that there would be severe bombings if the essay was not published in the papers. Several media outlets took Ted's promise and published the article in their paper. The FBI also subsequently tacked a one-million-dollar reward onto the publication for anyone aiding in the capture and arrest of this man. Around this time, Ted's brother David was alerted by his wife to the possibility that Ted could be this UNABOMBER. At first, David refused to believe it, but as he read the publication, he came to realization that the grammatical word flow of the paper followed the same word flow of previous works of Ted. With this in mind, David hired a personal investigator to follow his brother closely while also hiring the services of attorney Tony Bisceglie as his contract with the FBI. In 1996, Bisceglie sent a copy of Ted's dissertation from UC Berkeley, provided by David, to the FBI. As the FBI compared the essay with the dissertation, they came to the realization that the same man had authored both works. After the head of the investigation, Terry Turchie was alerted to the high probability that the FBI had found their suspect, he signed a search warrant for the cabin of Ted. David led authorities to Ted's cabin where authorities prepared to swarm the cabin. Fearing a fire fight with potential explosives would ensue, the FBI took every precaution in surrounding the cabin. However, Ted surrendered without incident and authorities took him into custody on April 3, 1996. After searching the cabin extensively, the FBI found numerous journals that confirmed every bombing Ted had authored. Additionally, the authorities found several components of the bombs that had previously exploded, along with a fully assembled bomb. Regardless of the rumors spreading as to what else Ted Kaczynski might have been involved in, the authorities were confident of one thing: they had found their man and the senseless bombings that had plagued their city would no longer dampen the nation. Shortly after being incarcerated, Ted was indicted on ten counts of illegal activity relating to bombs while also being charged with the murder of the three fatalities. After an extended trial, Ted was convicted of all his charges and sentenced to eight life sentences within the super-max prison located in Florence, Colorado. Despite an initial attempt to commit suicide, Ted has remained an active prisoner in the prison to this day.

Charles Manson

Throughout the history of crime, there have been many a man who worked alone and committed his evil deeds in the privacy of his personal life. However, there were various groups who worked as a team, influenced and inspired by a motivating leader who spurred his followers on to their vicious crimes. One man who used the group variation in his pledge to begin his genocide was Charles Manson.

Leader of the infamous "Manson Family," Charles made his living from organized crime and dreamt of the day when he would rule the world from wherever he desired. In his own imagination, Charles was certain there was an apocalypse on the verge of overtaking the world, and his organized crime would simply lay the precedent for this world-wide attack. Contrary to most of humanity's opinions on the potential of a worldwide siege, much less one at the hands of a fictional character, Charles welcomed the apocalypse with open arms and hoped that his work would not be in vain.

Unfortunately for Charles, justice found his evil actions to be well-beyond the measure of lucidity, and Charles was caught shortly after he started his killing spree. After fighting the court system for as long as he could, Charles faced the judge and was handed multiple life sentences, which he lived out to the age of 83, when cardiac arrest claimed his life.

The life of Charles Manson is a perfect illustration of what happens when one man becomes far too concerned and overcome with achieving world-wide dominance. So overcome, that he's willing to allow his world to be overcome simply for the pleasure of ruling the entire population. A body now resting in the depths of a grave, Charles Manson's legacy lives on; a legacy filled with hatred and death, and certainly no desire for humanity to repeat. In the end, Charles' life will serve no means other than to warn those behind him of the dangers in arrogance and using one's fellow mankind to achieve his sinister plot.

The life of Charles Manson was ushered into the world when he was born in Cincinnati, Ohio to Kathleen Manson-Bower-Cavender, a sixteen year old girl who had been kicked out of her own home and was now living with Colonel Walker Henderson Scott Sr. Scott Sr. was the apparent father of Charles, but Charles would never know this man. Prior to Charles' birth, Kathleen and Scott Sr. had been living together, Scott Sr. dishonestly convincing Kathleen that he actually did serve in the military despite the fact that Colonel was really just his name. Around the city where Kathleen and Scott Sr. resided, his name was was respected due to the fact that his dishonest tendencies went further than his home. Scott Sr. was known as a con artist, and his wife paid the price for this lifestyle. When Kathleen found out that she was pregnant, she told Scott Sr., sure that he would be excited of this new development in their quest to build a family. While Scott Sr. seemed initially excited at this opportunity, he told Kathleen that he had been instructed to return to the military but would be back in a few weeks.

After these "few weeks" turned into a few months, Kathleen realized she had been the latest victim of his dishonest lifestyle and would be left to parent this new child alone. Three months later, Kathleen would give birth to Charles on November 12, 1934, a child who would remain nameless for the first two weeks of his life. With Kathleen unsure of what to name her new son, Charles was referred to as "no name Maddox" for the first two weeks of his life, before Kathleen finally settled on Charles. Shortly after Charles' birth, Kathleen married a new husband, William Eugene Manson, and connived him to adopt Charles as his legal son. Manson worked locally as an employee at a dry cleaning outfit near the Manson residence. Kathleen proved to be an incompetent mother, often going bar-hopping for days at a time in the company of her brother, Luther. During these trips, Charles was bused around to various babysitters until his mother would return from her drinking binges. Charles' childhood was filled with sadness as he was neglected of the cares of a true mother and the absence of a father figure in his life. Unfortunately, Charles' life would become far worse before the year had ended.

After only eight months of marriage, Kathleen was given notice that her husband, William Manson, would be divorcing her. The court battle proved to be short, and soon William and Kathleen were no longer married. This separation proved to be immensely difficult for Kathleen to deal with, resulting in her adopting the life of a criminal. For the next few months, Kathleen would resort to robberies and petty thefts as a means of deriving an income for herself and her grossly neglected son, Charles. This string of petty thefts culminated in the large robbery of Frank Martin, a friend of Kathleen's brother, Luther. The pair had gone to Martin's house for a wine tasting and had immediately noticed the immaculate wealth Frank appeared to be privy to. After calling Luther, the trio attempted to rob Martin but were caught shortly thereafter, leaving a trail of obvious clues from the scene of the crime. For the next seven weeks, Kathleen would be housed in a women's jail cell until standing trial and being sentenced to five years in prison. Her brother, Luther, received ten years in prison. Kathleen's sentence being lighter due to the fact that she had a child who was still underage. For the next five years, Charles would be housed with his uncle and aunt in McMechen, West Virginia where his uncle attempted to give him a foundation to do right and not follow in the paths of his mother and father. Unfortunately, this foundation would prove to break away and Charles would go beyond the lifestyle and crimes of his parents.

In 1942, Charles' mother was paroled from prison, and the two were reunited, a time Charles refers to as being the happiest moment of his life. For the next few weeks, Charles and his mother continued to live in the area until his mother was evicted from her house, and the two were forced to move. Kathleen found work in Charleston, West Virginia, and the two moved to a small apartment in West Virginia shortly thereafter. In Charleston, Kathleen found friends of the same likes that got her placed in jail in the first place and was soon running around and drinking in the same lifestyle she had thought to have left behind. With no mother on the scene, Charles was left to do as he pleased and was soon staying home from school or going to friend's houses during school hours. Kathleen did work during the day but proved to be no match against the will of Charles, and he was left to do whatever he wanted to. Soon, Kathleen was robbing stores again and the subsequent arrest for grand larceny followed her like her past.

After the arrest was made, Kathleen was found not guilty based on lack of evidence. Charles knew his mother could not maintain her current lifestyle in West Virginia, so he convinced her to move with him to Indianapolis, Indiana. Kathleen agreed, and the two were soon boarding a bus that would lead them to a new lifestyle in Indianapolis. After the two arrived, Kathleen found part-time employment and joined the local chapter of Alcoholics Anonymous. During one evening of rehabilitation, Kathleen met Lewis, a man she would begin dating before being married shortly thereafter. Lewis proved to be no father to Charles, and the life Charles had lived in West Virginia soon began to tug on his emotions. Charles succumbed to these desires and was soon stealing from local stores, following the blueprint to the life his mother had led and continued to lead. However, Charles took it a step further and began robbing homes as well, doing all of his work during the day when the tenants would not be home. Kathleen decided she was unable to tend to both her job and Charles, so she began to explore the options of placing Charles in a foster home. After a search that lasted nearly two months, Kathleen found that no foster home was of good enough quality for Charles or, with knowledge of his past, was unwilling to accept Charles. Faced with no other options, Kathleen took Charles to Terre Haute, Indiana where she enrolled her struggling son in the Gibault School for Boys. Unfortunately, this home would have little to no effect on Charles' future or morals.

The Gibault School for Boys was run by Catholic priests who tried their best to influence the young men in their care to change from their devious ways. Most of the boys obeyed. Charles did not. After a few long weeks in the home, Charles fled from the boys' home and returned to his mother. Kathleen was having nothing to do with a runaway son however, and immediately returned him to the boys' home. Back at the boys' home, Charles was given strict punishment for his usurping of the rules and was not allowed to see anyone from off of the campus for the next two months. For Christmas, the boys' home allowed the young men to go to their relatives' home for a few days if they wished to do so. Charles chose his uncle and aunt in McMechen and spent the time there. However, while with his uncle and aunt, Charles attempted to steal a gun from a local hunting store. The attempt was futile, and Charles was taken into the local police station where he was driven back to the boys' home. Charles remained at the boys' home for the following six months but all the while was making plans to run away. His plan came to fruition in early October when he fled from the home and returned to Indianapolis.

In Indianapolis, Charles did not go home to see his mother. Rather, he began living in a small hotel room where he spent the days sleeping and the nights robbing local restaurants and convenience stores. A careless and young thief, the authorities had no trouble finding their suspect, and Charles was soon being enrolled in a new boys home called Boys Town in Omaha, Nebraska. Charles could have been sent to jail, but a local judge had compassion for him once he heard the story of his incompetent and unloving mother. At Boys Town, Charles met another rebellious youth named Blackie Nielson and began making plans to once again leave the boys' home. After securing a car, the duo left the boys' home in the blanket of the night's darkness and fled to Peoria, Illinois. Blackie's uncle was living in Peoria at the time and made his living as a professional and very competent thief. Charles was enthralled with his quick and efficient tactics in robbing a store and begged Blackie's uncle to allow him to "study" under him. Blackie saw the potential a trio of thieves could have, so he immediately began teaching the duo the principles of his trade. The team of thieves was effective for almost two months until Charles made a blundering mistake and was caught during a robbery of a local store. The police began looking at the life of Charles Manson and soon found that he was involved in a previous robbery that involved a casino and gun crime. The casino incident happened when Charles and Blackie had broken out of the boys' home and were in dire need of money. Charles was charged as a minor with theft and was sentenced to serving the remaining days of his childhood at the Indiana Boys School, a rigid and strict juvenile detention center that had been successful and breaking the criminal paths most of its attendees were traversing. This home would do more damage on Charles than construction, however. At the home, Charles was repeatedly raped, two of these coming at what Charles asserted was the encouragement of an officer at the school. Through these multiple times of being raped, Charles was forced to derive a self defense strategy that he referred to as the "insane game." Under this method, Charles would begin screeching aggressively and flailing his arms. By doing this, Charles took on the appearance of being crazy and irrational, thus ending the threat of violence against him. During his few months at the school, Charles would make several attempts at fleeing from the school. However, this reform school was far more secure than his previous schools and his attempts were futile. However, Charles would soon meet some other individuals who, as a team, would be able to circumvent the security of the school and escape.

In 1951, Charles and his two friends from the reform school successfully escaped the school and began making their way to California. The three stole multiple cars and were almost out of Utah when they were suddenly pulled over and taken to the police station for questioning. At the station, they were informed that by driving a stolen vehicle across the state border, they had violated the Dyer Act and were at risk of jail time. The judge decided that jail time would not be helpful in this situation and instead, split the trio of boys into various reform schools across America. Charles would be placed in the National Training School for Boys, located in Washington D.C., the strictest reform school in America. At this school, Charles was forced to take an IQ test where it was found that he was above the national average with a score of 109. However, Charles was completely illiterate. Without the ability to read, Charles' life was severely hampered, and his officers had more mercy on his punishment. Additionally, the officer interviewing Charles found that he was severely antisocial and did not enjoy being around other people. This officer felt that through the correct instruction and care, Charles could be rescued from his life of crime. The state agreed and transferred Charles to the Natural Bridge Honor Camp, a place that would allow him to have unlimited visitors and extended time away from the camp if he behaved well. Shortly after he was settled in the camp, Charles' aunt plead with the government to allow her to take Charles back home, asserting that she would act as his primary guardian and would find him suitable work. The judge agreed to a hearing where he could be better informed about this situation. However, shortly before the trial was to begin, Charles was discovered in a horrible sex crime, one that would leave his aunt heartbroken as she could not take him home. Charles was taken to the Federal Reformatory located in Petersburg, Virginia. While at this school, Charles was continually in contention with his officers, committing "eight serious disciplinary offenses, three involving homosexual acts." Charles had been given an opportunity for redemption, an offer he had squandered and would now pay the penalty for.

Upon discovery of Charles' disobedient stay at the National Training School for Boys, Charles was sent to a reformatory in Chillicothe, Ohio, a reformatory school that was of the utmost security. Charles was supposed to remain at the school until he turned 21, but a change in behavior led to an early release. In May of 1954, Charles left the reform school under good terms with his officers and began living with his uncle and aunt in McMechen, the only family members who were willing to take him in. Charles' life took serious advancements in 1955 when he was married to a woman named Jean

Willis. Previous records do not give any information as to how the two met, but rumor holds that it was while Charles was held in the boys' home. Charles left his uncle and aunt's home and began making his way across the United States to Los Angeles. To do so, Charles stole yet another car and was charged yet again with driving a stolen car across a state border. Charles was promised a shorter sentencing if he succumbed to a psychiatric testing, a deal he took immediately. The nurse who reviewed Charles' case and his psychiatric files recommended that he be given a probation rather than actually serving jail time. The judge agreed and would have accommodated such a request had Charles actually appeared in court. Rather, Charles was at home, refusing to attend court, and was subsequently arrested and returned to the courtroom. In court, the judge revoked his initial sentencing of probation and sentenced Charles to serving three years in prison at Terminal Island in San Pedro, California.

While in prison, Charles' wife, Rosalie, gave birth to a son, Charles Manson Jr. Rosalie subsequently began living with Charles' mother where she was able to help tend with the child. The two also accompanied each other to the prison when making their weekly visits to Charles. Charles was close to finishing his sentencing when he was informed that Rosalie was now living with a different man. Infuriated, Charles attempted to steal a car and escape prison but was caught immediately. Upon his trial, Charles was denied parole and instead given five years of probation. As a sick twist of irony, the same day Charles was sentenced to five years of probation, his wife's divorce letters arrived at the prison. For now, Charles' life had completely changed. While out of jail, Charles was now living a life solely for himself. His dreams of growing a family were demolished and his hopes of returning to a normal life with work had vanished with his previous wife. Rather than deal with his anguish through therapy, Charles would only drive himself deeper into his life of crime. The life of crime with Charles Manson was nearing its fruition.

In September of 1958, Charles began serving his probation. To make money, Charles began acting as a pimp, employing a 16 year old girl as his first "client." To derive additional income, Charles was able to convince his girlfriend to give him additional support from her parents. This girlfriend would go unnamed but was a constant source of financial support for numerous years after the relationship ended. For the next few years, Charles' life would be consumed with numerous periods in jail in addition to living a life of frivolous criminal activity. In 1959, Charles was charged with forging a U.S. Treasury Check and then attempting to cash it. The original check from which Charles drew the fake came from a stolen check, only complicating the matter. At first, the judge was contemplating sentencing Charles to 10 years in prison. However, Charles' sentencing was delayed when a young woman named Leona began crying in front of the judge, begging for her "boyfriend's" life. Upon further notice, this girlfriend was not the source of the financial income. The judge listened to her plea and allowed Charles to walk away simply because Charles and the girl were "deeply in love and would marry if Charlie were freed." The two would go on to be married, most likely out of an effort to go uncharged since the courts would then be futile in seeking Leona as a witness to testify against Charles.

Following the trial, Charles and Leona were accompanied by another girl, most likely the one supplying Charles with large amounts of cash, as the group began making their way to New Mexico. Charles was anything but dedicated to any of his relationships and actually convinced his own wife, Leona, to undertake the role of a prostitute to derive more cash for him. Federal investigators caught up with Charles and charged him with violating the Mann Act, an act of congress that is designed to protect people from slave or human trafficking. However, there was little evidence to support this charge, and Charles was freed shortly thereafter. Despite being freed, Charles surmised the authorities were most likely not finished investigating him. When Charles failed to report to his probationary officer, the federal investigators had enough of a charge to bring Charles in for questioning. In between being freed and subsequently arrested, the federal investigators had found new evidence that was enough to indict Charles in violation of the Mann Act. Leona was arrested shortly thereafter for prostitution and immediately confessed that Charles was her pimp. The investigators had enough evidence, and Charles was charged with violating the Mann Act and ordered to serve his 10 year sentence that he had gotten out of earlier. For one year, Charles would tie up the courts, attempting to have his sentence changed or reduced. However, these attempts would be futile, and Charles was left serving his second jail sentence. In jail, Charles was fortunate enough to be housed with Alvin Karpis, the guitarist from the Barker—Karpis gang. During his years in prison, Charles' mother remained staunchly dedicated to his well being and moved to cities near her son's various jails in an attempt to visit him regularly.

During the final days of filling his sentence, Charles was regularly assessed by a local psychiatrist within the prison. This psychiatrist took careful note that Charles was a "braggadocious man whose main calling in life was to bring attention to anything and everything he did—regardless of its contribution or detraction from mankind." Leona soon tired of the constant calls to the jailhouse and requested a divorce. Charles was relatively unaffected by this development, noting that he had only married her so that she would not be forced to testify against him. However, Charles was greeted with the divorce papers that included allegations that he and Leona had produced a child together. Charles readily admits that the two could have produced a child, and DNA testing between Charles Manson and the man who was rumored to be his son was inconclusive to either decision. In 1966, Charles was transported to Terminal Island, the prison where he had spent his first jail time. Charles was being prepared for early release, good behavior being the jail's reasoning for his release. At this point in his life, Charles' time had been spent largely in prisons across the United States. At the young age of 32, Charles had spent over 16 years in prisons and other reform institutions. Sadly, none of these encounters with the law, instructors, or counsellors had held any affect on his personal life. Charles still held careless abandon in his actions and had no compassion for the needs of others. Though his life was mainly petty crimes, the next set of crimes Charles committed would be his most deadly and would be the cause of his worldwide fame.

While in prison, Charles had become famous within the community for his good looks. After his release on March 21, 1967, Charles was followed around regularly by a group of women who referred to themselves as the "Manson Family." These women were mostly former prostitutes, but all were in love with Charles and were held within a tight bond of infatuation. Together, this group of people would inflict pain on thousands of people through the senseless killings of high profile people. In July of 1969, the group was the lead mastermind behind the killing of Gary Hinman. At the time of the murder, it was unknown who had done such a deed. However, one month later, the group murdered Sharon Tate and four of her friends in her home. Tate was a leading actress of the day and dearly loved by her fans across the world. Her death sparked international outrage and left investigators puzzled as to who was truly responsible for this crime. Only one day later, Leno and Rosemary Bianca were killed in the same manner the Tate group had been killed. The leading killer behind these murders was Tex Watson, a criminal who had served prison time for petty theft prior to becoming actively involved in the Manson Family. While Tex Watson was the main killer, the mastermind behind the entire series of attacks was Charles himself. Calling the acts a "premonition of things to come," Charles began ordering these killings in an attempt to "invite the leaders of the apocalypse to come." The highest profile the group tried to kill was President Gerald Ford. However, the perpetrator, Lynette Fromme, proved to be more irrational than competent and was caught long before he had the chance to kill President Ford.

The month of March in 1970 held many of the highest moments in Charles' life. His album, LIE was released, and on this album was the song, "Cease to Exist," a song that Charles wrote that was adopted by the Beach Boys and retitled, "Never Learn Not to Love." The CD was a dismal failure and Charles watched futilely as only 300 of the

2,000 copies produced actually sold. In addition to releasing the album, Charles also was in his final month of freedom. In the next month, Charles' life would catch up with him, and his crimes would seek the remainder of his life. On April 22, 1971, Federal Investigators found enough evidence to arrest Charles Manson on seven counts of first degree murder and another count of conspiracy to commit murder, a count that encompassed the murders of seven other people. With no defense willing to take his case, Charles represented himself and did a dismal job at seeking restitution as being insane. The courts found him guilty of all charges, and Charles was sentenced to death. However, Charles was elated in 1972, to hear that the death penalty had been ruled unconstitutional and would no longer be used in his state. After five years of attempting to change his death sentence to a short prison sentence, Charles was sentenced to life in prison with no option for parole. This came as a direct result of the new law, which stated "..."any prisoner now under a sentence of death may file a petition for writ of habeas corpus in the superior court, inviting that court to modify its judgment to provide for the appropriate alternative punishment of life imprisonment or life imprisonment without possibility of parole specified by statute for the crime for which he was sentenced to death." Charles' days in the courtroom were far from over, however. While many had thought he would live out his final days as a criminal within the California legal system, Charles was brought back into the courts to be charged with first degree murder, stemming from his first murder of Gary Hinman. Even with this new charge on his name, Charles continued to fight the legal system and petition for his release. All attempts at petitioning for his release would be immediately rejected.

Despite being a convicted criminal in the prison, Charles become an idol of many and was the coveted subject of numerous interviews in the 1980s. One interview, a 1986 CBS Nightwatch interview conducted by Charlie Rose won the Emmy Award in 1987 as the Best Interview. During these interviews, it became noted that Charles had tattooed a swastika on to his forehead, a symbol to the world of his fierce anti-semitism. Charles' anti-semitism was a source of conflict within the prison and culminated in a severe altercation on September 25, 1984. Charles had been in an argument with Jan Holmstrom when he insulted Holmstrom's religious chants. This infuriated Holmstrom, and he proceeded to douse Charles in paint thinner before lighting him on fire. Charles would suffer moderate to severe burns across his entire body, with the greatest being third degree burns on his back. This caused Charles to be taken to the California Medical Facility for months to recover before being taken to the Protective Housing Unit within the California State Prison. Charles' entire life story was published by NBC in 2007 when they aired the documentary, *The Mind of Manson*. The documentary proved to be pivotal in the world's perception of Charles, with many people realizing he was not the celebrity so many had praised him to be. Charles would continue to grow more disheveled in his appearance, a look corroborated by public opinion when an image was released in March of 2009 revealing a severely aged Charles Manson. Despite having a full beard and long, unkempt hair, Charles' swastika was still present and the hatred within his eyes had been replaced by a dull look with hints of fear.

Charles continued to live his prison life in complete solitary confinement until January 14, 2017, when it was revealed that Charles was slowly succumbing to gastrointestinal bleeding. The authorities took Charles to the hospital where it was revealed that Charles had little time to live. Charles would live longer than expected, lasting until late November. On November 15, 2017, Charles took a turn for the worse and was taken to a local hospital. No records were released in accordance with the federal laws of patient confidentiality. However, four days later, it was revealed that Charles had indeed died and would be cremated pending court rule. The life of one of America's most hated criminals had finally met its end, and Charles would soon meet his destiny. Following his death, Charles' body was fought over by numerous people, all of which were family members of Charles. One by one, these people were either deemed illegitimate in their search of Charles' body or became disinterested in the media storm that followed. Finally, after months of litigation, Charles' body was released to Jason Freemon who had Charles' body cremated and buried on March 20, 2018. Charles' life serves as an example to humanity that the scales of justice are not skewed in the end and that true justice will prevail, even through the disguise of a "family group" who destroyed countless lives across America.

H.H. Holmes

In the course of one's life, the desire to accomplish something or achieve a unique accolade sometimes causes mankind to go to unprecedented lengths to achieve the accompanying credit. For some, these lengths would include breaking the law; for others, these lengths throw any semblance of obeying the law to the wind. One man who seemed to kill for a living was Herman Webster Mudgett, more commonly known as H.H. Holmes, his alias. Herman lived a life that was completely consumed with killing people; people who posed a threat to him and his business. In all, Herman has confessed to 27 killings, though accounts from those closest to him hold that he killed almost 200 people during his time. Herman's killings were systematic, quick, and designed to carry a lesson to others; a lesson most people did not listen to or even hear. The life of Herman Webster Holmes gives mankind a vivid and graphic account of what happens when a man lets his potential glory supersede his compassion and love of mankind.

Herman was born to Levi Price and Tehodate Price on May 16, 1861, in Gilmanton, New Hampshire. Herman's parents were both a part of the great English Immigration that had occurred many years earlier. Herman had three siblings: an older brother, younger sister, and younger brother. Herman's family was devoutly religious, attending the local Methodist church on a continuous basis. During the week, Herman's family worked on their local farm where Herman was expected to do as much work as his siblings did, all being given equal chores around the home. As a child, rumors abound that told of Herman's father being aggressively violent towards his children and wife. While no physical proof exists to confirm this rumor, numerous first-hand stories exist from Herman's childhood that corroborate such a childhood. A childhood like this could have been what possibly led to Herman's graphic and violent adulthood where he showed little remorse for the killings and torture he committed. As a child, Herman was noted to have an odd obsession with killing the animals on his father's farm, often torturing them extensively before killing them. Herman's mother was especially nervous about this foundation Herman was laying and attempted to divert the interests of her brother towards something constructive. However, Herman refused all attempts that his mother made at interesting him in something more spiritual or constructive.

When Herman was 16, he graduated from high school and moved to Alton, New Hampshire where he became employed as a teacher. Oddly, his aid invested in children would bear no semblance to his murderous future. The following July, Herman married Clara Lovering, and the two birthed their first son, Robert Lovering Mudgett, on February 3, 1880. During these months of new beginnings, Herman showed no signs of being fascinated with death or torture, and his mother actually began to surmise that her attempts at diverting his interests as a child had actually been successful. In 1881, Herman met the qualifications to be a certified public accountant and began working as the city manager in Orlando, Florida. The following year, Herman moved his family to Burlington, Vermont where he enrolled in the University of Vermont. Here, Herman began pursuing a degree in medicine and surgery but was not pleased with the level of education he was receiving. The following year, Herman left the school and began attending the University of Michigan, once again moving his family to spend his school days with him. Still pursuing a degree in medicine and surgery, Herman succeeded at the University of Michigan and was awarded his diploma in June of 1884 after meeting the rigorous qualifications for the degree. Following his graduation, Herman began apprenticing under the watchful eye of Dr. Nahum Wright in New Hampshire, seemingly on his way to a successful career as a doctor.

During his final days enrolled in the University of Michigan, those sharing a house with Herman and his wife Clara began noticing that he was treating his wife differently. Whereas the couple had once held a seemingly romantic and loving relationship, the two seemed distant now with Herman often resorting to physical violence in his attempts at convincing Clara that his ideas were supreme to hers. The relationship began to show its strain and the housemates watched as the couple began to lose semblance as a true couple. Finally, Herman returned home one day after school to find that his once-beloved wife Clara had left for New Hampshire and would never see him again. It was around this time that friends and family of Herman's began noticing a change in him. Dr. Nahum Wright was the first to notice Herman's intense fascination in the cadavers located in his lab. Dr. Wright was the leading doctor in dissection during the time but even his fascination was no match for the delight Herman found in the human cadavers located in the lab. Coupling his CPA with the cadavers in the lab, Herman would often use the cadavers for defrauding life insurance companies, an act that was committed without the knowledge of Dr. Wright. Shortly thereafter, a young boy went missing in the same area as Herman and witnesses reported seeing Herman with the child shortly before he went missing. When contacted, Herman denied any wrongdoing and claimed that the young boy had merely gone home after he was done talking with him. The police were convinced with his testimony and refused to open an investigation into Herman. The locals were furious that more attention was not given to Herman but there was little that could be done without the police being on their side. With his reputation ruined, Herman left the area and moved to Philadelphia, Pennsylvania. In Philadelphia, Herman found employment at the Norristown State Hospital but was found to be touching some of the patients inappropriately while they were asleep, resulting in his immediate firing. However, no police investigation was launched into this accusation either. For the time being, Herman's charming personality was leading investigators astray. Sadly, this charming personality would also be responsible for the death hundreds one day.

After being fired from his position within Norristown State Hospital, Herman began working as a druggist at a local drug store in Philadelphia. This job provided Herman with a steady job for many months, but Herman made a drastic mistake when a child he had been mixing drugs for died immediately after consuming the drugs. Herman denied that the mistake had been completely on accident, but his name was ruined in the city and Herman was forced to move away. After leaving Philadelphia, Herman moved to Chicago, Illinois where he changed his name to Herman Holmes in an attempt to live his life anew. However, so much mystery still surrounded Herman and those closest to him were still content to maintain their friendship at a distance. Additionally, Herman began scamming people in the area and his name change was an attempt to disguise himself even more from those he had previously scammed. During this tumultuous time in his life, Herman was still married to Clara, despite her vow to never see him again. While still married, Herman married another woman, Myrta Belknap, in 1886, thus consummating his life as a bigamist. Myrta held obvious concern for being married to a bigamist and demanded that Herman consummate his divorce against Clara. Herman complied and filed for divorce a few days later, asserting successfully that Clara had shown infidelity from him by running away to New Hampshire without his knowledge or consent. However, with divorce needing to be an agreement from both parties, Herman's filing was futile unless Clara signed the papers. Clara refused, with rumors surfacing that allege her not even being shown the paperwork. Due to this, Herman lied to his wife Myrta and told her that the divorce was finalized. However, the divorce would never be issued, and Herman would die a bigamist.

Herman and Myrta had a child together, a daughter named Lucy Theodate Holmes. With no house to stay in, Herman began living with Myrta and their infant daughter Lucy in Myrta's home in Wilmette, Illinois. Shortly after becoming married, Herman began seeing another woman, Georgiana Yoke. While they would not be married until January 17, 1894, Georgianna would be Herman's third and current wife, consummating Herman as a bigamist with three wives.

Back in 1886, Herman had begun working at the drugstore of S. Holton in Chicago and purchased the drug store in 1890. Upon purchase of the building and land, the previous tenant of the drugstore went missing, causing many to believe Herman might have murdered her to recoup the financial backing he had submitted to purchase the store. However. this would never be proven, and Herman would never agree to such an accusation. In 1890, Herman began constructing a two story across the street from the drug store and labeled the new building as a "mixed-use building." The first floor would house a new drug store and the upstairs would be used for temporary housing, resembling a hotel. Two years later, Herman added a third level to the building with hopes of renting to more tenants with the coming World's Fair in Chicago. However, this portion of the hotel would never be completed due to architects never being paid by Herman. Herman accepted the law suit but continued to retain the money that was supposed to be paid to the architects. Additionally, the company supplying the furniture to the hotel ceased operations on Herman's order when they were alerted to the refusal to pay the architects. Later, during the police investigation of Herman, the house would be found to have many hidden tunnels and entrances, leading many to believe this building was constructed with the sole purpose of housing the murders Herman would complete later in his life.

Now residing in the house, Herman began murdering people seemingly whenever he felt the need to. The earliest known victim of his anger was Julia Smythe, one of Herman's mistresses. Herman's current wife knew of the affair but was content being his wife while Herman visited his mistress on many different occasions. When Smythe's husband found out about the affair, he moved away immediately and divorced Smythe. Herman housed Smythe in his house for a short while before murdering her when he grew tired of her companionship. This left Smythe's daughter Pearl alone for a short while before Herman killed her, not wanting the additional bills of another child in his life. Together, Julia and her daughter Pearl were killed by Herman on Christmas Even of 1891. The second known victim is Emeline Cigrande, another mistress of Herman. She had been living in the second portion of Herman's home until she went missing during the same week that Herman killed Pearl and Julia. Though Herman claimed that Cigrane had merely "left the area," it was later found that Herman had killed her shortly after murdering Julia and Pearl. During the same week of December, yet another woman went missing, Edna Van Tassel. Van Tassel was not a known mistress of Herman, but rumors abound placing her in the employment as a prostitute. Historians believe Herman lured Van Tassel to his home and had sex with her shortly before killing her and burying her with the other three victims. Altogether, Herman murdered four women during one week of December, and sadly, more women would join the group of the deceased. During this beginning of Herman's life as a serial killer, Herman maintained his life as a druggist and hotel operator, showing no change in lifestyle or remorse for his killings. He was so professional that all of his current wives went to their graves either never knowing of his wicked actions or not knowing of his deeds until the police would catch him many years later. For now, Herman's life was consumed with one person: himself. Many more people would pay the price of being labeled as a bother in the life of Herman Holmes.

Shortly after the Christmas of 1892, Herman began consorting with a fellow by the name of Benjamin Pitezel, a known criminal and fraudulent individual. Pitezel was a carpenter when he and Herman met, and the two developed a fast bond over their nefarious pasts and current illegal dealings. Herman employed Pitezel as a carpenter in his building, and in return, Pitezel was allowed to display and sell his new invention, a coal box, in Herman's store. Herman began tasking Pitezel with carrying out some of his most illustrious crimes, referring to him as "his creature." Around this same time, Herman was introduced to Minnie Williams, a woman he would soon employ as his local stenographer at his Chicago office. Through their relationship, Herman was able to convince Williams that she should transfer the deed of some property to a man Herman referred to as Alexander Bond. This "Alexander Bond" was actually just Herman, but nonetheless, Williams transferred the extent of her property in Fort Worth, Texas to "Alexander Bond," and Herman actually served as the notary for this transaction, effectively notarizing his own property transfer. Herman then proceeded to sign the property over to Pitezel to avoid any suspicion or inquiry into who this "Alexander Bond" was. Around this time, Herman and Williams began renting an apartment in Chicago, calling themselves man and wife, thus adding yet another wife to Herman's already extensive list. Shortly after moving into the apartment, William's sister Nannie paid the new couple a visit, giving her congratulations on their recent wedding and pledging her support for their future. Herman gave every indication of being appreciative for this kind gesture but in a surprising turn of events, ordered that Nannie spend the night with the couple rather than returning to her hotel for the evening. From that evening, all that remains is a letter addressed from Nannie telling of her plans to visit Europe with a man she referred to as "Brother Harry." This account could not be corroborated as neither Nannie nor Minnie would ever been seen again after that evening. When asked what happened to his wife and sister-in-law, Herman asserted that they had returned to their home in Fort Worth, Texas but no proof of this assertion could ever be found. July 5, 1893 would be the last day either of these two women would be seen alive.

Herman began to feel pressure from insurance companies across the nation, all seeking restitution from Herman's apparent arson many years earlier. Herman was not about to be held accountable for the millions of dollars he was being prosecuted for, so he left Chicago and fled to Fort Worth, Texas where he stayed on the property he had swindled from his late wife and sister-in-law. In Fort Worth, Herman had a new name and was intent on beginning his fresh start. His first action upon his arrival was to commence construction on a dwelling similar to the one he had just abandoned in Chicago. To receive the necessary supplies for the house he was beginning to refer to as his "castle," Herman began swindling merchants in the Fort Worth area, once again creating an illegal front to develop his building under. However, Herman would never be able to live out his dream of creating such a dwelling. On July 4, 1894, federal prosecutors caught up with Herman and charged him with the illegal activity of selling goods he had previously mortgaged with his local bank. After being transported back to St. Louis, Missouri, Herman used his charming personality to convince a local businessman to bail him out. However, while he was in jail, Herman befriended Marion Hedgepeth, a convicted man who was in the midst of serving 25 years in jail due to federal fraud. Herman needed nothing from Hedgepeth other than the name of a lawyer who could be persuaded to bend the law slightly. Hedgepeth readily agreed and supplied Herman with the name of his lawyer in exchange for $500 cash.

Despite having the government following him so closely, Herman had devised another plan that held the potential for great financial benefit. Herman was convinced that if he took out an insurance policy valued at $10,000 and then fake his own death, he could remove the constant presence of the federal government while also receiving a huge amount of cash; enough to last him until his death. Hedgepeth had instructed Herman to consult the legal services of Jeptha Howe from St. Louis. Upon consultation, Howe revealed that he would be very eager to help Herman with his plan, also adding that he saw no way in which the insurance company would ever find out about such a deal. However, the plan failed shortly after Herman faked his own death. The insurance company had heard of Herman's previous illegal activities and refused to pay the policy value to the benefactor. Herman knew there was little he could do to secure the cash other than produce a body, so he decided to let the matter drop and attempt the same scheme with his good friend Pitezel. Pitezel agreed that such a plan would be ingenious and immediately took out the same insurance policy, listing his wife as the benefactor. Using the same lawyer, Jeptha Howe, Pitezel took out the life insurance policy and found a suitable location in Philadelphia in which he would fake his own death. With the first plan failing, Herman made this plan more elaborate, arranging for Pitezel to be employed in a lab as an inventor and then be subsequently killed after an explosion erupted within the building. The plan was ingenious, leaving no trace of a body while also giving structural damage that would prove the death to the insurance company. Herman was tasked with finding a cadaver that would look similar to Pitezel. However, Herman grew jealous of the money and instead, knocked Pitezel unconscious and set him on fire. Pitezel died in the fire and the insurance company agreed to pay the life insurance policy to Pitzel's wife. However, the money would never make it to his wife; rather, Herman would collect each monthly payout. Pitezel's wife was still under the impression that her husband was merely hiding and said nothing about not receiving the insurance money. However, while Herman was manipulating Pitezel's wife so aggressively, the manipulation would soon turn into murder, and Pitezel's wife would be devastated.

Shortly after the "staged" explosion, Herman convinced Petezel's wife to allow him the custody of three of their five children. All the while, Herman and Petezel's wife began having an affair without the knowledge of Herman's wives. Herman proceeded to move Petezel's wife to Canada where he would leave her and move on to Toronto. In Toronto, Herman proceeded to murder two of the children Petezel had granted him custody of. To murder them, Herman persuaded the two children into the trunk of his car and then fixed a gas line to a hole he had drilled in the trunk. The girls were subsequently gassed and then buried nude in the basement of the house he was currently renting in Toronto.

While Herman was attempting to yet again start a new life in Toronto, a Philadelphia police officer had been investigating Herman since the event of the explosion that killed Petezel. Unaware to Herman, Petezel's wife had gone to the police and informed them of her suspicions that Herman had killed her children. Upon securing admission from the Canadian police, the Philadelphia detectives, lead by Frank Geyer, began investigating Herman's home in Toronto. One day, they noticed an odd odor emanating from the basement and proceeded to dig under his basement in an attempt to unearth this mysterious odor. Frank writes "The deeper we dug, the more horrible the odor became, and when we reached the depth of three feet, we discovered what appeared to be the bone of the forearm of a human being." Geyer found the bodies and proceeded to return to the United States where he secured an arrest warrant and arrested Herman Holmes on November 17, 1894. The following year, Herman's murder trial commenced, beginning with the murder of Benjamin Pitezel. The trial went well, and the judge found Herman guilty and sentenced him to death. Seeing he had little time to live, Herman began confessing to numerous murders. Some of these murders could be confirmed, but many of the people he admitted to having murdered were actually still living. For this reason, many of the confessions had to be banned from the court, the judge fearing that the dishonesty would prolong the death sentencing. Herman had little to wait before being put to death. On May 7, 1896, Frank Geyer hanged Herman Holmes at the Moyamensing Prison in Philadelphia. Those present at the hanging note Herman's calm expression right up until he passed away. The actual hanging of Herman took almost 20 minutes to complete. Herman stayed alive throughout the whole process until finally passing away after 21 minutes of hanging alive. At his request, Herman was buried in a cement coffin 10 feet below the surface of the ground.

Harold Shipman

Within the archives of serial killers in the world, most of the victims being targeted were targeted for biases and personal reasons. However, some victims received their death sentence merely because they were wealthy and the murderer was lusting after their wealth. Some, however, were murdered because they fell into the pattern of methodical murder being carried out by the murderer. The victims of Harold Shipman are an example of such a group. Harold Shipman, a prestigious medical doctor who had been trusted by both patients and medical personnel, was found to have murdered a number of his patients; estimates place his victim count in the low 200s. The common question asked among all families of the victims in a murder case is "Why?" and this series of murders was no different. While Harold would be captured during his time and would spend time in a prison for the remainder of his life, the question of why he committed such actions was never answered and is left to the speculation of the media and other sources. For some, his death marks a bit of discontentment, knowing that such a murderous villain would never receive the full punishment for his actions and that with his death, the answer to why he committed such crimes would also die. Harold Shipman's life is a perfect example of the heartbreak and misery that is afflicted on humanity when the helpless are taken advantage of. Harold chose to murder those who were the most helpless among him: those seeking his help and placing their lives in his care. Despite the tragedy his life created, Harold may serve as an example to those who are considering taking advantage of the helpless, an example that proves that when the helpless are harmed, a world of justice rises to their aid. Though Harold's murderous life caused grief in the families of almost 250 victims, his crimes led to reform among medical doctors worldwide and because of his crimes, the world has seen sweeping change that has left its patients safer because of it.

Harold Shipman was born on January 14, 1946 to Harold Fredrick Shipman and Vera Brittan in Nottingham, England. Growing up, Harold would be kin to two siblings, a brother and sister whose ages are unknown. Harold's parents instilled a strong work ethic in their children and stood for little foolishness as the children were growing up. As a mere lorry driver, Harold's father was forced to budget his money wisely, and as a result, the family practiced frugality extensively. Despite their poor conditions, the Shipman family was happy, and Harold's parents sought to provide their children with the most fulfilling and profitable childhood. In addition to their busy work lives, the Shipman family was deeply involved in their local Methodist church and were faithful attendees at every service. This deep-rooted Christianity seemed to have an adverse effect on Harold, however. At a young age, Harold rejected the words of religiosity that were spoken at his local church and despised the "fake belief" in God he witnessed at the church each week. Harold's personal life was not always dark, however. At a young age, Harold was enrolled in a local rugby team where it was found that Harold excelled quite well. During the vast majority of his childhood, Harold would spend many evenings playing rugby for various teams in the area surrounding Nottingham.

When Harold was eleven years old, he took the traditional testing offered by the government, the eleven-plus. For students to move on past their current studies and begin their career studies, all students were required the pass the eleven-plus. Harold breezed through the test and began his work at High Pavement Grammar School in Nottingham, England. It was at this school that Harold began demonstrating his athletic prowess that extended far beyond merely rugby. On the dare of a female friend, Harold tried out for the track team and was accepted as a distance runner. For the next few years of his schooling at the High Pavement Grammar School, Harold would become the best distance runner the school had ever seen and was elected vice-captain of the athletic association at the school. While Harold maintains that he participated in sports at this school for their athletic appeal, it is thought that Harold might have been using sports as a way to take his mind off of a home life that was breaking Harold's heart. During high school, it was found that Harold's mother was suffering from lung cancer. Harold was forced to watch his mother suffer daily from the debilitating disease, a torturous experience that left Harold scarred. On June 21, 1963, Harold watched helplessly as his mother breathed her last breath and passed away. Harold's world instantly changed, and friends and family recall a sharp change in his demeanor. Harold vowed to become a doctor that would rid the world of cancer so that no one else would have to endure the same tragedy he had just endured. While part of that vow would be completed by Harold, his becoming a doctor seemed to only give him access to patients where he could inflict the same pain that he had suffered. What had once been a dream to help people would somehow morph into a systematic killing of people who had trusted their life to him. However, Harold's life for now was focused on excelling in medical school.

Three years after his mother passed away, Harold found a new love in his life when he married Primrose May Oxtoby, a woman who would remain his wife even after he was convicted of his numerous murders. The marriage with Primrose was a fruitful and happy marriage that produced four children. Harold found new joy in Primrose and often commented on her smile. For the time being, Harold had found new joy and was pulled from the precipice of depression that had threatened to steal his joy and drive for a career. However, his joy restored, Harold entered Leeds School of Medicine in 1966 and began pursuing the career that would allow him to fulfill his promise to his mother.

For four arduous years, Harold fulfilled his duties at Leeds School of Medicine and met the requirements for graduation in 1970.

Following graduation, Harold found employment at the Pontefract General Infirmary, a hospital located a short distance from his house in Ponefract, West Yorkshire. The first few years of his employment were filled with mediocre tasks designed to familiarize him with the processes and surroundings at the hospital. Finally, after meeting the qualifications for promotion, Harold was promoted to general practitioner and transferred to the Abraham Ormerod Medical Centre located in Todmorden, West Yorkshire. While Harold had done nothing to alert his superiors to a possible character flaw during his first four years as a nurse, Harold began making mysterious mistakes during his time as a general practitioner—mistakes that should have alerted those around him to far more than a simple addiction. One year after assuming the position of general practitioner at Abraham Ormerod Medical Centre, administration was alerted to Harold and an alleged misuse of prescription drugs. After a brief investigation, it was found that Harold had been forging prescriptions to fulfill an addiction to the drug pethidine. Harold was dealt with severely and forced to pay a fine of 600 pounds. Additionally, Harold attended a drug rehabilitation center in York under his own advisement and seemed to be completely addiction free. In addition to being fined heavily, Harold had also been fired by the Abraham Ormerod Medical Centre and was forced to seek additional employment. After one year of unemployment, Harold was hired at the Donneybrook Medical Centre as their general practitioner in 1977. This medical center was located in Hyde and was not turned away from Harold's previous allegations. Serving as a general practitioner allowed Harold the luxury of developing a client base that he could someday penetrate as a personal doctor.

In 1993, Harold left his work as a general practitioner and started his own work as a surgeon in an office on 21 Market Street in downtown Hyde. Through his many years as a general practitioner and his few years as a surgeon, Harold became a trusted name within the community. The citizens of Hyde loved their personal doctor and families trusted Harold with their patients, young and old. However, unbeknownst to the citizens, Harold had been slowly killing many of the patients he had been trusted with in this city. For the time being, no one knew of his evil deeds. His days of being presumed innocent were at their end.

In 1998, some people within the community began to grow suspicious of their beloved doctor. One of Harold's secretaries, Linda Reynolds, had begun wondering why Harold seemed to lose so many of his patients. After talking about this concern with Deborah Massey, who was an employed mortician at Frank Massey and Sons Funeral Parlour, Linda discussed her findings with John Pollard who was the coroner for the county. After Pollard looked into the findings, he noticed that Harold had been needing a large number of cremation forms co-signed by Linda Reynolds, his secretary. Notably, the cremation forms were all for older women who had not been Harold's patients for a long period of time. Pollard alerted the local police to the matter and recommended that they launch an investigation into the pattern that was beginning to develop. However, the police quickly dismissed the claims, citing lack of evidence for the reason they could not arrest Harold. The police readily admitted that the pattern was "concerning" but that no charges could be brought on such a limited time basis. Upon Harold's arrest years later, the *Shipman Inquiry* would find that the officers investigating the odd pattern were grossly inadequate and were not experienced enough to be investigating an allegation of that magnitude. Sadly, the incompetence of the police department in Hyde would lead to more people being killed by Harold. Between the dates of Harold being investigated and Harold actually being arrested, Harold would kill three more of his patients.

Five months after being initially investigated, a taxi drive named John Shaw began wondering whether or not he should talk to the police about his findings that Harold could be involved in at least 21 murders. After wrestling with the idea for a while, Shaw approached the police, who had five months earlier been investigating Harold for a similar crime and alerted them that he had evidence that Harold was involved in at least 21 murders. The police jumped on this evidence and Harold was immediately made the chief suspect. Still lacking enough evidence to arrest the man, police began investigating the deaths of Harold's formed patients. The last known victim was Kathleen Gundy, one of Harold's patients whom had last been seen by Harold. As police investigated the death certificate, they found Harold to have written "old age" as the means of death. However, the police were alerted by a frantic daughter, Angela Woodruff, who was informed that her mother's previous will had been replaced by another will that gave Harold Shipman the entirety of Gundy's estate. When examining the new will, police found it to have been written on a typewriter, but they were unable to discount its validity. Police were certain that Harold had killed Kathleen and upon investigation of the body, found that heroin had been injected into her veins shortly before her death, most likely hastening her death. When police questioned Harold and asked him about the heroin, he informed them that Kathleen had been a heroin addict for many years, providing proof on his computerized medical journal. However, upon closer inspection, police found that Harold had written these medical entries in one day and had written them well after the date that was entered. With this evidence in hand, police arrested Harold on September 7, 1998 and charged him with murder and forgery. Upon investigation of the house, a typewriter matching the one used to forge Kathleen's will was found. Harold had long been enjoying his spree of killing his older patients. That spree was over, and Harold was in his new home: the jail cell. Now all that was left was finding out who exactly he killed, how he did it, and why any man would ever undertake such a horrible atrocity.

With Harold in jail, the investigation could begin in a more effective manner. After consulting with Harold's secretary at his local surgery clinic, the investigators were able to derive the names of 15 women whose deaths seemed to be in a pattern. The process of investigating these women's deaths was quite long, however. With the women having been dead for a number of months, their bodies had been buried, and any attempt at performing an autopsy on these bodies would likely gather no further evidence. However, when examining the medical journal found in Harold's house, investigators found that Harold had given all of these women a large amount of diamorphine shortly before they died. Harold would then sign the death certificate and simply record that the patients had died due to old age or poor health. This investigation would be the basis for the book, *Prescription for Murder*, that would be written by Brian Whittle in 2000. With this evidence in hand, the investigators arrived for the trial of Harold Shipman on October 5, 1999. The trial was held at Preston Crown Court and was expected to be quick, considering the vast amount of evidence the investigators had to present. The trial began with Harold begin charged with murder in the 15 cases where it was found Harold had given a lethal dose of medication. Harold's lawyers were adamant that the Kathleen Gundy case should be tried separately, seeing that this case was the only case in which Harold had a clear motive to kill her. Harold's lawyers were going to attempt to plead for malpractice on the remaining fourteen cases, but nothing became of the plea. The trial lasted only six days and following the case, Harold Shipman was found guilty of all 15 counts of murder and one count of forgery. The sentencing was administered by Mr. Justice Forbes who sentenced Harold to a life in prison and an added recommendation that Harold never be released for his atrocity against humanity. Harold Shipman's career woven with murder had finally reached its end.

Following the trial, those associated with Harold began removing him from any association with him. The General Medical Council formally struck him from their record only ten days following his sentencing. Harold had held hope that he might someday be released on good behavior. However, that hope was demolished when Home Secretary David Blunkett confirmed the whole life sentencing that had been administered by the judge and charged that Harold should never be released, a command that must be obeyed. Ironically, the power to levy such prison sentences would be lost months later, Harold Shipman being the last known convict to face this charge. Despite the possibility that he could have been released on good behavior, the investigators claim they had a bevy of additional information that would have led to future charges. Seeing Harold was already going to be spending the rest of his life in jail, they decided not to clog the courts with their additional trials. Throughout the entire trial, Harold maintained that he was innocent and that the trial was a complete mockery of the legacy he had attempted to create. His wife was additionally supportive of his innocence and quietly supported him throughout his tenure in prison. Harold Shipman would go down in history as being the only doctor in Britain to ever be convicted of killing his patients. Many more would be suspected and would undergo trials, but Harold would remain the only doctor ever convicted.

Harold's tenure in prison met its end on January 13, 2004 when he hanged himself in his prison cell using his bed sheets and the bars on the window. Those affected by Harold's devious actions voiced their discontentment with Harold's "easy" death. David Blunkett, the home secretary who had confirmed Harold's life sentencing, commented: "You wake up and you receive a call telling you Shipman has stepped himself and you think, 'Is it too early to open a bottle?' And then you discover that everybody's very upset that he's done it." Harold's death came as a shock to everyone but was noted as being coincidentally close to the time when his insurance payout would have expired. This allegation was corroborated by a probation officer who noted that Harold had mentioned wanting to kill himself numerous times, all with the motive of giving his wife the financial security the insurance payout would achieve. However, additional evidence surfaced showing that Harold's wife might have begun to lose her confidence in her husband's innocence, prompting him to kill himself rather than lose his one supporter. Regardless, Harold Shipman was dead and his deathly legacy on this earth was complete; the name Harold Shipman would forever be remembered as a man who took advantage of those who trusted him with their life.

The investigation into how many people Harold actually killed continues to this day. In 2001, a detective from the same city as Harold's first stint as general practitioner assessed that Harold had killed a minimum of 215 of his patients during his career, the youngest being a four-year-old girl. While a doctor, Harold had signed the death certificate of 459 people but some of these people were indeed nearing death and were not victims of Harold's systematic killing. Those nearest to Harold during his tenure as doctor were all investigated for their role in the death of Harold's victims, but none would be charged. Harold had worked alone all those years and now, Harold must bear the horrible reputation of a traitor-doctor, alone.

Aileen Wuornos

When looking at the range of crimes afflicted against humanity, it is often the case that serial killers held an agenda of sorts when enacting their devious plans. However, a select group of serial killers enacted their plans with one mindset: prejudice. While prejudice has been the motive for numerous notable genocides, it has often been examined more in the sense of racial tensions and equality within the workforce. The hatred fueled by prejudice has led some people to un-warranted measures: killing those they hate the most. Aileen Wuornos is a worthy example of someone who allowed the prejudice of hatred towards men to turn her life into that of a serial killer. Though Aileen had a childhood that lent itself to hatred towards men in general, her past was no excuse for her actions as an adult and the courts would side with Biblical precedent in pursuing the death penalty against her. That being said, Aileen's life is an example of the pressures that can be placed on a child who is mistreated and abused. Aileen would also become a victim of rape and assault years before her hatred of men led her to kill. In a sad sort of irony, Aileen's vengeance against men would lead her nowhere ending with her early death as a convicted felon. Truly, the act of forgiveness is what could have made Aileen's story and life so much more full. Given the choice between forgiveness and revenge, Aileen chose revenge and because of it, left numerous families grieving before eventually leaving her own family grieving in her loss. The life of Aileen Wuornos is an example to humanity of failing to forgive. Through it, those following can see the failure revenge brings and the empty success it offers.

Aileen Wuornos entered the world as Aileen Carol Pittman on

February 29, 1956 in Troy, Michigan, to Diane Wuornos. As a grim premonition of her future outlook on men, Aileen was birthed into this world without a father present. Aileen would never meet her father and would grow up hating his existence and the plight he left his family in by deserting them. Diane had married her husband Leo Dale Pittman on June 3, 1954 before divorcing after a short marriage of almost two years. The divorce was formally recognized on December 20, 1955, leaving Aileen two months short of having a father. Leo would move on to perform egregious sex acts against children, leading to a lengthy sentence in prison. While incarcerated, Leo was diagnosed with schizophrenia, a condition of the mind that would affect his daughter Aileen as well. During the last month of his incarceration, Leo shocked the prison guards and his family and eventually committing suicide by hanging in his prison cell. Sadly, Aileen's early years as a child would have no semblance of normality. With her biological father having deserted the family before committing suicide, Aileen was given no foundation to base a positive image of men. This image would be further depleted when Aileen's grandfather would take advantage of her youthful innocence and immaturity. For now, Aileen was stuck in the tracks of an abusive mother who neglected her children to go spend evenings with other men. Shortly before Aileen turned four, her mother decided that tending to her children was beyond her capabilities and abandoned them. Aileen had one younger brother named Keith, and both of them would be legally adopted by their grandparents on March 18, 1960.

The rest of Aileen's childhood is a sad image of the sexual atrocities enacted against children so commonly in present time. Aileen began to learn that her body could be sold to gain monetary return, and when Aileen turned eleven, she began having sex with other young men at her school. In return, the boys would give her food, alcohol, drugs, and cigarettes. Further reducing her image of men, Aileen began to engage in sexual activity with those men closest to her, the closest being her brother with whom she had sex with on a regular basis. Sadly, the grandfather who had rushed to her rescue when she was abandoned by her mother began to assault her as well.

Often, he would get drunk at a local bar before returning home and beating Aileen. Prior to her beating however, Aileen was forced to strip naked, allowing her grandfather to fulfill his sexual pleasures while succumbing Aileen to a perverted sense of submission. When Aileen turned fourteen, her life changed: she became pregnant. Aileen had been raped on many occasions before but none had resulted in pregnancy. This changed shortly after Aileen was raped by one of her grandfather's workers who had come to their house to do repairs. Aileen was immediately shunned by her grandfather as he was embarrassed to have an unmarried pregnant woman in his care. On March 23, 1971, Aileen birthed a young boy in the care of a pregnancy shelter. The boy was immediately placed into adoption and Aileen returned to her dark home where her life was trapped in a world where sexual promiscuity was her only escape. After giving birth, Aileen began to slowly retract from society, dropping out of school and ceasing to attend any social functions. In 1972, Aileen's only sense of hope was lost when her grandmother succumbed to liver failure and died. Without her grandmother's support, Aileen was rejected by her grandfather and was soon kicked out of the house. To this point, Aileen was dejected and felt as if being unwanted was worse than dying. After being arrested many years later, Aileen would confess that she contemplated suicide on many occasions. She never carried out the thoughts of suicide but her life was none the happier. Sadly, Aileen's life was only going to get worse from here.

After turning 15, Aileen was deemed competent to live on her own after her grandfather had kicked her out of the house. Now, without a grandmother, house, or purpose in life, Aileen began contemplating where she could live and how she would support herself. With no other options available, Aileen began living in the woods behind the house where she had grown up while also selling her body as a prostitute to stay alive by any means possible. A young girl who had once shown much promise and had as much potential as any other girl was now destined to live the life no one should have to live: a homeless girl selling her body just to stay alive. From here, Aileen's life would enter a steady downward spiral that would continue until her eventual incarceration.

In 1974, Aileen's already dismal life took a decline with the engagement of criminal activity. At the age of 18, Aileen was pulled over for driving erratically. Upon investigation, it was found that Aileen was driving while under the influence of drugs leading to her immediate arrest. In addition to driving under the influence, it was found that Aileen had produced and fired a pistol from her car as she was driving while also shouting expletives. These actions led to subsequent charges of disorderly conduct and illegal possession of a firearm. After posting bail, Aileen returned to a friend's home where she spent the rest of the week. Aileen then refused to attend her hearing which led to being charged with failure to appear. For Aileen, her life was at a crossroads – the crossroads of correcting her life or continuing to run into the arms of those willing her to do criminal activity.

Two years later, Aileen set out for Florida, hitch-hiking her entire journey from Colorado to Florida. Once in Florida, Aileen met a man named Gratz Fell. As the two began to get to know each other, it became apparent that both shared interest in each other. However, Fell was 69-years-old and Aileen was only twenty. Fell was a yacht-club president and was interested in Aileen merely for her sexual services. Aileen was interested in the financial security a marriage with him would bring. The two began to know each other more and began dating. Within one year, the couple was married. Their marriage proved to be a calamity of sorts while also being a comedy for those watching. The entire city where the two were residing became privy to the couple's marriage and soon, their marriage was the laughingstock of the community. Aileen was anything but faithful to the marriage and was the center of many conflicts at the local bar. After one such confrontation, Aileen was jailed for assaulting a man and Gratz refused to bail her out. Upon her release, Aileen returned home and promptly accosted her husband. The confrontation turned violent and Aileen wound up hitting Fell in the head with his cane. After this, Fell had filed a restraining order against Aileen. With no place to live, Aileen returned to Michigan where she continued her violent confrontations. Wherever Aileen went, she seemed destined for violence, the only way she knew how to get her point across. On July 14, 1976, Aileen was once again jailed in Antrim County when she launched a cue ball at the head of one of the bartenders. Aileen was charged with both assault and disturbing the peace. For Aileen, her life rested on getting what she wanted and if she was denied anything, she responded in violence. Aileen's life took another tragic turn only three days later when she was informed that her last living immediate relative, her brother Keith, had died of esophageal cancer. Ironically, Aileen seemed unfazed by his death and was happy to receive the $10,000 payout from his life insurance. On July 21, Aileen and Fell formally annulled their marriage, ending the nine week nightmare that had no semblance of a true marriage. The marriage had lasted nine weeks and had been the closest Aileen had ever come to true love, though she was still far from it.

One month after receiving her brother's life insurance payout, Aileen was fined $105 for driving under the influence of alcohol and was told she must pay or go to jail. Aileen chose to use the month's payout of insurance money from her brother's death to pay for the fine. In addition, she decided to go on a shopping spree where she made many purchase of items she had always wanted to own herself. Paying in cash, Aileen purchased many valuable items, including a car. However, as previously mentioned Aileen was a poor driver and totaled the car only weeks after purchasing it. Within two months, the car was totaled, the money from the life insurance was completely spent, and Aileen was no closer to finding help with her anger management woes than she had been before. During this time, Aileen admits that a number of people reached out to help her, all help which she rejected. Aileen was living the life she wanted to live and no one was going to take that from her.

For the next five years, Aileen's whereabouts were not recorded and she had shed no light on her actions during this time period. Her next known location was found when Aileen robbed a convenience store at gunpoint on May 20, 1981. Aileen was an incompetent criminal and was found and arrested shortly thereafter. Sadly, Aileen had only stolen $35 and two packs of cigarettes from the store, but would be charged for much more since she had used a gun and had threatened the life of the employee. On May 4, 1982, Aileen was sentenced to one year in the state's prison and began serving her sentence immediately. On June 30, 1983, Aileen was released from the prison with the promise, "I'll be back, I swear." Federal prosecutors were perplexed at Aileen's apparent hatred towards law enforcement, yet she pledged to return. Nevertheless, Aileen made every attempt to return to prison, including forging multiple checks and attempting to cash them at a bank located in Key West, Florida. Only five months after being released from the prison, Aileen was named as the chief suspect in a crime involving the stealing of a gun and ammunition in Pasco County, Florida. The investigation proved inadequate, however, and insufficient evidence led to no charges being placed. The brief respite in her law-law-breaking habit did not take long, and on January 4, 1986, Aileen was arrested for stealing a car and assaulting an officer during her attempt to resist arrest. Additionally, police charged her with obstruction of justice after she attempted to claim that she was her aunt by giving the police officer her aunt's identification. When the police were investigating the stolen car, they discovered a box of ammunition and a stolen .38 caliber revolver. After a brief jail stint, Aileen was released but was soon brought back in for questioning after a man accused Aileen of pointing a gun at him during a car ride. The man alleged that Aileen had demanded he give her $200 or she would shoot him. After he refused to comply, Aileen ran from the car. When Aileen denied the allegations, police searched her car where they found that she had a .22 stowed under the passenger seat of the car. The man failed to press charges, but Aileen was given a stern warning that any future crimes would be met with severe punishment.

After Aileen was released from questioning, she went to a gay bar in Daytona where she met Tyria Moore, a hotel maid from the same bar. The two began living together shortly thereafter and Aileen produced most of the financial equity for the family through her work as a prostitute. Aileen and Moore proved to be a violent team and often fought people together. During one such altercation, Aileen and Moore broke a beer bottle over a bartender's head and were charged with assault. Despite their violent nature, Aileen and Moore claimed to be truly in love, a claim that Aileen would carry with her to her grave.

Around this time, Aileen began hating men with a more fervent hatred. This hatred led to her to believe she could enact revenge on this gender by killing males systematically. Between 1989 and 1990, Aileen killed seven men, all whom she claimed had been attempting to rape her before she killed them. Richard Mallory was the first of her victims, a 51-year-old male who owned an electronics store in Clearwater, Florida. His body would be discovered in December of 1989; roughly one month after Aileen had shot him twice in the lung. For the next few months, Aileen continued her nightly job as a prostitute before resuming her killing spree on June 1, 1990 with the killing of David Spears. Spears' nude body with six shot wounds would be found the following night along Florida State Route 19. Five days later, Aileen killed 40-year-old Charles Carskaddon by shooting him nine times in the head. Almost two weeks later, Peter Seims, a local charity worker with a Baptist Church, reached out to Aileen and attempted to help her find shelter. Seims had no idea of Aileen's violent past or that she was currently involved in a massive killing spree. On July 4, Aileen killed Seims and deposited his body in an undisclosed location, never to be recovered. Troy Burress, a 50-year-old salesman, was Aileen's next victim. He would be shot twice before dying and deposited in a forest near where Aileen and Moore were currently living. One victim who may have been investigating Aileen in his spare time was Charles Humphreys, a former chief of police who had held some connection to Aileen in his past police work. Whether or not he was investigating Aileen up to the time of his death will never be known, but what can be confirmed is that Aileen shot Humphreys six times in the head, killing him, before depositing his body in Marion County, Florida. Walter Jeno Antonio would be

Aileen's last victim. Antonio was a 62-year-old trucker who had solicited Aileen's services as a prostitute. After receiving her payment from him, Aileen shot Antonio in the head four times before depositing his body in his car and leaving the car in Brevard County.

Aileen seemed to be growing comfortable with the prospect of killing men, a transition that could have cost so many more men their lives if she had not begun to make critical mistakes. On July 4, 1990, Aileen and Moore were driving Siems' car when they hit another car. Fearing police would recognize the stolen car and link them with the murder, Aileen and Moore ran from the scene, leaving the car behind. However, they left more than the car behind; both left their fingerprints all over the car and Moore left some identification in the car. With these critical pieces of evidence, police were able to link the two women with the murders and immediately placed a warrant for their arrest. Particularly helpful in identifying the women, Aileen's fingerprints were already on file due to her prison time in Florida. After running for almost five months, Aileen was finally apprehended at the Last Resort Bar in Volusia County, Florida. Moore was arrested in Scranton, Pennsylvania where they were able to use Moore to get Aileen to confess to the murders, thus exonerating Moore from the murders. With a full confession on file, police began setting out to convict Aileen for as many murders as they could pin on her. Seeking the death penalty, law enforcement was out to make sure no more families were affected by Aileen's devious ways.

After one year of preparation for the trial, the federal prosecutors were ready and the trial commenced on January 14, 1992. Though more evidence existed, the only murder Aileen would be standing trial at the time would be that of Richard Mallory. The trial did not take as long as expected, and on January 27, 1992, Aileen was convicted of first degree murder of Mallory. Seeing there was no possible way for Aileen to be acknowledged from this sentencing as a "sane" woman, her lawyers petitioned that she was actually mentally unstable and was unable to stand trial. After seeking a psychiatrist's aid, the lawyers revealed that Aileen had been diagnosed with borderline personality disorder and antisocial personality disorder, thus arguing that she was not competent to complete these murders in full knowledge of the implications. The courts disagreed, however, and sentenced her to death four days later. The trials continued, and for the next three, Aileen would plead no contest; she asserted, "I wanted to confess to you that Richard Mallory did violently rape me as I've told you; but these others did not. They only began to start to." The courts appeared unfazed by Aileen's assertions and instead gave Aileen three more death sentences to compliment her previous one. Aileen continued to proclaim that Mallory had raped her and that she should not have been committed to death for that murder. During the next trial, Aileen pled guilty to killing Charles Carskaddon, but continued to request a retrial for her killing of Mallory. New records showed that Mallory had been charged with intent to rape in the past, possibly shedding light on Aileen's honesty. However, all requests for a retrial were denied on the grounds that she had three outstanding death sentences in addition to Mallory's death sentence. For the nine murders, Aileen would receive six death sentences; Siem's being the only murder that she would not be tried for due to the lack of a body. Following the trial, Aileen was evaluated using the Psychopathy Checklist and was found to be identified as a "psychopath," scoring 32/40. After the sentencing, Aileen spent the remainder of her life in the Florida Department of Corrections Broward Correctional Institution. In her last statement, Aileen confessed, "I killed those men, robbed them as cold as ice. And I'd do it again, too. There's no chance in keeping me alive or anything, because I'd kill again. I have hate crawling through my system. I am so sick of hearing this 'she's crazy' stuff. I've been evaluated so many times. I'm competent, sane, and I'm trying to tell the truth. I'm one who seriously hates human life and would kill again." On October 9 2002, Aileen was put to death using lethal injection at 9:47 A.M. Aileen had refused her last meal and her last words were, "I would just like to say I'm sailing with the rock, and I'll be back, like 'Independence Day' with Jesus, June 6, like the movie, big mother ship and all. I'll be back."

Elizabeth Bathory

When examining the lives of serial killers throughout history, serial killers from the medieval ages have been embalmed as fictional tales founded on truth. One such story would be the tale of Elizabeth Báthory, a tale that sadly is founded on the truth that she killed more than 600 people during her lifetime. Elizabeth was the unfortunate product of a medieval kingdom that was focused on the wealth of the royal family rather than focusing on sharing the wealth with those who needed it most. As a result, it is largely believed that Elizabeth held no qualms in killing the hundreds of servant girls who worked for her. Another element of Elizabeth's life that is often overlooked is her suffering imposed by epilepsy. A disease that leads to numerous seizures at the exposure to bright or repeating light, epilepsy proved to be the scourge of Elizabeth's life and could possibly have been a contributing factor towards her hatred and despondence toward humanity. Though Elizabeth facilitated her murders in the darkness of her kingdom and without the knowledge of the public or her family, Elizabeth would eventually be caught and tried for her devious actions. However, the balance of justice would be largely skewed, and Elizabeth would remain alive due to the prominence of her family's name and the tarnished image the trial would bring to the kingdom. Elizabeth Báthory's life is the perfect example of a life that could have influenced so many more had it not been affected by the parasitical nature of greed and pride. By coupling Elizabeth's pride with her greed for her own health and wealth, the monster of Elizabeth Báthory was born and will forever be remembered as a murderous machine that showed little remorse for the hundreds of lives she took.

The year of Elizabeth Báthory's birth is unknown to mankind. The records from both 1560 and 1561 show a birth in the royal family that could have been her. For this reason, historians have given Elizabeth the birth year of either 1560 or 1561. Elizabeth was born into the royal family located in the Kingdom of Hungry within the Ecsed Castle. Elizabeth spent most of her younger years playing in the fields of Nyíbátor, Hungry while her family undertook the royal proceedings each day. Elizabeth's father and mother were cousins, her father being Baron George VI Báthory and her mother being Baroness Anna Báthory. Elizabeth's father was birthed into the royal family of the Ecsed branch of Hungarian government while her mother was birthed into the royal family of the Somlyó branch. With the family being oriented so heavily in the Hungarian government, Elizabeth was immediately given royal prestige and was the immediate niece of Stephen Báthory, the current king of Poland who was also the duke of Lithuania. The governments of Lithuania and Poland had combined to form a commonwealth many years before Elizabeth's birth, resulting in a commonwealth called Transylvania. With the governments combined as such, Elizabeth was destined to spend her life in politics and in the constant light of the public. Her brother, Stephen Báthory, not to be confused with her uncle who was also named Stephen Báthory, would eventually serve as the royal judge of Hungary. Throughout Elizabeth's childhood, the drama and prestige of the government surrounded her, giving her a glimpse of the power she would one day hold.

Despite being surrounded by the luxuries of the royal family, Elizabeth was a slave to something else: the chains of epilepsy. Due to the epilepsy, seizures became a regular occurrence each day of Elizabeth's life, causing her to hate her life. Historians point to the marital relationship of her parents who were cousins as the likely culprit for the condition. While the epileptic seizures were traumatic enough, the treatment for the condition was almost worse than the actual condition. For those afflicted with epilepsy, the medicinal practice of the time involved placing blood from another person who was not afflicted by epilepsy on the person's lips. This practice particularly traumatized Elizabeth but was nothing compared to the second practice her uncle recommended. In this practice, Elizabeth was forced to drink the blood of another person who did not suffer from epilepsy. In addition to drinking the blood, bits of another person's skull were added into the drink. Historians wonder if Elizabeth might have been attempting to salvage more blood and skulls in the future when she killed so many of her servant girls. While history will never know of the reason behind this, what is known is that Elizabeth was forced to undergo horrific medicinal practices that left her scarred and traumatized.

At a young age, Elizabeth was forced to attend the Protestant church in their city. Known formally as a Calvinist church, the church was similar to many of the other protestant churches in the area, though the family would attend the church out of tradition instead of want. In her personal diaries, Elizabeth records that her family disagreed with most of what was taught from the church but attended out of fear of what the public would think if the family ceased attending. Additionally, the church showered the family with financial resources if only they maintained their attendance at the church. While Elizabeth would attend the church for her years as a child, it is largely believed she ceased attending after reaching adulthood.

Though Elizabeth was inflicted with her epilepsy and the traumatic solutions being forced upon her, Elizabeth's home life was also riddled with influences that were derived from Satanic practices. In some accounts, records hold that Elizabeth was instructed to torture animals at an early age and that her family held no remorse for killing people. Additionally, Elizabeth was taught Satanism from one of her uncles who was recognized as worshiping Satan on a regular basis. Further records show that Elizabeth was also taught witchcraft from her aunt, a witch that lived with the family. From just these accounts, the future of Elizabeth is given in a clearer light. With such influence from demonic sources, Elizabeth was following many of the principles she was taught as a child when she began her killing spree so many years later. When Elizabeth was 10, her parents deemed her old enough for engagement and gave her to Ferenc Nádasdy for marriage. Nádasdy was the son of a fellow member of the royal family, leading historians to believe that this marriage was arranged solely out of consideration for political ties. When the news of the engagement reached the public, concern was raised regarding whose name would be assumed to become the last name. Due to Elizabeth's prestige and greater social standing, the couple would assume Elizabeth's last name of Báthory rather than assuming Nádasdy's last name. This engagement was greatly clouded, however, when news arrived that Elizabeth was pregnant with another man's child. At just the young age of 13, Elizabeth had been impregnated by a peasant boy whom had been a close friend of Elizabeth's at the time. Shortly after Elizabeth gave birth to the child, it was given to a woman who was a close friend of the Báthory family and the matter of unwed impregnation did not deter from the engagement of Elizabeth and Nádasdy. To ensure the child was given the greatest care, the royal family paid this woman to take care of Elizabeth's child, and the child was eventually moved to Wallachia, a region of land in Romania.

When Elizabeth turned 15, she and Nádasdy, who was 19 at the time, were married on May 8, 1575. The wedding was a pompous time of jubilation, and historical records account that over 4,500 guests were present at the wedding. After the wedding, Elizabeth left the castle her family was residing in and took up new residence at NádasdyCastle in Sárvár, the home of her new husband. The months directly following the marriage were difficult months for Elizabeth. While Elizabeth had envisioned starting a family together and spending much time with her new husband, her married life held quite the opposite with Nádasdybeing called upon to spend most of his time in the royal court. When he was not studying, Nádasdywas busy studying law in Vienna. To keep her busy during these tumultuous months, Elizabeth began studying foreign languages. In less than two years, she mastered four foreign languages. Additionally, Elizabeth began studying defensive strategies for war, a study that would become invaluable years later when she would be placed in leadership of the defense of the castle due to her husband's prolonged tour of war.

When Elizabeth and Nádasdy were married, the gift from Nádasdy to Elizabeth's family was a large castle located in the Little Carpathians in what is now Slovakia. This present particularly delighted Elizabeth's family and many members of the immediate family moved to this castle. The castle held special prominence in the Nádasdy family as his mother had purchased the castle and given it to Nádasdy for his 16th birthday. The castle exists to this day and is a major tourist attraction in Slovakia.

With war imminent, Nádasdy was called on to be the chief commander of the entire Hungarian army. Special instructions outlined an attack in which Nádasdy would begin attacking the Ottomans as many times as necessary to force a retreat. It was now that Elizabeth would begin to utilize the many days of studying defense and management. Immediately following her husband's departure for war, Elizabeth was placed in control of the financial dealings of the estate at Nádasdy Castle. During this long tenure as leader of the castle, Elizabeth was also in charge of being responsible for the people within her area. Often, Elizabeth would have to make medical decision and financial decisions for the Hungarian and Slovak people located in her area. Eventually, the war ended, and her husband returned but the moments of leadership would be put to use again shortly.

From 1593-1606, the empire was engrossed in the Long War and Nádasdy's services as a commander were once again called upon. During this absence of her husband, Elizabeth was tasked with more than simply managing the finances of the castle: now Elizabeth was in charge of the defense of the castle. This would be particularly important due to the strategic location of the Nádasdy Castle in regard to its proximity to Vienna. During the previous war, the Ottomans had attacked the village of Čathtice which was located close to Vienna, leaving Elizabeth worried they would attempt another attack shortly. Thankfully, no such attack would occur but in the preparation of such an attack, Elizabeth had divided the castle's army into two groups, demanding that one section of the troops be ready always. After the war ended, Elizabeth's husband returned home and relieved her of her leadership efforts.

During her times as leader of the castle, Elizabeth was sometimes asked to rule in the decision of several women who had been abused. If one were to view her atrocities later in life before being told of her decision, they might be tempted to assume her decision would favor the party opposing the abused women. However, Elizabeth always ruled in favor of the women being abused and always dealt harshly with the parties responsible for the mischievous deeds. Elizabeth gave every indication of being compassionate when in all truth, she was simply devising a plan that would bring pain to the lives of hundreds of girls.

In 1585, Elizabeth gave birth to her first daughter, Anna Nádasdy. It was not her first child, as she had given birth to a son many years prior, but it was the first child to be birthed between Elizabeth and her husband. Elizabeth would go on to give birth to four more children during her lifetime. Some historians allege that Elizabeth and Nádasdy had another son who died at a young age but no records exist to corroborate this fact. While no records of his birth exist, the name György Nádasdy exists, possibly denoting another child who died earlier than the other children. Still, historians are hesitant to give ownership of this child to Elizabeth considering how prominent all of her other children were versus the discrete records of this child. Shortly after the birth of every child, they were turned over to governesses who took care of them in their daily needs. This meant that the children had very little interaction with their mother, though this was not an odd nature considering the time. Just as Elizabeth had been cared for as a child, her children received all of their care from the crew of governesses who lived with the family.

In 1604, Elizabeth's life took a tragic turn when her husband of 29 years passed away. Medicinal records from the day seem to denote that Nádasdy's death was the result of an illness that originated in 1601. The illness originally began in the lower extremities of Nádasdy before slowly creeping up his body and eventually rendering him a paraplegic. In 1603, the illness had claimed all mobility from Nádasdy and he transitioned from a paraplegic to a quadriplegic. The slow death of her husband was traumatic for Elizabeth to watch and many family members noted that she took on a dark aura as her husband's death grew nigh. Finally, on January 4, 1604, Nádasdy passed away, leaving behind his wife and four children. Shortly before his death, Nádasdy passed all of his earthly possessions and the care of his family to a trusted friend of the family, György Thurzó. Of particular irony, György Thurzó would later be the lead investigator into the life and crimes of Elizabeth. With her beloved husband now deceased, Elizabeth slowly sank into a depressed state, the once stunning and brilliant Elizabeth Báthory never to return.

As history tells, the reports of Elizabeth's atrocities surfaced in 1602, two years before Elizabeth's husband would pass away. However, with the Báthory family going through such a trial, the kingdom thought it wise to dismiss such claims and let the family enjoy their final days with Nádasdy. For a short while, these reports subsided; however, the reports soon began to surface again and in a much more aggressive fashion. Finally, after enduring reports for eight years, King Matthias II confided that he would begin an investigation into Elizabeth and commanded the family friend György Thurzó to the investigation. Thurzó began his investigation by hiring the efforts of two notaries in his quest for evidence. The quest lasted two years and at the culmination of two years, the notaries returned to Thurzó with testimonies from over 300 witnesses who claimed to either have been afflicted and tortured by Elizabeth or to have witnessed one of her devious acts. During the investigation, no stone was left unturned. Anyone who had held remote contact with Elizabeth was questioned. With primary testimonies originating from the Sárvár castle, Thurzó returned to King Matthias II with all but a confirmation of her guilt. When examining the testimonies, it was found that Elizabeth had assaulted and tortured women and girls who were primarily between the ages of 10-14 years old. It was found that Elizabeth had enticed these girls to enter her care through promises of employment as maids and cooks in her kitchen. Once employed, these girls would begin to trust Elizabeth until she would eventually kill them and use their bodies for what seemed to be Satanic practices. In addition to the girls seeking employment, Elizabeth also found her victims through the parents of girls seeking to achieve courtly etiquette. During medieval time, it was common practice for girls to attend lessons in a castle on how to be more ladylike. These girls were especially vulnerable, with many of them coming from the homes of poor paupers. When their daughters were not returned to them, the paupers would question but would be given limited answers and told that their daughters were now serving in the castle as maids. While examining those afflicted is traumatic enough, studying the methods with which Elizabeth carried out her devious actions is even more traumatic. Often, Elizabeth would torture her victims through: beatings, mutilating their bodies, intentionally freezing or starving her victims until death, or drawing blood from their bodies until they died. When performing the investigation, Thurzó found that all acts of terror and torture were carried out by Elizabeth. She had done these actions alone and now she alone would stand trial for her deeds.

When reading the report, King Matthias II was shocked to find that Elizabeth had also experimented with the responses of animals to the girls. In some cases, Elizabeth would sear the bodies of the girls, while alive, before immediately placing the girls in extremely cold water. Additionally, Elizabeth had also attempted to skin girls alive by covering their bodies in honey and allowing ants to cover their bodies. Perhaps the height of the report was the section that entailed the alleged cannibalism of Elizabeth. On many occasions, servants and maids reported seeing Elizabeth cook the bodies of deceased servant girls over a fire before ingesting the cooked flesh. Upon reading this, King Matthias II was outraged and immediately proposed that Elizabeth be killed. However, the royal court persuaded King Matthias II to hold a fair trial in the seclusion of the castle. After deciding to hold the trial, King Matthias II commanded Thurzó to return to Elizabeth's castle and bring her to his castle for the trial.

When Thurzó returned to the castle, he found Elizabeth in the act of torturing a young servant girl. Thurzó immediately arrested Elizabeth and took her, along with four of her servants who were helping her at the time, to the castle of King Matthias II for a quiet and speedy trial. However, while the trial was intended to remain quiet, Thurzó was so incensed by the actions of Elizabeth that he began announcing her devious actions to the whole city. This caused King Matthias II to be forced to hasten the trial and give her a just punishment. Elizabeth was placed in jail, awaiting her trial to be held on January 2, 1611. The long period of Elizabeth's secret reign of terror had come to its conclusion.

The trial began on January 2 and extended through January 7. Each day, numerous witnesses were publicly questioned and with each witness, the public's disdain for Elizabeth grew. The climax of the trial occurred when one of Elizabeth's personal servants provided a list of over 650 girls who had been allegedly killed by Elizabeth. With this information, death seemed to be the only just punishment for Elizabeth. However, the royal family still worried about the precedence being set by killing a member of the royal family, not to mention the negative image this would cast on the family. King Matthias II proposed that Elizabeth be placed in a nunnery and spend the rest of her life as a nun. This seemed to be a plausible solution until the nunnery was told of Elizabeth's actions. After hearing of Elizabeth's atrocious actions, the nunnery refused to allow Elizabeth acceptance and commanded the king not to bring her. With the option of placing her in a nunnery removed, King Matthias II resorted to placing her in solitary confinement in the middle of the castle's dungeon. Placed under the watch of a guard for every hour of the day, Elizabeth would spend the remainder of her life in a small cell that had no windows. The only connection Elizabeth would have with the outside world would be a two-inch slat on the floor that allowed for ventilation and food delivery. The person who had so long trapped other girls in her castle and held no regard for their life was now trapped in a cell, never to see another ray of sunshine.

In prison, reports of Elizabeth's behavior held that she was reserved and offered no explanation for why she committed such atrocities. Despite attempts to offer her reconciliation, Elizabeth refused to apologize for her actions and eventually refused to talk about them at all. On August 21, 1614, Elizabeth began to complain of being cold and feeling numbness in her fingers. To this, her guard replied "It's nothing mistress. Just go lie down." Elizabeth complied with his orders and nothing more was heard. The following morning, guards noted there had been no movement in the cell and upon opening the cell, found Elizabeth dead. The public rejoiced at her passing, though some continued to complain that she had received a much nicer death considering the torture she put her victims through. Initially, Elizabeth was buried in a local church but upon discovery that a murderer was being buried in a sacred burying ground, the locals forced the family to move her burial plot to another location. The family settled on burying her in Ecsed, the place where she had been born. A life that had caused so much grief had met its ending and left nothing but a gloomy legacy of murder and selfishness in its wake.

Gilles de Rais

When examining the crimes of criminals from the beginning of time, there is a certain level of subjective acceptance that is used when assessing the crimes. For many, the crimes that amass the records would be deemed as immature or inconsiderate but would not lead one to hate the person who perpetrated the crime. On the other hand, there are a few crimes that have sparked severe anger towards the perpetrator, sometimes deeming capital punishment carried out by civilians when the government fails to meet the citizens' expectations. One branch of crime that is often deemed grossly inappropriate and worthy of severe punishment would be crimes against the defenseless, namely children. Within the metric of self-justification, many criminals compare their crimes in an effort to desensitize the nature of their crime. Crimes against children, however, are one crime that cannot be desensitized and leads to hatred from almost every source. One man who partook in gross crimes against children was Gilles de Rais; a medieval knight who would later became a lord shortly before commencing his crimes against children. Gilles was alive during the 1400s and took advantage of his great influence to feed his satirical sense of amusement. Despite his heroics alongside Joan of Arc in their leadership of the French army, Gilles preyed upon the defenseless and left horrified parents in his wake when the news and details of his crimes were brought to light. While the majority of Gilles' life was dedicated to hurting children and feeding a selfish and sick desire, Gilles' crimes did bring about reform to the treatment of children and served as a precedent for future rulings involving similar crimes. The life of Gilles de Rais serves as an example to what can happen when one allows his selfish desires to supersede the care and consideration of others. Gilles de Rais will forever be remembered not for his heroics on the battlefield but rather for his cowardly acts of self-pleasure, labeling him Britain's first serial killer.

Gilles de Rais was born one night during the year 1405 in modern day France, known as Brittany at the time. Due to the lack of historical records from this time of medieval history, very little is known regarding the childhood of Gilles. From the historical documents of the day, it has been found that Gilles belonged to the family of Guy II Montmorency-Laval and Marie de Craon. Together, Gilles and his parents resided in the family castle located in Champtocé-sur-Loire. It is largely believed that Gilles was a very smart child, often speaking in different languages and mastering the difficult language of Latin at a very young age. From his pre-pubescent years, Gilles began illuminating and translating manuscripts for his father. Aligning his education with the education of the other French children, Gilles' parents split his education between years of actual schooling and military schooling. The French army was the stabilizing force of the 1400s due to their strong military development programs within various schools across France. The de Rais family was affluent, influential, and largely believed to be among the leading families in France at the time. In addition to being highly intelligent at such a young age, Gilles was also noted as being very arrogant and obstinate as well. However, he demonstrated sound leadership and those around him accepted his demeanor as merely accompanying characteristics of leaders. In 1415, tragedy struck Gilles' family when both of his parents were killed in the same day from unrecorded causes. This left Gilles the sole heir to a large fortune, instantly propelling him to new heights of leadership and promise. Acting as his guardian for the remainder of Gilles' years as a child, Jean de Craon took in Gilles along with Gilles' younger brother René de La Suze. Due to René's young age, he was excluded from the benefits of the inheritance. Despite de Craon's care, this man would actually prove to be a great detriment to Gilles' life.

Jean de Craon was Gilles maternal grandfather, giving the two an instant bond. Furthering this bond, Jean gave Gilles whatever his heart desired, including women. Jean de Craon was a known swindler of the time but his financial prowess helped him maintain his following of people and influence. When Gilles turned twelve, Jean attempted to merge Gilles' love of both women and finances together through the marriage of Jeanne Paynel. However, Paynel, despite being an affluent heiress, was only four years old and her parents refused to allow her to marry a twelve year old lad who was obstinate. Not to be discouraged by his first failed attempt, Jean organized the marriage of Gilles and Béatrice de Rohan, another rich girl who was the niece of the Duke of Brittany. Eventually, this marriage too failed and Gilles was left largely frustrated with his failing grandfather. Against the wishes of Gilles, Jean eventually organized a successful marriage between Catherine de Thouars, the daughter of La Vendée and Poitou, two influential and affluent leaders within Brittany. Though this marriage was excruciating for Catherine to undertake, it gave Gilles the two elements he sought in life: a woman to bear his child and the financial security Catherine's inheritance promised. The two would have one child nine years following their marriage – a daughter named Marie. Seeming that Gilles' life appeared to be leading him towards happiness and wealth, Gilles was noted as being increasingly depressed and angry. Gilles had the leadership and financial security seemingly all men desired at the time; yet, he was very unhappy. Despite growing more miserable by the day, Gilles continued his pursuit of more leadership and would soon achieve the highest civilian area of leadership available in the young government of Brittany: commander of the Royal Army. For Gilles, the days ahead would hold increased leadership, financial affluence, and growing fame. However, they also held a dark transition in Gilles life when he would finally find an element that he could derive happiness from: the demise of the defenseless.

In 1364, the War of the Breton Succession ended, but there were still frequent attacks towards members of the government of Brittany, specifically the Dukes of the House of Montfort. These attacks would bring an opportunity for Gilles to demonstrate his military prowess and strategic planning. Until this point, Gilles had worked simply within his own castle, feeding off of the financial stability his marriage and inheritance brought. However, his military services were called on as the attacks intensified. At the age of sixteen, Gilles took his place as an aid for the House of Montfort, thus aligning himself with the Dukes of the House of Montfort. This move proved to be largely profitable for the lad who was repaid for his sacrificial and dangerous actions through various land grants that Gilles was able to convert to financial gain. Once again, the life of Gilles found its centric principle in deriving as much financial wealth as he could. A miser of sorts, Gilles was known for showing no philanthropic effort towards the citizens of his city. Yet, he remained in the forefront of leadership for the government and city. Gilles' life of leadership within the military continued with being granted commander of the royal army in 1425. This promotion came about as a result of meeting Charles VII at an undisclosed location in Saumur. In this meeting, Charles VII made mention that he had witnessed Gilles' tremendous military leadership during the attacks on the Dukes of the House of Montfort. During this meeting, Charles VII offered Gilles the position of royal commander with the only requirement being that he had to take lessons on the courtly manners that would be expected of him. Gilles accepted the offer and began learning the courtly manners through daily lessons of the Dauphin. During his first battle as royal commander, Gilles led the royal army in capturing the prestigious English sea captain, Blackburn. This move delighted Charles VII and Gilles' position as commander was solidified.

Gilles would continue to serve as the royal commander from 1425 through 1435. During many of his battles, Gilles was noted for the reckless abandon with which he approached each battle. During the Hundred Years War, Gilles' aggressive leadership would come into play mightily. It was during this period that one of the strongest battle duos of the medieval age was created. In 1429, Gilles was introduced to Joan of Arc, the heroic female leader of a small portion of the army. Joan of Arc needed more military aid to continue her siege of the

English troops, a move Gilles was more than willing to make. In addition, Gilles provided his own leadership and the two went on to defeat the English and Burgundian troops in sequential battles. Gilles was actually standing next to Joan of Arc for the entire Siege of Orléans, though his name is not found in most history books due to the atrocities he would commit later in his life. Following the victory at the Siege of Orléans, Gilles was given the distinguished honor of being one of four lords that would bear the Holy Ampulla as it made its move from the Abbey of Saint-Remy to the Notre-Dame de Reims, in celebration and tradition of Charles VII being consecrated as the next king of the French people. This move only bolstered his position within the French army and led to what his troops noted as being an increased sense of bragging. To further his pride, Gilles was actually certified as a Marshal of France on the day of the consecration of King Charles VII. Such a move distinguished Gilles and his fame continued to seep throughout France. When looking back on the life of Gilles de Rais, perhaps the greatest moment of his life was the victory he held at the Siege of Orléans. It seems that the majority of Gilles' accolades stem from this moment. One such accolade would have been the addition of royal arms to Gilles' personal coat of arms. Such an allowance effectively crowned Gilles as an honorary member of the royal family, an honor received by few but coveted by many. The addition, a fleur-de-lis growing, spelled various words that Gilles thought best exemplified himself. These words and phrases included "...high and commendable services, the great perils and dangers, and many other brave feats." It was easy to assert that Gilles was quite pleased with his bravery against the English during his tenure as royal commander. Gilles' relationship with Joan of Arc significantly soured following the war and culminated with Joan of Arc burning at the stake alone. In fact, Gilles was not even present at the burning of Joan of Arc. Such a move was cowardly, but none-the-less distanced him far enough from Joan of Arc to risk being burned at the stake himself. When Gilles' guardian from many years before died on November 15, 1432, he let his discontentment with his grandson be known through his will. In medieval times, the greatest possession one could give his offspring would be his sword and breastplate. Such a gesture denoted respect and admiration. Gilles should have been the first in the family line to receive such an honor but his grandfather thought differently, given Gilles' latest financial mistakes. Gilles had begun spending his money aggressively and recklessly, a move that his grandfather found contrary to the family faith. With this in mind, Gilles was overlooked for the sword and breastplate, both of which were given to his younger brother de La Suze. Angered by such a move, Gilles refused to attend his grandfather's funeral and instead began making even more frivolous purchases. It was now that Gilles' actions would begin to transition and the first audience of such a transition would be those closest to him: his family.

In 1435, Gilles left his position as commander of the royal army to focus on both a play he had written himself and a chapel, known as the Chapel of the Holy Innocents. The play became one of the most extravagant performances of its time as well as the most expensive production of the time. Regardless of having little financial backing when the play was being written, Gilles carried on the production and made hasty and costly acquisitions for the performance. However, Gilles soon ran out of money and was forced to sell all of his property just to carry on the performance. With the performance not even being close to production, Gilles' family began to seek the aid of the government in receiving an order for Gilles to stop spending money. The order came eventually but not before the play had been performed once already. Throughout the performance, unlimited food and drink was provided for the spectators at the personal expense of Gilles, while the cast discarded every piece of costuming after the performance per the wishes of Gilles. Despite losing his fortune to a dismal play, Gilles remained hopeful and desired to spend more money. The government had announced that Gilles was not to be sold anything else due to his habit of being a spendthrift. This ruling held no enforcement in Brittany, however, and Gilles merely moved to this location when he was unable to make purchases in Orléans.

Gilles soon began exploring the world of the occult, asking all people who knew how to summon demons and the principles of alchemy to come to his castle. During one such moment of summoning, Gilles was attempting to speak with a demon named Barron but was unsuccessful after three attempts. The man aiding Gilles in this attempt commanded Gilles to bring a cup full of the body parts of a child. Gilles returned shortly thereafter with body parts, presumably from his first victim; unfortunately, the demon was never summoned and Gilles was left financially broke and spiritually broken.

With his life turning negative and casting dark shadows, Gilles began assaulting children on a regular basis, without the knowledge of another human. Even with reports stating that Gilles began his assaults in 1432; historians believe that his first assault actually occurred in 1437 and spiraled quickly from there. In Machecoul, the grave of forty naked children was found, prompting an immediate outcry from the citizens. However, nothing was done and Gilles merely assured his constituents that he would investigate the crime himself. Gilles' first identified victim appears to be twelve year old Jeudon. This boy held contact with Gilles through a furrier named Gillaume Hilairet. At this point, Gilles was performing these assaults with the aid of his cousins, Gilles de Sillé and Roger de Briqueville. This duo of men would systematically provide Gilles with numerous children each day so that he could perform his self-pleasure acts on them before killing them. During a routine kidnapping of a child, the two men would dress the child in rich clothes to make it seem as if he was being adopted into Gilles' family. Gilles would then force the child to consume a large glass of alcohol. Following the meal, the child would be led to a room where Gilles had instructed servants to only allow admission to himself and his two cousins. Once in this room, Gilles would reveal his sadistic plan to the child, attempting to generate shock within the child. In his confession, Gilles would admit that this was his favorite part of his ritual. Gilles would then strip the child of his clothes, hang him from the ceiling with rough rope, and then perform a variety of sex acts on the child. Gilles admits that the cries of plea and desperation from the child were his greatest source of pleasure. After fondling the child, Gilles would bring the child down from the rope, assure him everything would be fine, and then proceed to either kill the child himself or have his accomplices kill the child. Such sadistic routines are graphic but were sadly carried out every single day by Gilles. In a latter portion of his testimony, Gilles recounted how he would kiss the children after they had been killed. If the child was handsome or pretty, he would have the child sliced open so he could admire the internal organs, an act that he stated brought him utmost joy. Following the ritual of killing the child, Gilles would burn the child's body, piece by piece, in the fireplace of his room. Dissecting the child before-hand allowed the smell to be contained and allowed Gilles more sadistic forms of self-pleasure. Though Gilles was deeply embedded in his daily ritual of killing children, the end of this horror was close at hand and soon, Gilles would be experiencing a portion of the torture he had put these children through.

In May of 1440, Gilles made a critical mistake when he assaulted and killed a son of the local cleric. This prompted a thorough investigation that when completed, found Gilles charged with the death of over twenty children. Gilles was immediately arrested and brought in for a trial. During the trial, the accounts of the killings became so graphic that the judge ordered the accounts to be removed from the royal record. At the culmination of the trial, Gilles stood guilty for the death of over 80 children. While only 80 children were identified, the estimate of murders rests just over 600 children. With the judge convinced of Gilles' guilt, he ordered that Gilles be hung along with his two cousins. Following a long parade, Gilles was brought to the Ile de Biesse for his death. In accordance with his request, Giles was hung prior to his two accomplices being burned and his body was removed before the fire incinerated it. His body was buried in the Notre-Dame des Carmes while his accomplices' bodies were permitted to burn before being subsequently spread across the plain of Rais. The life of Gilles, pure evil, had finally met its end and the death he had inflicted upon so many was inflicted back on him.

Ed Gein

Within the recess of crime history, the confessions of notable criminals are often examined to determine validity and possible causes of their crimes. Within these confessions, the liabilities of insanity or intentional harm are carefully examined to determine whether or not the perpetrator of the crime is fit to stand trial and receive the proper justice for his crime. Often, criminals have escaped the full judgment from their gross transgression by means of insanity, pleading not guilty due to their inability to control their actions. While some of these admissions of insanity are false and prevent true justice from being enacted, there are some whose admissions of insanity are true and should be dealt with appropriately. One such case would be the mysterious case of Edward Gein, a supposed murderer who also exhumed more than forty graves during his tenure as a criminal in the 1900s. However, when standing trial, Ed began to show a troubling series of behaviors that documented his insanity. Perhaps stemming from the loss of his only true friend, his mother, Ed was responsible for exhuming a number of graves in an attempt to retrieve body parts from the individuals. When police would search Ed's house many years later, they would find the extent of these body parts – Ed having replaced commodities in his house with the fragments from women's bodies. Additionally, Ed was found to have eaten the flesh of numerous persons whose graves he exhumed. Throughout the life of Ed, the sad truth of the mentally insane is shown. The product of a controlling mother, Ed became trapped in a world where his only friend was his dying mother. As a result, his mother left him completely unstable and helpless upon her death. With the knowledge of Ed Gein, humanity can more appropriately handle the mentally insane and offer them the security they need.

On August 27, 1906, Edward Theodore Gein was born to a poor couple, George Philip Gein and Augusta Wilhelmine Gein. Ed had an older brother named Henry George Gein. From his youngest years, Ed remembers the dismal state of his house and the instability his dysfunctional family offered. The relationship between Augusta and George became fodder for hatred and the two began living distant lives. They would never divorce, but Ed's parents were anything but the semblance of a happy family who cared for their sons. Ed's father George held numerous jobs that were indicative of an unskilled laborer including tanner, insurance salesman, and carpenter. For a short while, George owned and operated a small grocery shop that provided substantial income for the family. However, for unknown reasons, George sold the business and moved his family out of the city limits to a 155 acre farm that left his family sheltered from any involvement with the public of his city. The house and farm would remain in the Gein family until Ed's eventual arrest. Perhaps showing the source of Ed's instability, Augusta, Ed's mother, demonstrated severe obsession over her sons and ruled every aspect of their lives. Under no circumstances were her sons allowed to have any friends, leading to the Gein boys living an anti-social life founded on a hatred for society. The only times Ed was allowed to leave the security of the farm was when he was forced to attend school. The farm was large enough that Ed was kept quite busy with his daily chores around the house. Nevertheless, Ed often questioned his lack of friends and surmised that his mother was correct in assuming that all outside influences of his life were evil and sadistic. Despite her tendencies towards shunning all friends from her sons' lives, Augusta did hold strict religious standards, conforming to the Lutheran principles of the faith. Each day, Augusta prioritized sessions of teaching with her sons in which she would reveal the atrocities of the present world, painting every woman outside of herself to be a prostitute. Additionally, Augusta told the most graphic stories from the daily news to her sons, frightening them enough that they vowed to stay on the farm. Though Augusta was attempting to save her sons from the world's horrors, she was in affect breeding the horrors that her son would eventually carry out.

Augusta read passages of scripture that held graphic accounts of victims and rape, murder, and sexual misconduct throughout her teachings. Ed was given the opportunity to attend school and this would remain as the only time his mother allowed him to stray from her watchful eye. At school, Ed was known for being unfriendly and residing within his own world. Often, Ed would begin laughing during class lectures, seemingly amused by jokes he would tell himself. Classmates of Ed recall him being a smart lad but lacking any of the basic social skills needed to survive in a public school system. During several instances, Ed would attempt to be friendly to a fellow classmate, only to have his brother reveal his "sin" to his mother. Ed would then be severely punished until he ceased the relationship with the classmate. Ed's teachers were compassionate towards his situation, often attempting to talk to Ed's mother and convince her that a few friends would be beneficial to Ed's social ineptness. However, Ed's mother refused to allow Ed the privilege of friends and Ed continued to spiral into a state of being anti-social. Possibly telling of a condition much deeper than simply being anti-social, Ed remained close to his mother despite her control over his life. Classmates recall Ed being extremely gullible and appeared to have absorbed his mother's teaching with fervency. And thus would conclude Ed's childhood; a lad who held extreme potential and was smart enough to succeed but would remain trapped within a world of safety created by his mother. However, the world would eventually be introduced to the horrors being created within this "safe" world.

Ed and Henry continued to maintain their odd life, living with their parents well beyond their years of high school. Overall, the two men were content and the typical contention between members of the family became a regular aspect of their life. However, their lives changed when Ed turned 36. Ed's father had long been an alcoholic. The persistent drinking caught up with him and he passed away on

April 1, 1940. After performing an autopsy on George, doctors concluded that he had passed away from heart failure, the direct result of years of drinking alcohol. Henry and Ed were sad to see their father pass away but his consistent negativity and abuse were not missed. George had been the family's sole source of income and as a result, Ed and his brother were forced to begin taking jobs around their city in an attempt to pay the monthly bills. The community accepted the two men and noted their honesty and strong work ethic. Additionally, Henry and Ed proved themselves reliable to the members of the community and soon, the two held consistent jobs around the city. For Henry, his jobs consisted of manual labor while Ed focused more on babysitting. Ed seemed to relate with children on a more consistent basis and as a result, Ed became a trusted friend of the families he babysat for. While Henry and Ed were glad to be doing work again, Henry began to grow un-approving of his brother's deep respect and resolve for his mother. Augusta still abused her sons and let it be known that she did not approve of them working. However, even though all of this, Ed maintained his servitude to his mother and answered every call for him that she made. To try to dissuade his brother from his respect for his mother, Henry began belittling their mother every time he was with Ed. Often, Henry would also wage verbal altercations with their mother in an attempt to show Ed her fickle nature. Nevertheless, Ed would not be reasoned with and continued to regard his mother as the supreme authority in his life. Finally, Henry's frustration with his mother and Ed reached its maximum capacity and Henry moved out of the house. Without his mother's knowledge, Henry had begun dating a divorced woman who had two children and eventually moved in with her. Ed was deeply hurt by his brother's actions but did nothing to dissuade his brother from his decision to move out. Now, the only true influence in Ed's life was his mother, the one who had created his world for him.

Four years after the passing of their father, Ed and Henry were attempting a control burn on the edge of their property. Marsh vegetation had begun creeping upon the property line so Henry proposed burning the plants to recreate the property line.

Unfortunately, the fire soon ignited more of the plants and Ed and Henry were unable to control the fire. While both refused to call the fire department, the flames soon reached high enough to create a glow seen from the city and the firefighters arrived on the scene to extinguish the flames. Shortly after the fire department left the house, Ed made a call to the police station regarding his brother Henry being missing. After the police searched the property for hours, they finally found Henry's body, overturned in the soil and battered with bruises. Surprisingly, Henry was not burned in any way. After the coroner investigated the death, he found that Henry had passed away from a heart attack and listed the means of death as asphyxiation. However, police paid no mind to the bruises upon the head of Henry and no autopsy would ever be performed. Despite the lack of police intervention into the death of Henry, many locals held suspicions of foul play and held Ed as the primary suspect. It was known that Henry and Ed held a married relationship and the locals wondered if Ed blamed Henry for the fire. No proof of this allegation would ever occur and Ed would never confess to the crime.

As Ed and his mother continued to live in their large house alone, the two became closer despite Augusta's continual berating of Ed. The death of her son Henry had been quite traumatic for Augusta and the added stress led to a stroke that paralyzed her. Ed rose to the challenge of caring for his mother and would do so dutifully until her death. Often, Ed would push his mother's wheelchair and the two would go on long walks. During one of their walks, Ed and his mother witnessed their senseless neighbor, Mr. Smith, beating a dog to death. A woman came from Mr. Smith's house and began yelling at him for killing the dog. After the ordeal was over, Ed was shocked to see the dog lifeless. His mother was also incensed but not at the death of the dog; rather, Augusta was incensed that a woman was living with Mr. Smith, a woman Augusta would begin referring to as "Smith's Harlot." As Ed continued to care for his mother, it became apparent that her health was deteriorating, quickly. The episode with "Smith's Harlot" detracted from her energy substantially and soon, Augusta looked to be nearing her death. On December 20, 1945, Augusta had a second stroke, one that would leave her an invalid. Unable to speak, Augusta laid motionless on her bed each day, staring into the empty space above her. Ed was heartbroken by his mother's deterioration but was committed to care for her until her death. That day came on December 29, 1945, when Ed returned to his mother's room to find her cold to the touch. Ed was heartbroken. His one friend that he had for his entire life was now gone, never to be seen again on earth. In his biography of Ed Gein, Harold Schechter notes, "Ed had lost his only friend and one true love. For the first time, he was absolutely alone in the world." Sadly, Ed would turn to sadistic and terrifying means in an effort to bring his mother back. The life of Ed Gein was poised to take a dramatic downfall.

Following his mother's death, Ed continued to manage the family farm, tended to the livestock, and general upkeep. However, he could not bring himself to enter the room where his mother had passed away. In fact, Ed was too heartbroken to enter any of the rooms where his mother would spend long periods of her time. To calm himself, Ed closed the rooms he associated with her and boarded them from the outside. These rooms would never be entered again until the house was put up for auction many years later. In his spare time and at night, Ed would sleep in a small room that was located next to the kitchen. Without his mother's instruction, Ed was lost within his own world. To provide himself with a therapy of sorts, Ed began buying subscriptions to magazines that focused on death and various cults that celebrated death. It is believed that around this time, Ed began exhuming graves and was unaffected by the thought of death. Additionally, Ed began to develop an interest in the mutilating practices of the Nazi doctors years earlier. To provide an income, Ed began working for the city on their road crew and also helped in the seasonal work of threshing crops within the area. When finances grew tight, Ed sold 80 acres of the family farm. However, Ed's problems were about to include legal aid when his atrocities came to light.

On November 16, 1957, Bernice Worden, a hardware store operator from Ed's town of Plainfield went missing. Police did not think anything of her store not being open due to the current deer season. However, when her son, the police chief of Plainfield, went into the store a short while later, he found traces of blood but no signs of his mother being there. After examining the receipt log, Worden's son found that the last customer served was Ed Gein. Police found Ed at an adjoining grocery store and subsequently arrested him. After police began searching Ed's house, they came upon a horrific discovery. The first thing police found when examining the property was the body of Worden in a shed behind the house. Worden had been decapitated and was strung over a beam dangling, as a deer waiting to be processed would be. Police were horrified at the discovery and immediately began searching the house. It would be here that the police made the most grisly of discoveries. Within the house, the police found: chairs with human skin stretched as the cushion covers, wastebaskets made of human skin, various pieces of clothing such as leggings fashioned from human skin, masks made from female heads, the decapitated head of Worden, a belt made of nipples, a drawstring fashioned from a pair of lips, a lampshade that had been comprised solely of a human face, and the face of Mary Hogan, a woman who had gone missing months earlier. The search for Worden was over but police were not faced with a greater problem: identifying the bodies that had been destroyed. After being questioned, Ed rather bluntly told police where he had found his bodies: the local graveyard. After a lengthy period of questioning, it was found that Ed had scoured the graveyard every night for fresh graves of women that looked like his mother. From these bodies, Ed was rescuing any piece of usable flesh that could be added to his masterpiece: a woman's body fashioned from the various body parts. Ed had such an attachment to his mother that he was set on creating a "suit of her" that he could crawl in to whenever he was missing her. Police were almost too shocked to be incensed at Ed but the anger soon set in. During one interview with police, Ed ignited the anger of his interviewer so much that his interviewer smashed Ed's head into the side of the concrete wall. The grizzly details of Ed's life were about to be presented to the world.

The trial began on November 21, 1957 with Ed being arraigned on one count of first degree murder, the murder of Mary Hogan. However, Ed's lawyers had him tested for insanity and the results showed that Ed was suffering from schizophrenia and unable to be convicted. The judge ordered Ed to spend the remainder of his life in a mental correctional institution so that he would cease from being a threat to public safety. Almost eleven years later, the trial continued to press on, with lawyers arguing over whether or not Ed knew the consequences of what he was about to do prior to killing Worden. Ed was deemed to be not guilty with reasoning of insanity and was ordered to remain at the Mendota Mental Health Institute. His belongings were set to be auctioned until a fire destroyed his house and all of his belongings – the result of arson. On July 26, 1984, Ed passed away as a result of lung cancer. The media began using his life for their own financial gain, his story becoming the source of many new television show capers and movies. His confession has actually been featured on numerous heavy metal rock albums. After being buried in the Plainfield Cemetery, Ed's grave began to be vandalized on such a regular basis that officers were forced to leave the grave unmarked and merely in the same vicinity of his brother and parents. To this day, the gravestone of Ed Gein resides in the Waushara County Sheriff's Department. The horrific life of Ed Gein was now complete, a dismal reputation and memory being the only feature left in its wake.

Alexander Pichushkin

"Some people steal to stay alive, and some steal to feel alive. Simple as that." The quote by V.E. Schwab rings true as much today as when it was penned in her book, *A Darker Shade of Magic*. Corroborated by the fact that many high profile criminals have spoken of the high they received from committing their crimes, the true thrust behind many elements of crime is the adrenaline rush or even sexual pleasure derived from committing the crime. Moreover, many criminals grow proud of their crimes, leaving behind a small trademark within their crimes to be found. For some, this trademark was an intimate object left on the scene of the crime; for others, it was the method in which the crime was carried out. For Alexander Pichushkin, the trademark chosen was the large vodka bottle left pressed deeply into the gaping hole created in the victim's head, compliments of Alexander Pichushkin's violent hammer attack. While psychiatrists point to Alexander's injury as a child as the source for his anger and eventual murders, a mental condition cannot be given sole blame for such crimes simply because this condition cannot receive the appropriate judgment issued. Known as "The Chessboard Killer," Alexander Pichushkin gave society a horror story that actually played out in Bitsa Park in Russia. Consumed with leaving his legacy in history as being the deadliest serial killer, Alexander gave no thought to the lives he was taking, or the families that would be robbed of the presence of their loved ones. Though his story is the tragic culmination of a man who dealt with his anger in the most inappropriate way, the story of Alexander Pichushkin serves as an example for humanity on the effects of not seeking help to appropriately deal with bitterness and anger.

Alexander Pichushkin was born on April 9, 1974 in Russia, the son of Natalya Pichushkin and an unknown father. At an early age, Alexander's mother knew him as a kind child who loved animals and sought to serve them. One of her earliest memories of her son was of his uncontrolled sadness over the death of his pet cat. From the looks of Alexander's early life, his mother had no reason to ever think that her son would grow up to be the second-deadliest mass killer in Russian history. However, tragedy struck Alexander's life when he was four-years-old; during a trip to the park, Alexander was enjoying time on the swings when he fell off as the swing was entering its highest peak. After falling through the air, Alexander smote his head on the ground before being hit in the forehead by the swing as it came back down. While Alexander's mother dismissed the injury as anything serious, family and friends began to notice a change in Alexander's behavior – he was becoming more aggressive and hostile by the day. Today, doctors surmise that Alexander most likely struck his frontal cortex and damaged it severely. Damage to this portion of the brain can be most severe, with those being hurt here often exhibiting strong and unfounded senses of aggression towards those closest to them. With Alexander being in the early stages of his brain development, doctors assume that the brain damage in fact worsened as Alexander's brain continued to grow. Alexander started growing hostile towards his classmates at school, and his mother decided he could not remain the local elementary school, but was rather suited to be institutionalized until his mental condition could be more readily understood. Additionally, Alexander's mother noted that he had been bullied at school, his most common nickname being, "That Retard." Alexander's mother feared what he might do if called that name again, leaving her only option to place Alexander in an institution for children with speech and mental disabilities. Sadly, Alexander's life would only continue to grow more tragic within the institution.

When Alexander turned twelve, his grandfather convinced his mother to allow him to move in with him. Alexander's grandfather saw a highly intelligent side of Alexander's brain, one that he felt the doctors were missing and possibly inhibiting. After Alexander moved in with his grandfather, Alexander's mother noticed an immediate change in his disposition. Alexander seemed more happy and began to study his subjects with more vigor. Alexander's grandfather had begun introducing him to more extra-curricular activities, activities Alexander began to undertake with a serious, yet enjoyable, mindset. One attribute of the leadership of Alexander's grandfather was his choice to not mask Alexander from his inherent disability. Rather, Alexander's grandfather was upfront with him regarding his disability and insisted that he focus on overcoming it rather than simply attempting various achievements from school. By doing this, Alexander began to accomplish elements of school while also overcoming his disability and hostility. However, this would not be the sole method through which Alexander's grandfather grew his grandson. When Alexander turned thirteen, his grandfather thought he was old enough to begin studying his favorite game: chess. Alexander immediately fell in love with the game and demonstrated a genuine prowess for it. Once Alexander's grandfather thought he had mastered the minimum number of elements from the game, he began taking Alexander to Bitsa Park where he allowed him to play chess against some of his friends who had been very experienced in chess. The men were amazed at Alexander's talent as he began beating everyone. When examining Alexander's love of chess, doctors and psychiatrists surmise that his love for this game stemmed from his ability to dominate the entire playing board at once. For Alexander, life was about dominating your enemies, and chess gave Alexander the chance to dominate the playing board and his enemy: his opponent. However, even outside of the school system, Alexander was not shielded from the bullying of his peers. Still referred to as "That Retard," Alexander attempted to focus his anger on the chess board and continued to dominate the board in every game he played.

As Alexander's fame within the small group of chess players in the park continued to grow, it seemed as if he had found a niche that could solve his anger problems. However, Alexander refused to confront the root of the issue and instead relied on almost a therapeutic sense of anger management through his chess games. Alexander's dominance in the chess games took a serious hit however when an integral force within his life was removed: Alexander's grandfather passed away. Simply succumbing to the rigors of old age, Alexander's grandfather passed away, leaving Alexander alone and without the only stabilizing and supporting figure he had held in his life. Alexander admits that during this time, he contemplated suicide on many occasions, simply wanting to be out of his dark life and back with his grandfather. Alexander's hostility started to return and his anger and aggression towards others began to get out of hand. To curb the violent outbreaks he had begun experiencing, Alexander began drinking vodka in great amounts, becoming drunk every night. In addition to depressing his anxiety and violent tendencies, the alcohol allowed him to harbor fantasies of his grandfather returning while numbing the pain of his loss. While drunk, Alexander would still maintain his rigorous chess schedule, often playing games while fully intoxicated. The vodka was a two-fold element of success: it both reduced the emotional loss his grandfather while also allowing him to fit in more with the regular chess players in the park. Most of these chess players drank regularly and often played drunk. The only difference between these players and Alexander was that Alexander could play at complete performance while fully intoxicated. In an odd sense of shielding the powers of the vodka, Alexander continually performed just as he would while intoxicated as if he were playing sober. However, the chess and exhibition games were not enough to dull the dark side of Alexander that was beginning to develop. He began to fantasize about having extreme and total control over humanity. Doctors surmise that Alexander's true source of power came from his grandfather, and without him, Alexander felt powerless, which was a position he could not be in and still succeed with his current outbursts of rage.

Most of Alexander's populous of friends were older men whom he played chess with. Many of these men saw the change in Alexander's behavior following the death of his grandfather. They noted that he often would become hostile in a chess game, treating the chess game as a life or death experience in which the loser was completely subject to the powers of the winner and would be put to death. While there were no deaths or even threats of death, those playing Alexander agreed that the anger within the match stretched far beyond pure competition. Alexander was facing an unseen enemy and was taking out his rage on his opponents in the game. Sadly, this anger would begin to be channeled towards the weakest among society, all in an effort to satisfy his hunger for complete control over humanity.

When chess failed to satisfy Alexander's hunger for control and dominance, he turned to another source of power: the fantasy of total control. In this fantasy, Alexander would walk around, pick an ordinary citizen, and imagine himself having the control of life or death over them, the definition of complete control in Alexander's eyes. However, this fantasy lasted a short while and before long, Alexander was contemplating how he could turn this fantasy into a reality. To achieve this, Alexander began threatening young children that lived around his house. To allow his self the pleasure of experiencing these thrills later in life, Alexander began documented the instances on his camera and would watch them later that night; the sadistic sex tape of a mentally deranged man who lusted after complete power and had to prey on those who could not defend themselves. One occasion, in which Alexander was assaulting a child, he walked around his house holding the child in the air by one leg. During the climax of his moment of self-pleasure, Alexander dangled the child outside of his window and repeatedly said "You are in my power now…I am going to drop you from the window and you will fall 15 meters to your death." Even though Alexander did not follow through with the death threat, he admits to watching the video continuously that night, often experiencing the equivalent to a sexual orgasm while watching the video. Despite the fact that Alexander was not physically hurting anyone, he was breeding such a love for hurting humans in his mind with these videos, sadly this love would soon facilitate itself and Alexander would begin his tenure as a murderer.

In 1992, Andrei Chikatilo was convicted of murdering 52 people in Russia. Alexander felt sure he could better this number, and while playing chess one day, contrived an idea that would make him the most famous serial killer in Russian history. Using a chess board, Alexander would seek to fill in every chess square, 64 total, before ceasing his murdering passions. Alexander's first murder had taken place years before when he was just a teenager. He had gotten into a fight with a fellow young man from his neighborhood, and after the two argued for a few minutes, Alexander proceeded to push the young man out of a window, causing the boy to die from impact. However, Alexander caught a break when the police ruled the death a suicide. It is unknown why Alexander ceased killing, perhaps due to his newfound love of chess at the time. Sooner or later, Alexander was once again set on returning back to his murderous ways. Alexander began targeting men he was well acquainted with: the homeless men of Bitsa Park where Alexander played chess so frequently. Alexander would entice the men to follow him, promising them the joy of drinking a bottle of vodka as they sat at the grave of his dog. When Alexander had given them a large amount of alcohol, he then waited for them to become intoxicated, at which point he would hit them repeatedly on the head with a hammer until they were dead. After his first murder in this method, Alexander began shoving the empty vodka bottle into the shattered skull, thus labeling the murder to himself. During the first few murders, Alexander would drag the bodies into the woods or dump them into a nearby sewer. Eventually, Alexander began just leaving the bodies where he murdered them, making Bitsa Park a horrifying place to be. During investigations into the murders, it was found that Alexander always murdered his victims from behind, ensuring they were completely surprised by the attack. This method allowed Alexander to ensure that he did not get any blood on his clothes. During these murders, Alexander notes that he experienced a certain level of thrill in ending the life of a fellow human being; "In all cases, I killed for only one reason," recounts Alexander, "I killed in order to live, because when you kill, you want to live. For me, life without murder is like life without food for you. I felt the father of all these people since it was me who opened the door for them to another world." In effect, Alexander was killing to curb his hunger of killing; however, this hunger only grew with each murder completed. In 2006, Alexander would murder his last victim – one of merely three women that he would murder. Marina Moskalyova was an employee at the same grocery store where Alexander worked, and through work the two became good friends. When Alexander asked Moskalyova to accompany him to his dog's grave for a drink of vodka, Moskalyova became suspect and gave her plans and Alexander's number to her son. When Moskalyova failed to return to her home that night, her son called the authorities and stated that he felt his mother had been murdered. After a short search of Bitsa Park, Moskalyova was found, along with a train ticket in her pocket which placed her at the train station at a designated time. After reviewing security camera footage from the night, authorities found her, accompanied by Alexander on the train. With this evidence, the police arrested Alexander and charged him with the murder of Moskalyova.

After being arrested on June 16, 2006, Alexander was convicted of 49 murders and three attempted murders on October 24, 2007. When Alexander learned that his murder count stood at only 49, he asked the courts to add an additional eleven murders to the conviction, to bring the total to an even 60, claiming it was not fair to the others to have died without reaching the goal he worked so hard for. Alexander was sentenced to life in prison and fifteen years of solitary confinement. To this day, Alexander remains jailed with limited contact to the outside world, still a self-proclaimed innocent who fears no man, and claims his deity as God.

John Haigh

With the justice system of England being among the greatest and fairest, the driving force of any trial is one word: evidence. Without substantial or proper evidence, the thought of even holding a trial is an ill point and those seeking a trial risk being prosecuted for false arrest. Simply put: a trial in England requires evidence and evidence that is indisputable. In some cases, tangible evidence has been destroyed but where the tangible evidence once stood is the shadow of intangible or emotional evidence. One case in which the accused sought to vanquish himself due to the lack of evidence was the murder case of John Haigh. John Haigh, a former mechanical engineer, had come under the assumption that the phrase *corpus dilecti* referred to the inability of the court system to convict a man without the presence of evidence. However, John was basing his definition of evidence off of the physical bodies he would murder; the thought of witnesses never crossed his mind and would therefore be the shortcoming of a man who was categorized with the most conniving of murderers. John Haigh was among the first serial killers in England, and to this day is remembered for being the most creative in his effort to destroy the bodies. Recalling the lab trials of his college days, John used sulfuric acid to disintegrate the bodies of his victims, thus leaving no trail of evidence. However, this very method would be his shortcoming and police would soon find the structure of his diabolical plan and prosecute him appropriately – hanging him till his death. When asked why he undertook such a plan and murdered nine people, John's response contained an allegory of a man who was discontent with his current wealth and desired the wealth of those around him, thus using jealousy to fuel his drive against those who possessed a life he desired. The life of John Haigh may serve as a blueprint of a life that was overtaken by the seeds of jealousy – seeds that grew into the monster responsible for killing nine people and melting their bodies in sulfuric acid.

On July 24, 1909, John Haigh was born and began his life as a normal child who enjoyed playing outside and tending to his various animals. Born in Stamford, a portion of Lincolnshire, England, John was born into a family of hard workers who enjoyed the middle-class. Despite John's parents bestowing the necessary funding and care to make his childhood a beneficial one, John states that his childhood was dark and absent of friends. This is corroborated by the fact that John held regular contact with only his dog and family. However, when John began to grow up, he began to fight against the very principles that had guarded his family for generations. The Haigh family was religious and belonged to the Plymouth Brethren, a group of conservative Protestants near the Haigh family. This religious dedication served as a stumbling block to John, a man who was constantly at war with the church leaders over their alleged hypocrisy. In attempt to bring this child back into the fold, John refused their offers and continued to reject the teachings every Sunday. Nonetheless, John's father continued to force him to attend church, convinced that his son was merely addressing his acclimation to puberty in such an aggressive manner. During his childhood, John alleges that he had numerous nightmares involving the religion of his parents; nightmares often including genocide or mass murder as some other religions had turned out to be. However, his father refused to lend ear to John's pleas and John was forced to maintain his membership within the church. Despite the disagreement with his parents over religion, John did agree with his parents on their love for music. As a mere four-year-old, John began demonstrating a love of music that would remain for the rest of his life. During his youth, John spent a majority of time listening to the live performances of works by such authors as Felix Mendelssohn, Johann Sebastian Bach, Tchaikovsky, and Antonio Vivaldi. Music proved to be the therapy he desired and his parents noted that John was more reserved and level-headed after listening to or playing classical music.

In school, John worked hard and made good marks, a fact that greatly pleased his parents. When John was only thirteen, he pledged to continue the family trade of mechanical engineering just as his father and grandfather had done. When John was of age, he began exploring various grammar schools within the area in which he could continue his education. This choice was largely made for him when he was awarded a scholarship to the Queen Elizabeth Grammar School located in Wakefield, England. John demonstrated his prowess and was awarded subsequent scholarships to various schools in the area. One of these schools was the Wakefield Cathedral located in Wakefield. At this school, John became more involved in the extracurricular activities, first joining the college choir as a choirboy. After graduation, John began working within the motor companies of London working as an apprentice in the motor concept portion of the companies. However, this job proved to leave John quite displeased with himself and he soon left the job for another job that allowed him more interaction with the general public. Holding his previous job for only one year, many employers were hesitant to hire a man who had previously quit his job and regularly voice his complaints with the job. Finally, John was offered a job that he felt suited his desires. The job he settled on would be insurance sales, a job that placed him on the doorstep of potential clients. John remained employed at this job for almost two years, but his jealousy of his employer soon resulted in getting fired. John had seen the office his employer held and the car he drove around, driving John to begin a systematic habit of stealing from the cashbox left at work. When found out, John was immediately fired, thus consummating the beginning of a life that would be dominated by the lust of jealousy and desire to accumulate wealth at any expense necessary, including human life.

In 1934, John, still unemployed from his bout with stealing from his former company, met and married a 23-year-old woman named Beatrice Hamer. Beatrice (more commonly known as Betty) lived near

John and was someone he enjoyed talking to about his troubles within his company. For a while, the marriage seemed to be a sweet one, but soon, serious cracks began to appear in the marriage, indicative of a marriage so quickly decided upon. Despite knowing the marriage would likely not last to the end of the year, John and Betty continued to live together as a married couple. The marriage lasted longer than most thought it would and two years later, John and Betty moved to London as John continued to search for work. His previous employer had told every company within the area about his theft, resulting in no one being willing to hire John. In London, John secured work as a chauffeur for the wealthy William McSwan. McSwan owned numerous arcades in the area and was known as a philanthropic individual in London. However, John left the work as a chauffeur (under good terms) for another job that offered more financial incentives but held less notability. In truth, John was trading his good work to be a con-artist. John began selling falsified stock shares under the name of William Cato Adamson, a supposed stock broker who held offices in Chancery Lane, London; Hastings, Sussex; and Guildford, Surrey. John posed as Adamson and claimed he was selling stocks that had been repossessed by the bank following the death of his clients. Thus, selling fraudulent stocks from illegitimate, deceased individuals allowed John to offer these stocks at a price significantly under the going rate. This reduced the suspicion most potential buyers would have held for such low-priced stock. However, John made a critical mistake when he misspelled the name of one of the cities his office was supposedly located in, misspelling Guildford as "Guilford" on a letterhead, a mistake noticed by a potential buyer. For such a notable and wealthy man to make such an elementary mistake caused suspicion and the client tipped off the police who subsequently arrested John. John received a four year sentence in prison for fraud, a sentencing that would cause him to miss more than simple financial gain.

Unbeknownst to John, his wife Betty was pregnant with their first child at the time of his sentencing. Regrettably, John would be residing in his prison cell when he received word that his wife had given birth to his child and she had immediately placed the child up for adoption. This move incensed John and he demanded an immediate divorce from Betty, a demand she easily met. Now without his child or wife, John would begin his spiral into greed and jealousy, a lust that would claim the life of many before eventually claiming his own life.

When John was rebased from prison, World War II was on the horizon and the English people were busy preparing for it, leaving John unable to continue his life as a con-man selling false insurance and stock. However, this would not stop John from perpetrating more crime, resulting in lengthy stays in prison. While in prison, John came to the conclusion that the only reason he was spending such a long time in prison was because he was failing to kill his victims, allowing them to report his crimes to the police. However, John was hesitant to kill someone and leave their body to be discovered, an action that would have immediately have pinned him to the crime. John's moment of discovery came when he read of a murderer named George-Alexandre Sarret, a man who had killed his victims and then disposed of their bodies in vats of sulfuric acid. John was convinced this was the best mode of disposing of the bodies and made preparations to accumulate sulfuric acid upon his release. In the meantime, John focused on developing a process from murder to body dissolution, a process he soon mastered. In 1943, John found himself released from prison and eager to attempt his new method of dissolving bodies. For a trial, John killed a mouse and put him in the acid, returning only 30 minutes later to find the mouse completely dissolved. This left John elated and certain that he had stumbled upon a process that could leave him guiltless and rich.

Upon his release from prison, John became employed at an engineering plant as an accountant. During a routine visit from the board of directors, John came into contact with McSwan, the man he had previously worked for as a chauffeur. John went out for dinner with his former boss and was subsequently introduced to McSwan's parents, Donald and Amy McSwan. In conversation, John found that McSwan was currently working for his father, simply collecting the rent from his father's tenants. As a result, McSwan was living a lavish lifestyle, a lifestyle John soon began to grow quite jealous of. One year later, John was unable to hide his jealousy for him and lured the wealthy son into the basement of his home. After pushing McSwan in front of him, John smote him over the head and rendered him unconscious. John then placed McSwan's unconscious body into a vat of sulfuric acid and left the body to dissolve. When John returned two days later, he found that McSwan's body had completely decomposed and was now a mere pile of sludge. John then dumped the solution, including John's body, down the sewer and reported to McSwan's parents that McSwan had fled to Scotland and had left his duties to John. McSwan's parents believed John and allowed him to remain in McSwan's old house and assume his job as rent collector. However, after one year, McSwan's parents began to question John more intensely, fearing why their boy had not returned from Scotland. Fearing the parents would alert the authorities, John brought McSwan's parents to the same basement he had killed their son in the previous year. Using the same method of murder, John rendered both parents unconscious and then dissolved their bodies in the sulfuric acid. John then assumed their lives, collecting their rents and all financial gain. While John was living a lavish life, compliments of the individuals he had murdered, this life would soon run short of money and John would be forced to murder more people to maintain his lifestyle.

With finances becoming scarce, John befriended a couple – Dr. Archibald and Rose Henderson. Using the pretense of real estate investment, John invited the couple to his house to see if they would like to purchase it. The couple agreed and had no sooner been shown to John's basement when they were given the same treatment of those murdered before them. After dissolving the bodies, John used Dr. Henderson's letterhead to forge a letter demanding that all of Dr. Henderson's possessions be given to John. John then proceeded to sell the items. However, John's lavish lifestyle could hardly be supported by even Dr. Henderson's wealth. Forced to kill yet again, John stalked numerous potential victims until he settled on Olive Durand Deacon, a 69-year-old woman who's deceased husband, John Durand-Deacon, had amassed a large fortune during his lifetime. Using the pretense that he was interested in Durand-Deacon's idea of artificial fingernails, John invited her to his basement where he shot her once in the back and disposed of her using his sulfuric acid vats. However, the acid had begun to lose his acidity and was losing its effectiveness in dissolving bodies. For this reason, all but Durand-Deacon's ankle would be dissolved, a mistake that would cost John his false guise of innocence.

Two days after Durand-Deacon was killed, her friend Constance Lane reported her disappearance to the police. Police discovered that Durand-Deacon had been visiting John and upon arrival at his house, found several of her items in his office, most notably her fur coat. When the police found a large vat of sulfuric acid in the basement, they began to grow suspect and investigated John's backyard where they found one item of interest on a rubbish pile: Durand-Deacon's ankle. With this price of evidence, the police arrested John and charged him with murder. Following a colorful trial in which John attempted to plea his innocence on the ground of insanity, the jury found him guilty despite a startling revelation that John drank the blood of his victims prior to dissolving their bodies. Following the jury's decision, the judge sentenced John to death by hanging. John's last known words were, "Make it a large one, old boy," in reference to a cup of brandy he was offered prior to execution. On August 10, 1949, the judgment of John Haigh was consummated and he was hanged on the gallows at the Wandsworth Prison, thus ending a life of jealousy and murder. While John had stolen the life from so many, he in affect had his life stolen from him from the very vice he would not give up: jealousy.

Richard Speck

One of the greatest attributes to the American justice system is the preservation of the sanctity of life. In crimes resulting in the loss of life, the justice system has the opportunity and obligation to retain the greatest gift any person is gifted with: life. However, under certain crimes, simple clerical error or unsatisfactory work on the behalf of the justice system has allowed criminals the right to enjoy their remaining days as a jailed person after they viciously removed this right from someone else. This malfeasance was present in the case of Richard Speck, a man from Kirkwood, Illinois who murdered eight women, among other crimes committed. While the nation was mostly in agreement that Richard should be killed and an initial sentencing culminated in his being sentenced to death within the electric chair, an unprecedented mistake made by the justice system caused Richard to remain alive. While Richard was awaiting a retrial due to the mistake in jury selection, the Supreme Court ruled that the death penalty was unconstitutional and Richard Speck was instead allowed to live out the remainder of his days alive. Richard would soon become a popular prisoner in the Stateville Correctional Center being known for his sexual promiscuity. Richard's sentence reversal serves as both a topic of hatred for some while being an example of the revised justice system for others. Although some may argue that the jury error allowed Richard more time to live, subsequently leading to his sentence reversal, others advocate that this was merely the justice system avoiding the grievous mistake to be made should Richard have been killed. Despite the fact that the argument is prone to subjective pretense, the life of Richard Speck showed a man who held no virtue and lived his life for the benefit of himself. Demonstrated in his life within prison years later, Richard Speck held no remorse for his killing spree and carried out his actions in the name of justice and self-pleasure. The life of Richard Speck serves as an example of the power and blindness a selfish attitude will bring about.

On December 6, 1941, Richard Speck was born in suburban Saint Louis, Missouri to Benjamin Franklin Speck and Mary Margaret Carbaugh Speck. Richard was born into a large family; the seventh child of the eight children Ben and Margaret would grow their family to be. There was a significant age difference between Richard, his younger sister, and their older siblings. At a young age, Richard and his father became very close, a tight bond unifying them in family love. Richard's father was a good man who feared God and advocated against any use of alcohol. However, the tight bond between Richard and his father became simply a legacy when Benjamin succumbed to a heart attack in 1947, when Richard was only six-years-old. For Richard, this death would have severe implications on his life. Richard was devastated, but being so young, struggled with the true gravity of the situation. In 1949, Richard's mother began dating another man but to the shock of her children, this man seemed to be contrary to anything their father had previously been. Alcoholic, abusive, aggressive, and curt were the words most used to describe Carl August Rudolph Lindbergh, the man who would eventually become their step- father. After Richard's mother married Lindbergh, the children noticed an instant change in the moral of the home, particularly in young Richard. Lindbergh held a blotched past that included various charges for assault and robbery. At this time, Richard and his younger sister were the only children still living with their mother, so following the marriage, Richard's mother brought her two remaining children with her to live with Lindbergh in Santo, Texas. In Texas, Richard started third grade at the local school. What should have been a fun and exciting time in any young man's life was quite the opposite for Richard. Routine abuse, both verbal and physical, plagued his life. The period of fourth through eighth grade was a particularly tumultuous time for Richard, most noticed in his deteriorating academic performance. Richard was at a cross roads in his life and unfortunately, he was about to take the wrong path.

When Richard entered ninth grade, his academic performance (which had been spiraling) sputtered before dying completely. A terrified public speaker, Richard refused to study and never wore his glasses required for reading, a refusal that cost him the ability to successfully read. Finally, after being fed up with school, Richard dropped out once he reached sixteen, the legal age to do so. Sadly, years earlier, Richard had traded academic success for an alcohol addiction beginning at age 12. When he was thirteen, Richard received his first warrant for arrest, a sad premonition for the future of his life. After developing his drinking addiction for three years, Richard reached a point at age fifteen when he was reaching intoxication levels on a daily basis. To pay for the cost of his alcohol, Richard was forced to seek employment at the 7-Up bottling company located in Dallas. Richard held employment for three years, the longest tenure at any job Richard would hold. In 1961, twenty-year-old Richard met Shirley Malone, a fifteen-year-old girl at the Texas State Fair. Richard and Shirley consummated their relationship after only three weeks of knowing each other and Shirley became pregnant, and the two married shortly thereafter. This life of frivolous decisions and reckless abandon would dictate most of Richard's life. With Shirley pregnant, Richard moved into his mother's apartment that was already housing Richard's sister, her husband, and Richard's mother. At this time, Richard's mother had recently separated from his stepfather, Lindbergh. Richard continued to brush with the law, mostly through public intoxication and disorderly conduct. One such incident landed Richard in the county jail where he would miss the birth of his daughter, Robbie Lynn Speck. However, Richard failed to tell his wife that he had been arrested, leading her to believe he was seeking employment and unable to come to the hospital. However, she would soon find out that he had instead been serving his sentence inside the county jail for punching a man during a bar fight. While she would claim not to be disappointed, she would soon find out this was who Richard truly was.

Shortly after the birth of his daughter, Richard told Shirley that he would be a different man for them, but that promise was short-lived. On July 8, 1963, Richard attempted to cash a forged check that he had stolen from a man he worked with. When the store refused to cash his check, Richard held the store at gunpoint, stealing cigarettes, beer, and a measly $3 of cash. The getaway was futile as police quickly found him and Richard received a three year sentence in the state prison. For these three years, Richard was to spend his time in the Texas State Penitentiary located in Huntsville, Texas. He behaved well in jail and was released on parole early after only serving a little over half of his sentence. On January 9, 1965, Richard attempted to rob a woman outside of a grocery store, after being back with his family for merely a week. Brandishing a 17-inch carving knife, Richard demanded the woman's money but was forced to run when the woman screamed and fled. Richard did not know his way in this new section of the city and was found by police with minutes of running away. Richard returned to the court system and awaited his next sentencing. Upon being sentenced, Richard was slated to spend the next 16 months in jail but a clerical error allowed Richard to be released only six months later. Sadly, this allowed Richard to be released from the judgment of his crime; the first of two times that Richard would not receive the full punishment for his trial.

Following the clerical error, Richard returned to civilian life after six months and promptly took employment with the Patterson Meat Company as a driver. However, after having six accidents within the first two months, Patterson Meat Company placed Richard on probation and informed him that one more violation of company policy would result in his firing. Richard did not take this threat seriously but was not surprised when he was fired one month later for arriving to work late. After being fired, Richard and his wife began experiencing more aggression towards each other, largely the result of Richard's instability and failure to hold a job. For this reason, the couple separated and Richard moved in with a divorced woman who had three children. This provided Richard with another job for the time being since the woman needed someone to babysit her children while she was at work. Richard was also quite intimidated by this woman due to her previous employment as a professional wrestler. One month after Richard and his wife separated, Shirley filed for divorce, greatly angering Richard. However, there was little he could do stop the divorce which became official, and Richard and Shirley were no longer married. Angry at Shirley's decision, Richard went to his favorite bar and began drinking heavily. This resulted in yet another bar fight in which Richard stabbed another man. Richard was initially charged with aggregated assault but was able to reduce this charge to disturbing the peace when his mother hired a smart defense attorney to represent him. Richard was ordered to pay a $10 fine and upon refusal to do so, was placed in police custody for three days. At this point, Richard began living his life in reckless abandon, doing what he pleased and when he pleased. Richard's first rash decision following the charge of "disturbing the peace" was to rob another grocery store. To do so, Richard purchased an old car and then robbed the grocery store of all of its cigarettes, stowing the cigarettes in the trunk of his car. With the cleared of cigarettes, Richard began selling the stolen cigarettes to customers in the parking lot of the very store he had just robbed. The police were soon told of his grievous actions and issued a warrant for his arrest. This led to Richard running from the law and fleeing Dallas, Texas where he had been previously residing. For the next few months, Richard would live in Illinois out of the sight of his mother and law enforcement.

In Illinois, Richard moved in with his sister Martha Thornton who was living in Chicago. The police were quickly alerted of his presence in Chicago and Richard was forced to flee to Monmouth, Illinois. In Monmouth, Richard worked as a carpenter for his brother. Unfortunately, he was soon incensed to hear that his wife had remarried another man after only being divorced for two days. Feeling betrayed and angry, Richard began spending day and night in the local taverns of downtown Monmouth. It did not take long for Richard to be involved in another bar fight which once again resulted in his being detained and questioned by police. On the other hand, nothing was said of his outstanding arrest warrant in Dallas and

Richard was released. Upon his release, Richard entered the home of Virgil Harris, a 65-year-old woman who lived in downtown Monmouth. When Harris returned to her home, Richard tied her up, blindfolded her, and raped her before stealing all of her money and running away. Richard stayed out of sight for a week but returned a week later and killed Mary Kay Pierce, a barmaid at Richard's favorite bar. Pierce's body was found behind the tavern. After being questioned by police due to his familiarity with Pierce, Richard claimed innocence and police were unable to uncover any real evidence of his interference. When police requested that Richard remain in Monmouth for questioning, Richard assured them he would stay put, but when police arrived at his hotel later, they found him missing. The only remaining items in the room were the stolen pieces of jewelry from both of the women assaulted.

On the run again from police, Richard sought asylum in his sister's residence in Chicago. When asked why he had returned so suddenly, Richard contrived a fib detailing how he was running from a crime lord who had sought his assistance, but Richard, portraying himself as a law-abiding citizen, had refused, and thus resulting in his stay in Chicago. Richard's brother in law was able to find a job for Richard in the U.S. Coast Guard on a lake freighter. After being fingerprinted and undergoing a physical examination, Richard began work on the *Clarence B. Randall*. During his first week of employment on the ship, Richard succumbed to acute appendicitis and was life flighted from the freighter to a hospital to undergo an emergency appendectomy. Richard was then forced to remain unemployed as he recovered from the surgery, living with his sister during these months of unemployment. After resting for three weeks, Richard returned to work on the *Clarence B. Randall* and would remain employed until an altercation with the captain which forced him to leave the ship. Richard returned to Chicago by train and told another fib in an effort to convince his sister to allow him to stay with them. His sister reluctantly agreed on the grounds that he finds a job. Seeking employment, Richard returned to the National Maritime Union hiring hall in Chicago where Richard attempted to achieve his seaman's card. Richard was promised a spot on a ship but promptly lost that position when a man with more experience was hired in his spot. After Richard returned home, his sister informed him he must move out. Richard packed his belongings and returned to the hiring hall where he slept in the hall. On the morning of Tuesday, July 12, Richard was offered a position on the *Sinclair Great Lakes* as a seaman. After rushing to the dock, Richard was disappointed to find that his spot had been given to someone else. Frustrated and angry, Richard went to a local tavern and spent his remaining funds on alcohol. When his funds ran out, Richard found an elderly woman named Ella Mae Hooper and held her at knifepoint until she gave him the remainder of her money. After securing her funds, Richard raped her, tied her up, and left her in the kitchen of the Shipyard Inn. In addition to the stealing Ella's money, Richard also stole a small handgun from her house. After spending the money at a local bar, Richard left the bar and set out to complete one of the deadliest murder rampages that the nation would endure.

Located only 150-feet from the hiring hall where Richard had spent his last week, stood a building that housed eight student nurses. Armed with a switchblade and a gun, as well as being incredulously drunk, Richard broke into the home of the eight student nurses and placed all of the women into on room that had no windows or means of escape. After the women had been held in the room for more than three hours, Richard began leading the women out, one by one to the living room where he either strangled or stabbed the women to death. Richard followed this pattern for all but one of the eight women; the eighth woman was raped before being strangled by Richard. Although Richard had murdered the eight women who were residents within the house, he overlooked a nurse who was spending the night and had crawled under the bed. This would prove pivotal in the trial as she provided as definite identification of Richard as the murderer.

For two days, investigators pored over the crime scene, unable to determine who had perpetrated such a crime. Finally, a break was made when fingerprints found matched the fingerprints of Richard that had been taken only feet away at the hiring hall. After police issued a warrant for his arrest and asked for the public's help in finding Richard, the man who owned the hotel Richard was staying in phoned the police and informed them of his whereabouts. When Richard saw the police arrive, he attempted suicide (unsuccessfully) and was arrested immediately when police entered his room and found him crouched in the bathroom. Taken to the Cook County Hospital to recover from his attempted suicide, Richard confessed to the crime of murdering eight women. When informed of the confession, Illinois Supreme Court Justice John J. Stamos stated, "We don't need it. We have an eyewitness." Seemingly, Richard was on his way to the electric chair and the public's opinion largely supported this measure of punishment. On April 3, 1967, Richard's trial began, and after being identified positively by the remaining nurse from the house, the trial hastened to its finish. After only deliberating for 49 minutes, Richard was sentenced to the electric chair by Judge Herbert J. Paschen. Richard appealed this decision and was granted an immediate stay. However, the appeal was heard on November 22, 1968 and immediately upheld. While it seemed that Richard had no hope of living past his death sentence, Richard became the subject of confusion when it was found that an error in the jury selection process required a re-trial. The re-trial was held on June 28, 1971 and while his conviction was upheld, the courts reversed his death sentence due to the improper jury selection. Additionally, *Furman v. George* became a pivotal court case in 1972 and deemed the death penalty unconstitutional. For this reason, Richard was sentenced to 1,200 years in prison with no option for parole. Richard began his stay in Stateville Correctional Center and soon became known for his brazen admission of murdering women. Once, when asked about the murder, Richard responded, "Sure I did. It just wasn't their night."

On December 5, 1991, only one day from his 50th birthday, Richard succumbed to a heart attack and passed away at the age of 49. Fearing protests, Richard's family held a private funeral and cremated his body, spreading the ashes in an undisclosed location.

Richard Ramirez

Within the realm of serial killers and thieves, the element that differentiates these crimes is the motive, or more appropriately, the engine behind the man or woman killing the lives in a senseless fashion. In many cases, jealousy, hatred, and mental illness are the chief culprits, but in a select number of cases, the motive lies within a surprising faction: religion. Most religions promote peace and love towards mankind, but there exists a fraction of religions that allow for and sometimes advocate for the death of innocent human beings. One of these religions would be the diabolic worship of Satan, also referred to as Satanism. Through a quick study of the worship of Satan, one would find that death is the hymn of this religion and the murder of innocent lives is completely accepted as the focused missionary work of the religion. One advocate for such worship was Richard Ramirez, known more commonly as the "Night Stalker" for his murderous escapades by night. While Richard's murders are atrocious enough and left little grace to be given to the man, the accompanying crimes (including rape and sodomy), left humanity furious that such a man ever graced the same earth as the innocent lives he took. Sadly, Richard would never be held fully accountable for his crimes, succumbing to B-cell lymphoma while awaiting his death within the California gas chamber on the Californian death row. Some would advocate that the true judgment for his crimes was not met, but the true justice for Richard was found not solely in his consequences, but in the trial in which he was exposed as a malicious killer and sentenced to death. Richard Ramirez, though a dedicated worshiper of Satan, stood responsible for his crimes and was held accountable for his actions. Though he would never feel a fraction of the pain he inflicted on so many people, Richard's consequences for his actions were served through his guilt, despite his assertions that he felt no wrong for what he had done. Through the protection of a brave police department, the heinous actions of Richard Ramirez were brought to completion and justice was restored to the state of California.

Born on February 29, 1960, Richard Ramirez was born to Julian and Mercedes Ramirez as the last child in a line of five children. Both of Richard's parents were hard working immigrants who had held hard working jobs in Mexico before trading their hard life for a more challenging life as immigrants in the United States. While Richard's father was a hard worker and provided for his family, he suffered from an unknown illness that resulted in fits of rage. These fits of rage usually ended with Richard receiving an abusive blow from his father, all setting a foundation for the abuser Richard would one day be. However, these abusive settings were not all that Richard experienced as a child. On two separate occasions, Richard experienced traumatic head injuries that left him unconscious; for instance, a dresser fell on his head when he was only two-years-old, and on another occasion, Richard fell off of a swing and the swing struck him on the forehead. In result of these experiences, Richard began noticing slight tremors until he began lapsing into epileptic seizures almost every day. Because of this, Richard was forced to remain in his bed for many days at a time. During these extended stays in bed, Richard's cousin Mike Ramires returned and told young Richard graphic stories of when he was a U.S. Army Green Beret in the Vietnam War. Mike had seen his fair share of graphic war and felt the need to recount all of these experiences to young Richard. When Richard turned twelve, Mike began showing Richard pictures that gave his army stories new life. In many of the pictures, Richard was able to see Vietnamese women that Mike had either killed, raped, or in some cases, both. In one picture, Richard recalls seeing his cousin holding the severed head of a Vietnamese woman who Mike had raped prior to killing her. In addition to facilitating a love for violence and murder, Mike also taught Richard the unknown joys of smoking marijuana and how to roll his own joints. Often, the two could be found smoking and fantasizing of sexual violence together. Sadly, these moments would have a profound influence on Richard.

When Richard turned thirteen, his daily habits included smoking marijuana and listening to Mike talk about war. Richard's father had turned violent and Richard was beginning to feel the brunt of his father's rage. Seeking reprieve from these violent outbursts, Richard began sleeping in a cemetery located near the family's house. Family and friends report that Richard also began to exhibit a love for the dead during this time. Shortly before Richard's fifteenth birthday, he watched in horror as his cousin Mike, the one he had grown quite close to, shot his wife in the face during an argument over food. Richard was taken aback by his cousin's actions and sought to erase the image of his dead cousin's wife from his memory. Richard had thought he loved violence but the actual scene frightened him terribly. To escape the terrors, Richard began using LSD regularly and sought the powers and worship of Satan. It is unknown who introduced Richard to Satanism but what is known is that Richard developed a life-long dedication to Satan through his cousin's violent stories. Richard's cousin would be found not guilty under reason of insanity and would serve a meager four-year sentence in the Texas State Mental Hospital. Despite bring horrified by his cousin's actions, Richard continued to let him tell him stories of his violent outbursts, unaware that he was changing, never to return to his sanguine self again.

Richard left school in ninth grade and moved to California with his cousin Mike. Mike eventually ended up moving out of California, but Richard would remain in California until his death years later. For the next few years, Richard did odd jobs around his house and spent considerable time in jail, under the allegation of selling drugs. When Richard turned 24, his crimes transitioned from drug smuggling to senseless killings, and all at what he alleges was Satan's bidding. Richard's first victim of murder would be a nine-year-old Chinese girl who was living in the same apartment complex as he was. When the girl, Mei Leung, came outside one day, Richard pulled her into his apartment and raped her before stabbing her to death. While Richard would never be convicted of this crime due to lack of evidence at the scene of the crime, DNA samples collected later would piece him to the crime. However, this would be well after Richard's death. Two months following his murder of Mei Leung, Richard murdered Jennie Vincow, a 79-year-old widow. The reasoning behind the murder of Vincow would never be understood, but the brutality of the murder led police to believe Richard held prior contact with this woman before she was murdered. Richard had cut her throat so deeply down her neck that police accidentally decapitated her when moving her body to a stretcher. Richard had made sure that his DNA and traces of evidence were removed from the scene; carelessly, Richard left a single fingerprint on the window screen when removing it to make his escape. Police would struggle to match this fingerprint with his profile for a while until his murders began to show a set pattern; police were able to identify him and confirm that this crime was indeed his undertaking. For almost one year following the murder, Richard remained out of sight from the police, still selling drugs and working odd jobs. However, Richard asserts that Satan told him to kill Maria Hernandez and in obeying this being whom he worshipped, Richard fired a .22 caliber pistol at Hernandez but inadvertently shot the keys in her hands, leaving Maria unharmed. When Richard noticed that she had not been harmed, he feared that Jesus Christ had stopped the bullet, causing Richard to flee into Maria's house. Inside the house was Maria's roommate Dayle Okazaki whom Richard shot once in the face, instantly killing her. After fleeing the scene, Richard rushed into the street in front of a car being driven by Veronica Yu. Pulling her from the driver's seat, Richard shot and killed Yu and drove away in her car. With two people being murdered in one setting and another murder attempted, local media rushed to the scene. When the story was relayed from Hernandez, police surmised they had the start of a rampant and viscous serial killer on their hands. Unfortunately, they would see much more death before they caught this viscous killer.

Ten days following the double murder, Richard resumed his killing spree, revisiting a home that he had previously burgled. Once inside, Richard shot and killed Vincent Zazzara before tying his wife Maxine to the bed. Once bound, Maxine was brutally beat by Richard and forced to reveal the locations of the valuables within the house. While Richard was attempting to find these valuables, Maxine loosened her bonds and found a shotgun under the bed. Unfortunately, the gun was not loaded, and when Richard returned, he brutally stabbed Maxine before gouging her eyes out and leaving them on the dresser for the investigators to find. While Richard was making his escape, he landed in the soft flowerbed outside of the window, leaving a fresh imprint of his Avia tennis shoes. During his killing spree, his Avia tennis shoes would eventually receive almost as much media attention as he was garnering. When the police saw the ballistics report from the bullets, they noted that they matched the bullets from the previous three murders, confirming that they were dealing with a serial killer who did not seem to have a designated "hit list;" he was picking his victims at random and in doing so terrified the Los Angeles area.

Two months following the murder of the Zazzara couple, Richard broke into the home of Bill Doi, a 66-year-old man who spent each day caring for his wife who was a quadriplegic. When Bill awoke to the sounds of Richard entering his home, he immediately investigated and was met by Richard who shot him in the face, killing Bill instantly. When Richard discovered Bill's wife Lillian, he raped her and proceeded to search the house for valuables. Richard would leave without killing Lillian, but her experience left her too traumatized to reveal any information of value to the investigators. However, the bullets found in her husband matched the bullets from the previous murders and police were able to tie this murder to the serial killing spree of the man they only knew as the "Night Stalker."

On May 29, 1985, Richard hot-wired a Mercedes-Benz and drove to an elderly lady's home which he chose at random. The home was owned by Mabel Bell and her sister Florence Lang. When Richard entered the house, the first item he saw was a hammer which he would utilize as his weapon for the night. After beating Bell senseless, he proceeded to rape Lang before drawing a pentagram on her thigh. Richard then tied both women together and shocked them repeatedly with the bare end of an electrical cord. Richard fled the scene, leaving Bell to die from her injuries and Lang to remain alive but mentally scarred. Richard alleges that he was again instructed by Satan to drive to Carol Kyle's home in Burbank where he tied Carol and her son up. After finding all of the valuables within the house, Richard sexually assaulted Carol before running from the scene. One month later, Richard broke into the home of Mary Louise Cannon and stabbed her until her death. Nothing of value was taken from the woman's home. Three days later, Richard burgled the home of William Bennett. However, at the time the burglary, only William's younger daughter Whitney was in the home. Richard knocked the young girl unconscious using a tire iron. Once she was unconscious, Richard attempted to shock the girl but was startled so much that he fled the scene, claiming to have seen Jesus Christ standing over Whitney's body. Whitney survived the attack, but would require over 450 stitches to close the deep cuts on her head. Two days post-burglary of the Bennet home, Richard broke into the home of Joyce Nelson where she was sleeping alone on the couch. Richard proceeded to punch her repeatedly and kick her, resulting in her death. However, Richard left an imprint from his infamous Avia tennis shoe on her face which police were able to identify as his. Though Richard was seemingly invisible at the time, he was running out of time and would soon be found by police.

On the same night that he murdered Nelson, Richard drove around until he found a house that looked valuable enough to burgle. The home was owned by Sophie Dickman who he raped and sodomized. In this particular burglary, Richard demanded that Dickman "swear on Satan" that she had told him everything, giving police the foundation of the profile they were looking for. From July 20 through August 24, 1985, Richard would burgle seven more homes and murder seven more people. Police were perplexed as to whom this individual was, but offered little news to the media with the fear that the media would reveal this information, thus potentially prompting Richard to alter his actions and give police less evidence. A potentially damaging reveal was made when Mayor Dianne Feinstein told the press that the perpetrator was wearing a size 11 1/2 Avia tennis shoe. This news held little pertinence to the public's opinion but was the one identifying aspect of the criminal thus far. When Richard found that his shoes had been identified, he proceeded to throw them off the Golden State Bridge into the river below. On August 24, Richard attempted a burglary at the home of Bill Carns and Inez Erickson. Richard shot Carns in the face but failed to kill Inez. Following his escape, Inez would provide police with a detailed description allowing them to pinpoint Richard's profile from his earlier days in prison. After a long search, the police had an identity they could release to the public. In a press conference, the police chief asserted "We now know who you are, and soon, everyone else will. There will be no place you can hide." On August 31, Richard was walking about Los Angeles, unaware that he had been identified, when a group of pedestrians began yelling in his direction the word "Night Stalker!" Richard fled the scene but was soon captured and beaten senseless by the group of citizens. Police soon arrived and Richard was taken into custody. The "Night Stalker" was finally found and would be headed to trial for his egregious actions.

After the trial began on July 22, 1988, Richard watched as a jury became filled with hatred towards his senseless killings. On September 20, 1989, the trial reached its end and Richard was found guilty of all thirteen counts of murder, eleven sexual assaults, five attempted murders, and fourteen burglaries. Richard was sentenced to death in the Californian gas chamber but would await the long process of appeals before his death. On June 7, 2013, still awaiting his death, Richard succumbed to the rigors of B-cell lymphoma and passed away at the age of 53. Richard Ramirez served 23 years on death row before being killed by his drug abuse in his younger years. The terrifying life of Richard Ramirez had reached its end.

Gary Ridgway

The systematic killing of humanity has forever been a process dealt with severely by the justice system of the United States. In many of these cases, abuse as a child was present and was found to have laid a foundation of hatred that would be the fuel for the serial killing. One case that held such facets was the killing spree conducted by Gary Leon Ridgway. Known as the Green River Killer, Gary would lead a life that was founded on hatred towards his mother and sex workers. During his confession of the crimes, Gary revealed to investigators that he had been abused as a child by his mother, an act that caused a burning hatred to form in his mind and eventually lead him to kill over 70 women in the United States. However, Gary's actions were his own choice and for this, the justice system of the United States handed him 48 life sentences to accompany one life sentence that he had received from a previous murder. Gary escaped the death penalty by entering a plea bargain in which he confessed to more crimes that he had committed, Gary today resides in a maximum security prison located in the state of Washington. The life of Gary Ridgway shows humanity the type of monster the seeds of bitterness can grow. Gary's choice to enact revenge upon innocent lives for the wrongs of his mother caused heartbreak in countless individuals and a life sentence for himself.

Born on February 18, 1949, Gary Ridgway entered the home and care of Thomas and Mary Ridgway in Salt Lake City, Utah. Gary was the middle child in a family of three sons; however, he remained distant from his family and would never facilitate a fond relationship with them. Friends and relatives note that the family was extremely dysfunctional and had strange habits. Mary Ridgway was a stay-at-home mother while Thomas Ridgway worked as a bus driver. When Thomas returned home from work, Gary recalls him exhibiting extreme hatred towards the sex workers who frequented his bus each day. Ironically, Gary also remembers his father using their services on a frequent basis. During his childhood, Gary was plagued with wetting the bed until his early teen years. Every night, Gary would wet the bed, and every morning his mother would personally wash him. For this reason, Gary experienced puberty with his mother touching his genitals on a regular basis, a condition that left him sexually scarred and fantasizing of both killing and having sex with his mother. In addition to wetting the bed, Gary also suffered from dyslexia and was not a proficient student. During his freshman year of high school, Gary failed every class, resulting in him to be held back a year. Additionally, Gary began exhibiting strong hostility towards those around him, inciting fights on a regular basis. When he was 16-years-old, Gary lured a six-year-old boy into the woods and stabbed him repeatedly in the stomach, resulting in the child suffering a lacerated liver and broken ribs. Gary would never be prosecuted for this crime as the child would not reveal his attacker until years following the incident.

When Gary graduated from Tyee High School in 1969, he immediately married the woman he had been dating throughout high school, Claudia Kreg. Not having any employment opportunities as a high school graduate, Gary joined the United States Navy and was deployed to Vietnam. Upon arrival in Vietnam, Gary began work as a janitor on a supply ship but was also involved in fighting combat during his tenure as janitor. In addition to his work, Gary took advantage of the lack of security in Vietnam and raped numerous Vietnamese women. He had also been frequenting the areas of the local sex workers and utilizing their services. After numerous sexual bouts in Vietnam, Gary found that he had gonorrhea but was unfazed by this complication and continued to have sexual intercourse with sex workers on a regular basis. During his stay in Vietnam, Gary received word that his wife Claudia had begun sleeping with another man and was seeking a divorce. Before the end of the year the divorce was finalized. Shortly after, Gary returned to the United States and began dating Marcia Winslow. The two would be married eventually but this marriage would be plagued with Gary's sexual escapades and run-ins with the law.

Around this time, Gary began exhibiting a strong sexual desire for women. Gary's first two wives would recall how much Gary demanded sex from them. During one event, Gary held Marcia in a chokehold, demanding that she have sex with him when she refused his initial offer. Despite his strong inclination towards sex, Gary became a steady church-goer and demanded that his wife adhere to any principle taught by his pastor. Gary recalls that he became strongly bi-polar during this period of his life, often taking a break from reading his Bible to cry aloud. It was not uncommon for Gary to cry during one of his pastor's sermons. However, Gary's love of sex with other women and his adherence to the Biblical principles of purity were not aligned, leaving strong arguments with his wife. As the pleasures of sex within his bedroom began to wane, Gary began requesting that his wife have sex with him in public, park benches being his favorite spot. When his wife refused, Gary would seek the services of the numerous sex workers in the area. Ironically, many of the areas where Gary insisted he have sex would eventually be the resting place for many of his victims. Gary's wife, Marcia, was bringing him adequate sexual pleasure at the time, so he felt no need to admit his infidelity to her. Unfortunately, she knew of his infidelity and would soon file for divorce.

After Gary and Marcia divorced, Gary's sexual desires became unquenchable and his life became nothing more than a desire to have sex at whatever means required. This desire would lead him to perform the most egregious actions a man could perform against a woman: rape and murder. Though the number is disputed, law enforcement asserts that Gary murdered 71 women and teenage girls. This number is corroborated by Gary though he later would remark that he had lost track of the exact number of women he killed. The greater number of these murders would occur between 1982 and

1984, with many of the women killed being sex workers in the area. Gary's target female included girls who had run away and had no place to spend the night. Regardless of the age of the women, the common denominator between all of the women killed was their instability of life; Gary was seeking the most vulnerable among the Seattle area. A true act of cowardice but an act that would grant Gary the sexual satisfaction he desired. As Gary continued to murder women more rapidly, his body count was exceeding how many could be placed in a certain area without attracting the surveillance of the police. Initially, Gary dumped the bodies of the women into the Green River, prompting the nickname, "The Green River Killer." However, Gary was forced to re-think his location when police began patrolling the Green River area more thoroughly. To throw police off the trail, Gary would often cross the surrounding borders of the nearby states and dump bodies in those areas. This caused the police organizations from several states to be called upon, thus leading to a sooner arrest of Gary. What had once been thought of as a good idea to throw police off his trail, would eventually lead to his demise.

After Gary killed his victims, he would often have sexual intercourse with them before dumping their bodies. In most cases, the bodies were found nude and posed in various sexual poses. On a few rare occasions, Gary would return to the scene of his crime to have sexual intercourse with his victims, well after they had been dead. When asked why he returned to the scene since it might risk his being caught, Gary noted that despite the risks, it was still less risky than attempting to rape women while they were alive. To reduce the risk of the police being able to identify the bodies and more importantly, him, Gary would often dump trash on the dump sites, rendering the bodies impossible to identify.

After Gary's arrest, he revealed to the police his tactics for luring the women to a place where he could kill them. Gary would create a boy, referring to him as his son, and tell the women that he was interested in starting a relationship with the woman in order to give his son a caring mother. These women, in their various states of vulnerability, would often consider Gary's plea an honor and concede to his request. Once Gary had them in his truck, he would either kill them there or return to a site in the woods to kill them. As his actions became better known, Gary's choice location for murder was his truck, with his main method of killing the women being by strangulation. During his first murders, Gary simply used his hands to carry out the heinous crime, confiding in prosecutors that he loved the feeling of "women thrashing about for their life." However, using his hands allowed these women to hit him, often causing blood. For this reason, Gary began resorting to using ligatures, tight bands that allowed the murder to be carried out more quickly and without the risk of being hurt in the process.

When police in Washington began noticing more bodies being found in the Green River area, they feared they had a serial killer close by. To combat this unknown killer's future attacks, police created the Green River Task Force to conduct investigations on the murders. Police realized that even though they had no new information on this "unknown killer," they were sure a serial killer was on the loose. With most of the victims being found nude, the police asserted that they were seeking a man who was not merely killing women out of pure hatred but rather including a sexual fantasy in his murders. To better understand the mind of such a man, police interviewed Ted Bundy, a serial killer from earlier who had been captured and was waiting on death row. Bundy had recently become a born again Christian and was interested in helping the investigators catch the unknown man behind these murders. It was on Bundy's suggestion that police began watching the sites of the women found murdered and asserting that the killer would most likely return to have sex with the victims. Sadly, the sites they were watching had already been frequented by Gary, but Bundy was right, Gary was returning to the scene of the crime. The only problem was that police were arriving far too late to catch Gary in the act.

In 1982, police arrested Gary under the suspicion that he had been utilizing prostitutes, but no evidence had been found so Gary was released. When police questioned Gary again in 1984, he agreed to a polygraph test which he subsequently passed. However, Gary remained a distant suspect in the Green River killings. In 1985, Gary sought more stable love in his life and began dating Judith Mawson. In 1988, the two were married. Despite Gary's brazen killing during this time, Mawson was completely unaware that Gary was killing these women. In all their years of marriage, the only odd scenario that Mawson could remember was that there was no carpet on the floor of Gary's house when she moved in. Police surmised that Gary most likely used this carpet to transport a murder victim sometime in his life. In 1987, Gary was once again called before authorities who took a DNA and saliva sample from him. Gary was immediately released and police noted his polite and courteous manners during the ordeal. This would mark the first time Mawson would be alerted to Gary's status as a suspect in the Green River killings, which Mawson had never heard of on account of her not watching the news. During Gary's marriage with Mawson, he claims his love for her was true and that he honestly had less of an inclination to kill women during this time. This claim is corroborated by the fact that Gary only murdered three women over the duration of his relationship with Mawson. Even so, three women was still too many and Gary's days of innocence were growing short. When Mawson was told of Gary's reluctance to kill women during their marriage, she replied, "I feel I have saved lives by being his wife and making him happy." This happiness would not last long, however, and the public would soon become acquainted with the man who had stolen happiness from countless lives.

In 2001, detectives ran a sample test using the saliva and DNA samples taken years earlier from Gary. The samples matched the semen found in one of the victims and detectives rushed to locate Gary; the man they now confirmed was the "Green River Killer." After locating Gary at the Kenworth Truck Factory, police rushed to the scene and arrested Gary for the murder of four women (the only women they had solid evidence for at the time). Later, police would be able to match paint flecks found at the scene with paint used at the Kenworth Truck factory years earlier. This revelation would lead to three more charges of murder being added to Gary's name.

After two years of deliberation, the Seattle news revealed that Gary had been moved from maximum security jail to a more moderate security jail that was closer to where the trial would be held. Three months later, the trail commenced and Gary was presented a plea deal that would trade his impending death penalty with a confession to 44 additional charges of murder. Additionally, Gary would have to lead prosecutors to the remaining dump sites of his victims, a request Gary readily agreed to. After police were able to locate 44 additional bodies, the plea deal was finalized and Gary was ensured he would spend the remainder of his life in prison. On December 18, 2003, Gary was sentenced to 48 life sentences without the possibility of parole. Gary was also charged with tampering with evidence and given an additional ten years of prison time for each body, bringing an additional 480 years of sentencing to his current 48 life sentences. While evidence continues to be unearthed regarding Gary's crimes, no new trials have been opened considering Gary's life sentences already in existence. To this day, Gary resides in a maximum security prison and maintains that his life's career was murdering women. Though still alive, the life of Gary Ridgway has affectively been limited and the justice of Gary's crimes has been served.

Albert Fish

If there was one thing that drove serial killers to complete their evil deeds, it would be their obsession with control. Most serial killers killed from a lack of control the perpetrator exhibited or experienced earlier in his or her life. However, there are a select number of cases that deal with a very different motive for murder: cannibalism. The act of eating raw meat or the meat of human beings, cannibalism is a barbaric form of self-pleasure that is facilitated through years of sexual fantasies and sexual abuse. In this case, the act of cannibalism was bred through extreme abuse as a child. Albert Fish is an example of a man who, already from a family prone to mental illness, was abused at an orphanage. Also exposed to horrific actions of self-gratification through barbaric traditions, Albert would become known as "The Boogey Man" and would abuse and kill over 100 children in his time, also taking part in eating these young children on many occasions. However, this abuse can never be an excuse for the actions of Albert Fish. Many will make the decision to overcome their unfortunate childhood moments of horror and become stronger in the process. However, some will succumb to the strength of greed and take advantage of the weakest in society. By doing so, those like Albert Fish are demonstrating how weak they truly are—so weak that they have to choose their victims from the pool of the weakest possible. The life of Albert Fish should serve as an example to society of the horrors one can inflict simply because he or she is unable to overcome the abuse inflicted on them.

Born on May 19, 1870, to Randall and Ellen Fish, Albert was the youngest of four children and was birthed into a home where an odd foundation had been laid. Albert's father was older than Albert's mother by 43 years and was 75 when Albert was born. For this reason, Albert grew up in a home where his father and mother were estranged and his father was not a constant in his life. The Fish family resided in Washington D.C. where Albert's father worked as a riverboat captain. His father, 80-years-old at the time, succumbed to a heart attack and passed away on October 16, 1875 when Albert was only five-years-old. With no source of income, Albert's mother was unable to properly care for Albert and considered placing him in an orphanage. Thus, at the young age of five, Albert was placed in the Saint John's Orphanage near the family house. Albert would be abused on a regular basis at this orphanage but would never divulge this information to his mother. In addition to being abused, Albert was also privy to sexual acts between many of the boys in the orphanage. After a period of beating, Albert began to actually enjoy being abused. Albert would recall, "I was there 'till I was nearly nine and that's where I got started wrong. We were unmercifully whipped. I saw boys doing many things they should not have done." Psychologists point to this transition as the defining moment in Albert's life precluding his sexual misconduct. Just as Albert's life was seemingly plummeting beyond repair at the orphanage, his mother was able to secure a job working for the government and began making enough money to resume her care of Albert. However, Albert's mother noticed the drastic change in her son. No longer was Albert consumed with nature as he had been prior to being admitted to the orphanage. Now, Albert seemed only excited by one element: sexual fantasy. Two years after Albert resumed living with his mother, he entered a relationship with a boy he had met at the telegraph office. This relationship would prove to be the most detrimental to his life and would lead Albert deeper into his dark world. Shortly after they began dating, his partner demonstrated the practice of eating his own facies and drinking his own urine. These two conditions were known as coprophagia and urolagnia respectively. These actions in themselves would have horrible effects on Albert, permanently damaging his mind and altering his behavior.

As Albert began to slip farther and farther into his life of same gender attraction, he made regular appearances at the baths in the

Washington D.C. area where he often just stared at the bodies of boys as they undertook various stages of undress. Additionally, Albert began transferring his sexual thoughts from his mind to paper as he wrote obscene letters. Albert would then find classified ads listed by women in the area and would send these obscene filled letters to these women. However, Albert would leave the letters without a return address, rendering the women helpless in finding the man responsible for such an atrocity.

When Albert turned twenty, he moved away from his mother to a city farther up the East Coast: New York City. When confessing to his crimes years later, Albert would admit that these months in New York City would be the first times he listed himself as a prostitute while also raping young boys on a regular basis. With the law centered on other crimes, Albert was left to his own life and made raping young men a regular occurrence. After living alone for eight years, his mother became worried that he would marry a male, a horrid crime at the time. To prevent this from happening, Albert's mother found a woman who was interested in becoming wed. This woman, Anna Mary Hoffman, was nine years younger than Albert but still agreed to marry him. Once married, Albert and Anna would go on to parent six children, giving the illusion of a pleasant home life with a healthy marriage. However, the home life was anything but pleasant. Albert regularly left home unexpectedly, often going to the home of one of his "clients" for a night of sexual pleasure between two lovers of like gender. Additionally, Albert continued to molest children while being employed as a house painter. Often, his jobs led him to homes where he would have unlimited contact with the children in the area. Throughout these years, Albert held numerous boyfriends, many at the same time. During a weekend getaway with one of his boyfriends, Albert and his boyfriend visited a waxworks museum. In this museum, one exhibit featured a bisected penis. Albert recalls being completely engrossed by the penis and wanting to know more about the practice of sexual mutilation. Upon leaving the museum, Albert pledged to become as well aquatinted with the practice as possible. However, this would have to wait as he was arrested in 1903 on charges of grand larceny. Upon sentencing, Albert was sentenced to a prison sentence at the Sing Sing Correctional Facility in New York.

After Albert served his sentence in the prison, he was released and began working on the barges in Wilmington, Delaware. While employed in Delaware, Albert became friends with Thomas Kedden and their friendship blossomed into more and soon the duo entered a violent and sexually driven relationship. At the time, Albert claimed that despite the sexually graphic nature of the relationship, Kedden was completely competent and consented to the various sex acts being performed on him. However, future records would show that Kedden was actually quite unstable mentally and possibly suffering from Down syndrome. Despite Kedden's obvious incompetence, Albert continued to force the man to perform sex acts on him. After having sex with Kedden for ten days, Albert forced him into his car and drove him to an abandoned farm house. Here, Albert systematically tortured Kedden daily and often at night as well. For the next two weeks, Albert would torture Kedden each day, exhibiting an unwavering spirit in spite of the man's pitiful pleas for mercy. Finally, after two weeks of sexually graphic torture, Albert reached the climax of his torture by slicing half of Kedden's penis off and managing the wound by simply tying a napkin to the severed penis. Recalling this moment, Albert noted "I shall never forget his scream or the look he gave me." Albert's original plans were to kill Kedden at the farm house but a heat wave in the area forced Albert to leave Kedden alive. After tending to Kedden's severed penis, Albert kissed Kedden goodbye, placed a $10 bill in his underwear, left him tied up, and fled from the house. Albert would never hear from or see Kedden again in his life. "Took the first train I could get back home," recalls Albert. "Never heard what became of him, or tried to find out." When Albert returned home from his sexual escapade, his wife greeted him by informing him that she would be moving out of the house and seeking a divorce. John Straube had been boarding with the family for the past three years and secretly has been having an affair with Anna Mary. Albert seemed unfazed by his wife's desertion, most likely cementing the fact that he held more of a desire to have a sexual relationship with a man instead of a woman. While Albert was not disappointed by Anna Mary's request for a divorce, he was dismayed to learn that she had taken all of the items from the house and had maintained ownership of the household. Additionally, Albert began experiencing hallucinations of the auditory senses around this time as well. Many times, Albert could be seen running around his neighborhood, convinced there was an unseen force chasing him. Once, Albert ripped up the carpet in his living room and rolled himself up into the middle of the carpet roll, all at the command of John from the Bible. Due to his unstable nature, friends and family began avoiding Albert as much as they could.

With his family leaving him to his own actions, Albert began to experiment with the thrills of self-harm. On 29 separate occasions, Albert stuck a needle in his groin and left it there to become embedded in his flesh. Years later, when Albert would be arrested, police would be shocked to find that Albert had 29 needles buried deep within the flesh of his groin and stomach. In addition to the needles, Albert also paddled himself with a paddle that had nails protruding from every side. This became a daily ritual until the pain became too great that Albert was forced to stand instead of putting any pressure against his rear end. Being unable to paddle himself, Albert began soaking a wool cloth with lighter fuel before placing it in his anus and lighting it on fire. Such odd habits drove most friends away and the only people left within his daily acquaintances were his children. To his credit, Albert never harmed his children but did ask them to paddle him on more than one occasion.

When the self-harm and self-mutilation was not enough to derive adequate satisfaction from, Albert began indulging in a practice he had often held tremendous interest in: cannibalism. To ease himself into the practice of eating the flesh of another human, Albert started by eating raw meat. Often, Albert would feed his children these same meals of raw meat. After acquiring a taste for raw meat, Albert was served his first meal of human flesh by one of his friends only months later. Two years following his introduction to self-mutilation and cannibalism, Albert lost his temper with a mentally handicapped child in downtown Washington. D.C. and stabbed the child. This would be the first in a long line of children that Albert would either permanently handicap or kill with his grotesque methods of torture. Albert's tools of death, which he referred to affectionately as the "implements of Hell," were a butcher knife, a meat cleaver, and a handsaw. Albert began choosing his victims carefully, only choosing the disabled or African-American children under the pretense that no one would miss such children. When he grew wary of showing his face in public due to the outcry over the unsolved murders taking place, Albert convinced other children to friends to his house where he would strangle the children before separating their bodies with his tools.

Five years into his murderous escapade, Albert walked past the Kiel home where Beatrice Kiel was outside playing. Albert attempted to convince her to join him, offering her a small sum of money if she would aid him in looking for rhubarb. Right as Beatrice was about to accept his offer, her mother came outside and grew horrified when she heard the offer made by Albert. Beatrice's mother immediately forced him from the property and demanded that he never return. However, Albert would return to the barn later that night before being discovered and run off by Hans Kiel, Beatrice's father.

Albert maintains that his mutilation of children was completely out of obedience towards God, a claim he would maintain until his death years later. Supposedly following the will of God, Albert convinced two young men to accompany him to his apartment where he was supposed to cook them food. While Albert was in the kitchen preparing to kill them and cook their flesh, one of the lads dislodged Albert's mattress under which laid the tools Albert used to mutilate his victims. The boys grew fearful of the tools and fled from the house, leaving Albert extremely angry that his plot had failed. In 1928, Albert was alerted that a family was attempting to hire their son out to a business firm for schooling. Albert thought this the perfect opportunity to subside his urge for human flesh so he immediately made arrangements to meet with the family and potentially hire the son. Once at the house, Albert introduced himself as Frank Howard and asserted that he was interested in hiring their son, Edward Budd, for his business firm. However, Albert later confessed he fully intended to murder Edward, hang him until his blood was drained from the body, and then eat him. However, upon arrival, Albert noticed that the family had a young girl named Grace as well. After the family consented to allow their son Edward to be put under the tutelage of Albert, Albert made arrangements to return Edward a few days later. One week later, Albert called on the family and apologized for failing to return for Edward. It was at this time that Albert requested that the family allow him to take Grace to his niece's birthday party, a fictitious gathering designed to allow him to murder Grace. The family agreed and kissed their daughter Grace good-bye, unaware they would never see the girl again.

When Grace failed to return home the next evening, the family grew worried that something rash had happened. After a few days, the family realized that their greatest fears were confirmed: Albert had kidnapped Grace. The search began and would sadly continue for years. In 1930, Albert's ex-wife convinced police to arrest Charles Edward Pope under the false allegation that Pope had helped Albert kidnap Grace. However, Pope was found not guilty and the realization that the family might never see Grace again began to surface. Six years after her disappearance, a mysterious letter was sent to the Budd family, outlining the alleged kidnapping of Grace. As the parents read horrified, the letter outlined the barbaric practice of killing and cooking Grace many years earlier. The writer of the letter, thought to be Albert, showed no remorse for the egregious act he had just committed, and ended the letter with: "I choked her to death then cut her in small pieces so I could take my meat to my room, cook, and eat it. How sweet and tender her little ass was roasted in the oven. It took me nine days to eat her entire body. I did not fuck her though, I could have had I wished. She died a virgin." The parents handed the letter to the police and prayed that the letter was not true. However, Grace's body would never be found and Albert would confess to this crime in an even more explicit fashion when he was arrested. While the police were investigating the letter, it was found that the letter had been written on private stationary from the N.Y.P.C.B.A. Company. Upon further investigation, similar paper was found at a local hotel. When police searched the room, they found that Albert had recently stayed in the hotel, evidence enough to arrest him. To catch Albert, the head investigator waited outside of the room until Albert returned later that night. When the investigator told Albert of the crimes he had been convicted of, Albert proceeded to produce a knife and attempt to stab the officer. Albert was easily disarmed and taken to the police station, never to see the light of day for more than ten minutes ever again.

During the beginning stages of the interviews, Albert was adamant that he had never intended to rape Grace Budd. However, in a private meeting with his attorney, Albert admitted that he had ejaculated while trying to kill Grace. Because of this information, the attorney was able to successfully argue that Albert had killed Grace out of a sexual desire instead of the desire to eat her. The trial began on March 11, 1935 and concluded on March 21, 1935 with Albert being sentenced to death in the electric chair. For one year following the trial, Albert stayed at the prison in Washington D.C. while the appeals process took place. On January 16, 1936, Albert Fish was placed in the electric chair and killed. The capstone to his horrid name, Albert was killed, never to take another life and never to harm another child.

David Parker Ray

In the fight against murder and more specifically, serial murder, it is a profound truth that the childhood of the eventual serial killers held the foundation for the mass-killing they would one day incur. If examined more closely, the lives of the serial killers held potential to be normal and contributing to society; however, many of these same children were abused as children, giving them the foundation of hatred and revenge upon which they would enact their crimes. One such case was the torture case of David Parker Ray. At a young age, David's parents divorced and he was removed from his house to spend the remainder of his pre-pubescent years without the support of his parents. Sadly, the abuse as a child for David did not come in the form of physical abuse. While his abuse was of a sexual nature, it was through pornographic magazines his father supplied him with that David became addicted to a sadistic form of sexual pleasure: torture. Through his father's supply of pornographic magazines, David became one of America's most proficient torturers and suspected serial killers. While no bodies would ever be found, David was known to be a serial killer, but the only thing saving him from jail being the lack of evidence. The life of David Parker Ray is an example for society on the importance of child rearing. The foundations created by parents will lead to men and women of integrity. Unfortunately, this was not the case in David's life and due to his parent's inept nature of parenting; David Parker Ray will forever be remembered as "The Toy Box Killer," a man who would rob the innocent joy from over fifty women and children while murdering many more.

On November 6, 1939, David Parker Ray was born in Belen, New

Mexico to two unnamed parents. During his childhood, David's parents fought incessantly over the smallest of arguments. These arguments would culminate in their eventual divorce and the legal battles regarding David's custody ensued. However, neither parent seemed to be suited to take care of the children, resulting in their kids being placed with their grandparents. David enjoyed his time with his grandparents, remarking with admiration on the freedoms his grandparents allowed him to have. However, this freedom was marred by the consistent visits from his father. In the case of David, his young life would have been better served if he had never seen his father again. David's father was a chronic alcoholic and showed no remorse in engaging in any illegal activity. During each visit, David's father would leave him with numerous pornographic magazines that he had read and was finished with. David recalls his first experience reading the pornographic magazine, "thrilling" being the word he used to describe the moment. After the thrill of pornography began to wane, his father began leaving him pornographic magazines that contained sadomasochistic pornography. This level of pornography depicted the sexual pleasure some men derived while inflicting torture on other people. The thought of torturing women began to please David and sadly, the foundation for his future escapades was laid.

During his high school years, David was incessantly bullied, noted for being grossly afraid of the women in his school. Due to his lack of a love life, David was often the butt of homophobic slurs and homosexual allegations. However, underneath the quiet exterior of a boy who was afraid and nervous around women was a man whose sexual fantasies included rape and torture. As David continued to grow deeper into the sadomasochistic pornography, he began drawing his own pornography, depicting several poses of torture he derived himself. David recalls one moment when his sister discovered his drawings and confronted him on his fascination with sexual bondage. However, David assured her that pornography was simply a "hobby" and that his respect of women was well maintained. David's view of women was tainted significantly though. Following graduation from high school, David would join employment at a local auto shop where he was employed as a mechanic. His work within mechanics led him to a short tenure in the U.S. Army as a general mechanic. Upon completion of this employment, David was then honorably discharged from the army and returned to civilian life to continue as a mechanic.

As a mechanic, David began to postulate a plan for achieving his sexual fantasy of rape and torture. Having no qualms about raping women or enacting physical violence against them, David began formulating a plan to transform a tractor trailer from a containment device to a torture chamber. To complete such a tragic transformation, David soundproofed the trailer and outfitted it with various torture devices. These torture devices included pulleys, whips, chains, straps, arm clamps, surgical blades, leg spreader bars, leather constrictors, and hand saws. David had been extremely thorough in outfitting the trailer; soon to be home to the horrifying crimes of sexual torture.

With his trailer completed, David began making preparations to victimize the women he had so long dreamt of. The majority of these attacks would occur in the state of New Mexico with David parking his truck in one location and bringing the victims to it. While David would be the sole party responsible for the torture, there were several people who agreed to lend their support in some facet to David. Oddly, several of the accomplices would be women whom David was currently victimizing – the threat of David's actions against women showing them no concern apparently. After a few attempts at torture, David added some more tools to the torture chamber: syringes, books on painful techniques, sex toys, and a homemade electric generator that was the chief method of David's torture sessions. To further terrify his victims, David fastened a mirror to the ceiling of the trailer so that his victims would be forced to watch the methods of torture as they also felt them. For most of his tortures, David strapped his victims to a table where he then proceeded to begin his torturing by removing bits of skin from the victim's body. In some cases, David would strap his victims to a table that bent the victims over and left their vaginal and gluteus area unprotected. David would then either rape them himself, have his friends rape them, or in some cases, allow his dogs to rape the victims. David's horrifying escapades had begun and would continue for numerous years.

At the height of the psychological portion of the torturing, David maintained that his greatest thrill came from seeing his victim's watch their own torture. In addition to the mirror that victims could watch themselves in, David also recorded every torture sessions and made his victims watch their own torture sessions; indeed, the most horrifying portion of the torture for the victims was rewatching themselves undergo the bouts of pain. For David, his plan seemed foolproof. In his own mind, he would never be caught. However, he was only moments away from making a critical mistake.

During one attempt at luring a woman to his trailer, David wore a police officer's uniform and attempted to arrest a woman. The woman complied when David arrested her under the false pretense of being a sex worker. David handcuffed the woman and took her to his car. David then drove her to his trailer where the lady soon realized how she had been fooled. Horrified, there was nothing she could do. David locked the woman in his trailer and for the first time in a while, moved his truck from its current location. After an hour's drive, David arrived in Elephant's Butte where he decided the locals would provide no resistance or interest in his truck. Once parked, David left the trailer for three days and began living in a hotel in the area with his girlfriend Cindy Hendy. On the third day of being kidnapped, the woman managed to free herself from the tractor trailer. Hendy noticed the woman escaping and began pursuing her but was forced to stop when she was stabbed in the neck with an ice pick by the woman. The woman successfully fled the scene, completely nude and still lugging chains and a shock collar. Not far from the trailer, a household opened their doors to the woman's frantic pleas for help and authorities were summoned. Upon their arrival at the tractor trailer, David was taken into custody and the trailer and its contents were seized.

With David in custody, multiple other women began surfacing, making claims similar to the one of the woman whom David had most recently accosted. Through the testimonies of the women, police arrested numerous accomplices of David, most of which were local law enforcement. Sadly, through the discovery of David, it was surmised that the bodies of the women killed had been disposed of in dangerous mines and were not able to be found. With no bodies, no charges of murder could be brought against David. However, a video tape found in the trailer provided police with ample evidence that David had been the mastermind behind the horrifying torture. In this video, David accosted and kidnapped Kelli Garrett in 1996. David had convinced his daughter to lure Garrett to his trailer by drugging her beer. With Garrett inebriated, David was able to render her unconscious and drag her into his trailer where he tortured her for three days. On several occasions during the torture, Garrett blacked out from the pain and shock. On the final day of the torture, David cut Garrett's throat and left her on the road, believing she was dead. Garrett, however, would make a full recovery and move away from the area. In a twisted sense of fate, Garrett's husband would believe she had been cheating on him and would divorce her immediately upon her return, despite the extent of her injuries. With the testimony of Garrett and the video of her being tortured, police believed they had the perfect case against David. However, they wanted to find a body and charge David with murder, convinced this was the only means of him receiving the death penalty they believed he deserved. Despite sending over 100 agents to David's property, not one body would be discovered during their searches. David would never stand trial for murdering a woman.

With the three women being accosted during separate times, the courts decided that they would hold three separate trials, one for each woman. However, one of the victims would die prior to the trial, rendering the trial unable to be performed. During the initial days of the interrogation, police offered David the opportunity at a 224 year prison sentence in exchange for vital information In turn, David would not be tried for murder, the police never revealing to David that they did not have a body. David took the offer and divulged the locations of many of his crimes. During this time, the police would charge several of David's accomplices, all who would go to prison for extended periods of time. Three years after being arrested for torture, David was being prepared for transport to the Lea County Correctional Facility. The state police were interested in interviewing him extensively prior to the trial beginning. David was beginning to show cooperation, leading the police to believe they would be able to find a body soon. However, David succumbed to a heart attack while on the trip and passed away before the police were able to rush him to a hospital. No foul play was suspected in David's death but the police were devastated that they would never receive a definitive location on the victims of David. The life of David Parker Ray, though once an iceberg of doom and tragedy crushing the lives of the young women it interacted with, was now unable to accomplish any more torture. The name of David Parker Ray will be forever remembered as a coward who preyed upon women as his means of sexual pleasure.

Edmund Kemper

Throughout the records of serial killers and high-profile murderers, one disturbing common denominator exists between most of the cases: necrophilia. Necrophilia is a fascination with dead bodies and more specifically, a fascination with sex acts performed on a dead body. With such people revering the body as a mere "temple" to themselves, it should be no surprise that these men and woman can take lives so arbitrarily. The surprising fraction of this group comes from those who can take the life of one of their family members. The ability to take the life of the closest individuals one can have on earth demonstrates a callous nature that is frightening even to the perpetrator. One case of a man who showed little remorse for killing his family is the case of Edmund Kemper III. During his life, Edmund took the life of his grandparents and mother in addition to seven other individuals. When considering the life of Edmund, the motive behind the brazen nature of his killings becomes very clear: pure hatred. As a victim of verbal and physical abuse as a child, Edmund enacted his revenge on his mother by brutally killing her parents before returning for her. The life of Edmund Kemper is an example of one whose hatred overtook his rationale and fueled an unquenchable anger, resulting in the senseless killing of ten people. By refusing to control his anger, Edmund weakened himself and is paying the consequences for his actions by serving eight life sentences. A bright life, once touted to be good enough for medical school, now lives behind bars, all because of an uncontrollable rage.

Born on December 18, 1948, Edmund Kemper III began his life in the arms of Edmund Kemper II and Clarnell Kemper. Edmund was the second of three children born to the couple and would eventually be the lone son in the family. Edmund's father had worked in World War II and was maintaining his employment in the army by testing nuclear weapons well after the war had ended. When Edmund's father decided he needed employment closer to home, he began working as an electrician for the city, a job his wife particularly despised. When Edmund's mother would belittle her husband's job by referring to it as a "menial" electrician job, Edmund's father would always respond: "...suicide missions in wartime and atomic bomb testings were nothing compared to living with her." All throughout Edmund's childhood, the hatred between his parents channeled to him, leaving Ed horribly neglected. At an early age, Edmund's parents noticed that Edmund had a particularly tall stature. When Edmund was only four years old, he stood greater than one foot taller than friends who were his age. In addition to his extreme height, Edmund's parents also noticed that Edmund seemed to be a very intelligent child. Despite these unique features found in Edmund's life, he began to startle his parents with his odd habits; most of Edmund's odd habits centered on cruelty demonstrated towards animals. In several shocking appearances, Edmund killed or tortured animals and often paraded around with his dead animals. On one occasion, Edmund buried his family's pet cat while it was alive. After he was certain that it had died, he dug into the fresh grave and removed the cat, whereupon he decapitated the cat and placed its head on a stick. After walking around with the head of the cat for a few hours, Edmund grew fearful that his family would see the cat and realize what he had done so he reburied the cat. When Edmund turned thirteen, he exhibited more cruelty towards animals when he killed another cat on the allegation that the cat liked his sister more than it liked him. While Edmund did not parade this cat as he done with the previous kill, he mutilated it and kept various pieces in his closet. Upon discovery by his mother, she forced him to throw away the pieces of the cat but did not chide him for his actions. Little did Edmund's mother know that these mutilations were laying the foundation for future mutilations which would be enacted against humans.

In his youth, Edmund was known for being both well acquainted and fascinated with death. In a sick ritual, Edmund would sometimes cut the heads off his sister's dolls. Additionally, Edmund's home-life began deteriorating and caused him to experience close brushes with death – both at the hands of his sister. When Edmund's parents separated, Edmund became so frustrated with life that he vowed he would get even with his parents one day. Due to the separation, Edmund was forced to reside with his mother who was also falling deeper into the depths of alcohol addiction. Clarnell thought little of Edmund and attempted to demonstrate this extreme hate daily through making fun of her own son. Alleging that she feared what Edmund might have done to his sisters, Edmund's mother forced him to reside in the basement of the house, only allowing him to come up for brief periods of eating and occasionally going outside. Often, Edmund would be made fun of by his mom for his exorbitant height. At this point, Edmund stood almost 6'5" and was unnaturally thin. As he grew older, his position with his mother deteriorated to the point of her referring to him frequently as "a real weirdo." As a child, Edmund's mother had refused to cuddle with him, citing a fear of him becoming gay. This refusal turned into a hate speech of sorts when she began asserting to Edmund that he was as bad as his father and that he would never find a girl who would love him. Such hate-filled words left Edmund even more resentful of his mother and caused the relationship to grow more distant. Edmund recalls that at these moments, he began to feel as if he did not have a mother at all, but rather a woman who was set on discouraging him from his potential. Sadly, she would succeed, costing her a price more valuable than she ever thought possible.

Shortly after Edmund turned 15, he decided his mother was unbearable and not worth the constant belittling. With no other options, Edmund ran away from home and moved in with his father. After his father had divorced his mother, he had moved to Van Nuys, California. Edmund hitchhiked to Van Nuys and found his father, who had recently remarried a woman with a son. Edmund's father was not pleased at the return of his son and Edmund soon found himself being depreciated by his father. After one month of living with his father,

Edmund was forced to leave his father's house and move in with his mother's parents in North Folk. Soon after moving in with his grandparents, Edmund realized that his grandparents were very much like his own parents, in that they belittled him. While the discouragement was not as frequent as it was in the homes of his parents, Edmund asserted that it was worse given his grandmother's "senile" mindset and her "constant emasculating of [him] and [his] grandfather." During the early days of his tenure with his grandparents, Edmund began demonstrating his disdain for them, often having loud arguments that would result in Edmund spending hours out of the house. On August 27, 1964, Edmund and his grandmother had launched into a particularly violent argument. Sadly, this argument would end far more violent than his other arguments had ever had. After the two refused to calm their argument, Edmund ran to his room where he had stored a hunting rifle. Edmund loaded the rifle and ran back to the kitchen where he proceeded to shoot his grandmother in the face. Edmund then fired twice more into her back to ensure she was truly dead and proceeded to stab her multiple times in the abdomen with a knife. When Edmund's grandfather returned from work later that day, Edmund shot him the instance he stepped from his vehicle. After stepping back and assessing what he had just done, Edmund thought it best to phone his mother and seek her wisdom in proceeding. Edmund's mother was understandably upset by the situation, but this murder was most likely precipitated on the foundation of hatred she had created with Edmund so many years earlier.

Once Edmund's mother was informed of her son's atrocity, she advised him to call the police and turn himself in. As a 15-year-old, Edmund had just committed a double murder and would now face a judge to assess his punishment. Prior to his sentencing, the judge had psychiatrist Donald Lunde assess Edmund and see what the motive for the death was. After a brief conversation, the motive became quite clear: pure hatred for his parents. "In his way," wrote Lunde, "he had avenged the rejection of both his father and his mother." Sadly, Edmund would now become a rejection of society, the news of this horrific double murder spreading quite quickly. Edmund was diagnosed with paranoid schizophrenia and sent to serve a five-year sentence in the criminally insane portion of the state prison system in California.

During his imprisonment, Edmund became the talk of the prison, namely because no one agreed that he should be imprisoned in the criminally insane unit. Every report that the psychiatrists detailed on Edmund stated that he was smart and demonstrated "no flight of ideas, no interference with thought, no expressions of delusions or hallucinations, and no evidence of bizarre thinking." The investigators were stumped. The reoccurring question became, "How could a man commit such an egregious act, be deemed criminally insane, and then make a complete turnaround?" This was the same man who had months earlier commented on his grandmother's death by saying, "I just wanted to know what it felt like to kill grandma." During subsequent IQ tests one week later, Edmund scored a 136 before subsequently scoring a 145. In addition to his excellence in intelligence, Edmund also began to prove his good behavior. At the climax of his good behavior, Edmund joined the Jaycees and became a pivotal member within the prison. Five years following his sentencing, Edmund was deemed fit for society again and was paroled on good behavior. Edmund was far from good and had indeed been acting out one of the longest lies a man could act. His face of vengeance and revenge would soon surface again, and police would be horrified upon discovery of the crimes he would commit.

In accordance with the state laws, Edmund was released into his mother's care and soon began experiencing the same belittlement he had experienced prior to his arrest. In addition to being forced to stay with his mother, Edmund was also forced to attend a community college. While he was rejected from his initial career path of being a police officer, Edmund began working with the police officers of his area and created many lasting relationships with them. After three months of living with his mother, Edmund had enough financial stability to move out of her house and in with his friend. However,

Edmund's mother still called him multiple times each day and often arrived at his house unexpected.

After Edmund began a new job with the Highway Department, he saved up enough money to purchase a Ford Galaxy which he began using to ferry young women back and forth to work. It gave Edmund great thrill to be in control of these women's destiny, though he would ferry many of them without hurting them before commencing on his murderous spree. After almost 150 women, Edmund began to have urges he could not resist, culminating in the murder of Mary Ann Pesce and Anita Luchessa. These two college girls had been hitchhiking and were picked up by Edmund. He then drove them to a forest that was miles away from where they had intended on arriving. There, he handcuffed both girls, strangled them, and raped them postmortem. Edmund had fantasized about raping a woman while she was alive but the risk of leaving a witness alive drove him to commit these acts after the women were dead. After having sex with both of the victims following their deaths, Edmund left the bodies at the foot of Loma Prieta Mountain. Police would find the skull of Pesce but nothing of Luchessa would ever be found.

Only five months following the double murder of Luchessa and Pesce, Edmund lured Aiko Koo, a 15-year-old Korean student in the area, to his car where he rendered her unconscious, raped her, and then killed her. Edmund almost made a critical error when he wound up locked outside of the vehicle. However, for unknown reasons, Koo let him back in the vehicle where he eventually then killed her. Edmund then took the body, stowed it in his trunk, and took it to his apartment where it would be dismembered and disposed of. Over the next two months, Edmund would kill and rape three more women. While these crimes are horrific, the climax of Edmund's murderous spree was on April 20, 1973, when Edmund had a violent argument with his mother. Edmund had moved back in with his mother and was awakened one night when she loudly announced her return from a party. Upon her arrival, Edmund's mother and he began to argue loudly, climaxing in Edmund retrieving a hammer and smashing it into his mother's face. After she fell unconscious, Edmund severed her head from her body and placed it on a shelf where he threw darts at it for hours. Later, Edmund took his mother's corpse to his room where he had sex with it. After dumping his mother's body in his trunk, Edmund called his mother's best friend, Sally Hallett, to the house where upon her arrival, he strangled her to death. Edmund then severed her head from her body and used the rest of the night to have sex with her corpse. When he had derived as much pleasure as he could from the moment, he called the police, turned himself in, and awaited their arrival.

Once in jail, Edmund was charged with eight counts of murder. Upon his indictment, Edmund immediately began yelling about wanting the death penalty, a call he would maintain until his incarceration. Five months after being indicted, Edmund was found guilty of all eight counts of first-degree murder and sentenced to life in prison. However, Edmund continued to clamor and request "death by torture." Because the state of California's death penalty was suspended at the time, Edmund never received his wish and was sent to the California Medical Facility for life, where he resides to this day. Whether or not insanity was a contributing factor in these murders will never be known. However, one would be foolish to overlook the hurt and devastation the rejection in Edmund's life caused. With two parents refusing to love him, Edmund took out his revenge on his parents in the most evil way: taking life away from those they most loved and in one case, taking their own life.

Andrei Chikatilo

If one were to stand back and observe the complete life of a serial killer, they would find the moment in this person's life where it all changed; where they went from being a person who loved life to becoming a person who sought to take the lives of others simply out of spite or enjoyment. In some cases, parental neglect would be the chief contributing factor. In other cases, a moment of rejection could have caused the turning point. In the case of Andrei Chikatilo, the clear turning point came when he discovered he was impotent. Such a disease, more commonly known as ED, affects millions of men in the world to this day. However, many of the men have sought help and aid in overcoming the disappointment from not being able to perform up to par sexually. Such would not be the case in the life of Andrei Chikatilo. Rather than seek help from a source who could give him wisdom, Andrei sought his sexual fulfillment from other sources, which ultimately culminated in his killing strictly for the pleasure of killing. In his life, Andrei killed over 55 people while sexually abusing numerous children. Following his final apprehension, Andrei would confess that during each of these murders, he experienced the sexual pleasure he had been denied his whole life. Such a revelation revealed the engine behind the drive Andrei possessed. However, the legacy of Andrei grows tragic, with the loss of innocent lives simply for the sexual high he experienced every time he killed someone. Through the life of Andrei, humanity can be reminded that greed and dissatisfaction rob more than simply the happiness of the person dissatisfied—they also rob the person's life.

Born into a small village outside of Sumy Oblast in the Ukrainian portion of the SSR, Andrei Chikatilo was birthed to two parents who worked hard, yet were unable to provide necessary requirements for care simply due to the stringent restrictions being imposed on the land from the hand of Joseph Stalin. Stalin's harsh sanctions on the people led to extreme hunger being experienced by the entire working class of the SSR. Andrei recalls being told by his mother that she had given his older brother Stepan to their neighbors to eat. Such a horrific story terrified young Andrei and he continually feared that he would be fed to the neighbors if he did not "earn his keep" at home. Despite their father's attempt to derive food for his family, they were often forced to eat the grass and leaves that collected outside of their hut. When Andrei turned twelve, he ate bread for the first time in his life, documenting how long and harsh the famine established by Stalin truly was. Andrei's father joined the Red Army during World War II and Andrei was left as a young five-year-old with only his mother for company. When the Nazi's invaded Ukraine, Andrei became acquainted with the horrors enacted by the Nazi army. Often, Andrei and his mother would be forced to crouch deep within ravines and ditches to avoid being spotted by the Nazi army. At the climax of the war, Andrei and his mother watched speechless from a ditch as their hut and only means of protection burned to the ground, compliments of the Nazi Army. Neighbors and family members helped restore their house, but Andrei was left without a bed, forcing him to sleep in his mother's bed. Andrei was only seven years old at the time and was still wetting the bed every night. After each bed wetting, Andrei's mother would beat him severely and rebuke him for inconveniencing her.

When Andrei was eight-years-old, his mother unexpectedly gave birth to a girl who would be named Tatyana. During this time, Andrei's father was a prisoner of war so there was no possibility of him being the father. Rather, the father was an unknown German soldier who raped Andrei's mother during a raid of their house. Shortly after, Andrei began attending school and was noted as being an extremely smart student despite being unnaturally weak. His unusual stature caused a great trial when students at his school began making fun of him and intentionally running into him, causing him to fall. Andrei was also prone to fainting due to his lack of nourishment. However, Andrei did his best to not allow these trials to stand in the way of his education, often taking his studies home and studying late into the night. In his second year of schooling, Andrei's mother noticed that he had a keen skill in memorizing large amounts of data. This habit continued into high school where Andrei's teachers all held Andrei as the model student. With the encouragement of not remaining poor in his sights, Andrei continued to study hard and finally graduated in 1954, the first from his family to complete their education. However, this time of joy and exultation was dampened significantly by the discovery that Andrei was impotent. Andrei had suspected it for years but found it true when he began attending dates with women but was unable to derive an erection during the date. The women remarked that Andrei was incredibly nervous, perhaps the result of his impotence. In a fit of anger once, Andrei leaped onto the back of his cousin and fell with her to the ground. As a seventeen-year-old man, Andrei noticed that he experienced a sexual orgasm as she struggled and writhed to free herself from his grasp. Sadly, this recollection would serve as the foundation for his future when Andrei would begin murdering for the sexual thrill he desired.

Once graduated from high school, Andrei attempted taking his education to college, but he was denied acceptance into Moscow State University on the grounds that he did not have adequate grades. While Andrei refused to believe this and asserted that the university was discriminating against him due to his father's status as traitor in the army, the truth was that Andrei had simply not performed well on the entrance examination, yet another failure in his life. Faced with the failure of entering a college, Andrei entered the labor force as an electrician in Kursk before subsequently joining a vocational school to become certified in communications. All throughout this journey to becoming a communications technician, Andrei was unable to maintain a serious relationship due to his sexual inability.

In 1957, Andrei entered employment with the Soviet Army when he was drafted by the government to work as a border guard in Central Asia. In 1960, Andrei became a bona fide Communist in order to be granted leave from the army sooner. Back in the Ukraine as a civilian, Andrei returned to his parent's home where his father had recently returned from his tenure as a prisoner of war. Once home, Andrei was humiliated to find that the entire village had found out that he was unable to perform sexually. Humiliated, Andrei recalls, "girls were going behind my back and whispering that I was impotent. I was so ashamed. I tried to hang myself. My mother and some young neighbors pulled me out of the noose. Well, I thought no one would want such a shamed man. So, I had to run away from there, away from my homeland." And run away he did. Following a period where he drifted from city to city, Andrei found work in Rostov-on-Don as a communications engineer. Two years later, Andrei married Feodosia Odnacheva, though this marriage was largely orchestrated by his sister and the two found little love for each other. When Andrei disclosed his impotence to his new wife, she contrived an odd manner in which she was still be able to conceive under the intimacy of Andrei. The plan worked and Andrei was soon a father to two children. Shortly after marrying his wife, Andrei took a position at Novoshakhtinsk as a teacher. Andrei proved to be a horrible teacher, unwilling to lend his students aid or even mark a semblance of classroom order. Tragically, his position as school teacher would prove more effective in his quest for sexual pleasure as his first known sexual assaults would take place here. Between 1973 and 1974, Andrei would sexually abuse numerous students, both in his classroom and in public settings. Often, teachers would walk past his classrooms, only to see Andrei fondling himself in front of the entire class. When his sexual obsession became clear to the faculty, the president of the school informed Andrei that he could either be fired or voluntarily leave. Andrei chose to leave and assumed a similar position at a nearby school shortly before leaving to teach in Shakhty.

In 1978, Andrei's sexual obsession led him to murder his first victim, a nine-year-old girl named Yelena Zakotnova. Andrei had lured Yelena to his house, telling her false tales of the piles of candy he had stashed in his house. After a failed attempt at raping the young girl, Andrei proceeded to stab her multiple times in the stomach, a process that culminated in his ejaculating. When Andrei realized that he was only able to achieve sexual pleasure through killing people, he began seeking out the weakest society could offer. Runaways, homeless people, prostitutes, and young children became his targets. Sadly, in the case of Yelena Zakotnova, the police falsely arrested and charged another ex-convict with her murder, despite the numerous pieces of evidence pointing to Andrei. This ex-convict was unjustly put to death for the murder of Yelena, thus costing the police an innocent life for their major oversight. Had police paid more attention to the details and less attention on the biased of previous criminal history, historians believe that they might have avoided the mass killing from Andrei.

In 1981, Andrei was fired from his teaching position for his numerous cases of sexual misconduct. However, no police reports were filed and Andrei was left free to roam the streets, without the knowledge of the police. Once again, gross oversight allowed Andrei to continue to murderous ruse instead of being brought to justice for his atrocities against humanity. Two days after killing Yelena, Andrei strangled Larisa Tkachenko and used his teeth to mutilate her body. Upon noticing her riddled body, Andrei had an orgasm and proceeded to writhe over her dead body. For the next nine months, Andrei ceased from murdering until his sexual tendencies overtook him and he began seeking out his next victim. Shortly after he left his house, Andrei met a young 13-year-old girl named Lyubov Biryuk. Andrei lured Lyuboy into the woods where he immediately stabbed her repeatedly in the stomach. Once dead, Andrei proceeded to gouge out her eyeballs, succumbing to the demonic tale that outlined demons watching their perpetrators through the eyes of the victim. When Andrei realized how easy it was to kill and how excited he became through killing, he began to use less discretion when choosing and killing his victims. In two months, Andrei killed five victims, all runaways from the ages of nine to eighteen. After Andrei killed another child in December of 1982, the police began to grow suspicious of the systematic killings within the area. The police deployed numerous detectives to the same crime scene, dead set on finding this perpetrator who was causing so much fear. The chief detective, Major Mikhail Fetisov, had his fears subsided when he noticed the similar markings on the eyes of the victims. In Fetisov's mind, there was no doubt a serial killer was on the loose and his identity was completely anonymous.

From June of 1983 to September of 1983, Andrei murdered six more women, all of whom were linked by the police to the killer of the previous four. With no identity known, the police began compiling a list of the supposed features possessed by their killer. After months of deliberating with psychiatrists and criminal psychiatrists, police correctly assumed that they were looking for a man who had been abused as a child and was facing some type of erectile dysfunction in his adult years. To close out 1983, Andrei brutally murdered 14-year-old Sergey Markov, stabbing him over seventy times in the process. In 1984, Andrei killed over twenty people; all while leaving no sign that he was at the crime scenes. The police in Russia were both stumped and terrified. The voracious and violent nature of the crimes committed by Andrei were terrifying the public, and the random nature at which he selected his victims was keeping many people indoors.

In late 1984, Andrei was arrested for stealing equipment from his employer whom he had held years before. Prior to his arrest, he had been seen walking around his village, talking to random women, and apparently seeking them out. In one occasion, he went about pressing his erect penis into un-consenting strangers. The police did nothing and refused to prosecute him further than the small theft. Andrei would serve a short three months in jail before being released, free to continue his murderous spree of sexual satisfaction. For the next two years, Andrei would limit his killing to random strangers and no more than once a month. For a brief period, he completely ceased from killing due to the national publicity he was receiving. However, the sexual urges started again, and in later 1986 Andrei resumed his murdering. In 1987, Andrei killed three more people, a feat he would return to in 1988. From 1988-1990, Andrei killed seven more known people. Andrei made a critical mistake on November 6, 1990 when he killed a woman and washed his hands in broad sight of a police officer. While the police officer did not arrest him at the time due to lack of evidence, but he did approach Andrei and get his name before allowing him to leave. When the police uncovered a body in the same area that Andrei had been in days before, the police officer named Andrei as the chief suspect and Andre was immediately put under 24-hour surveillance. After only six days of constant surveillance, Andrei was seen roaming about Novocherkassk and talking to young children. Police then arrested Andrei on suspicion of murder and found various weapons of murder while searching him. These weapons would be the chief exhibits of the trial which would commence two years later.

On April 14, 1992, the trial for Andrei began. The trial lasted almost six months and on October 15, Judge Akubzhanov stated the following: "Taking into consideration the horrible misdeeds of which he is guilty, the court has no alternative but to impose the only sentence that he deserves. I therefore sentence him to death." Andrei would be executed by firing squad on February 14, 1994.

Henry Lee Lucas

The lifespan of a serial killer contains one climax: when they were killing the most people while also remaining unknown to law enforcement. For most, that moment occurred shortly before being captured by the police, adding validity to the fact that men of evil grow confident and make rash decisions that cost them their freedom. One such case within history would be the case of Henry Lee Lucas, a man whose prestige as a serial killer comes from an un-orthodox element: his confessions or rather the timely nature and breadth of his confessions. Henry Lee Lucas was only suspected of murder when he began telling of countless other murders that he had supposedly been responsible for. However, after checking with various sources, it was found that Henry Lee Lucas had likely lied about these murders simply to meet the requirements of his plea deal. This would cause a false sense of closure around thousands of family members surrounding the victims while also causing a mountain of police work to be undertaken following the report that his confessions were false. While the count of his murders was a false tale, the fact that he was a serial killer was never a question to be answered. Henry Lee Lucas killed many people that only history will tell how many can be verified. Sadly, as is the case in so many serial killers, Henry was given a poor childhood that was filled with abuse and instability. The life of Henry Lee Lucas would culminate in his death while in prison; his life would serve as a precedent for others to note and derive corrective action from. From the life of Henry Lee Lucas, society can be given a clear picture of what a life void of a structured home and love can result in.

Born on August 23, 1936, Henry Lee Lucas was the victim of being born into a home where love was nowhere to be found. Sadness overshadowed the home, a dark preclusion to the death that would one day follow the sadness into the home. Throughout Henry's childhood, he was abused physically by his parents, two people who took their frustration of life out on him. Shortly after Henry turned 10, he was involved in a violent fight with a friend that resulted in a severe infection in his left eye. Doctors tried their best to save his eye, but the infection was too manifested, so Henry would go throughout his life with a false eye filling the void of his left eye that was removed. In a home void of love, Henry was forced to go to any length for attention, culminating in his reputation being founded on his odd behavior. Bordering on manic, friends described Henry as being a boy who would undertake any activity, regardless of how dangerous or frightening it was, simply to receive attention. Creating the foundation for his sexual fantasy someday, Henry's mother sought her living as a prostitute, often bringing the clients to her own home when her husband was not home. During these moments, Henry was always forced to watch his mother have her solicited sex. In addition to being a prostitute, Henry's mother was a cross dresser who forced Henry to participate in cross dressing in public.

When Henry turned thirteen, tragedy struck his home when his father passed away. Henry's father had been crippled for years, the result of a railroad accident that left his legs severed by a railcar. Adding to the tragedy of the situation, Henry's father died as a result of being locked outside on accident during a freezing blizzard. Unable to reach to doorknob, Henry's father had simply sat outside the door until he developed hypothermia and passed away. While his father had shown little interest in his life, Henry was devastated by the loss and ran away from home. For months, Henry lived homeless, floating from city to city in rural Virginia. During these months, Henry's sexual urges began to increase and overtake his emotions. When a young girl named Laura Burnsley refused to have sex with him, Henry resorted to strangling her, consummating his life as a serial killer. Three years later, Henry was charged with multiple counts of burglary in Richmond, Virginia, resulting in a four-year prison sentence. After spending three years in prison, Henry decided he could not remain a prisoner for the last year and made plans to escape the prison. His escape was successful but short-lived; the police caught him days later. Back in prison, Henry had an additional year of prison added to his sentencing, courtesy of his rash decision to run away. When he was finally released on September 2, 1959, Henry decided his life would be better served in Michigan, so the twenty-three-year-old man travelled to Tecumseh, Michigan where he would live with his sister.

In Michigan, Henry developed a relationship with a pen pal whom he had begun writing to while in prison. Shortly after, Henry proposed engagement via letter and his pen pal accepted his proposal. The two were set to be married when his mother cast a disapproving shadow on the relationship, accusing her son of being too hasty in his decision. Commanding him to return home, Henry's mother became incensed when he refused to move back with her. The argument turned violent and culminated in Henry stabbing his mother in the neck with a knife. According to Henry's personal perspective of the story, "All I remember was slapping her alongside the neck...then I noticed that I had my knife in my hand and that she had been cut." Henry fled from the scene of the crime and his sister Opal would return to find their mother still alive, but she had lost a large amount of blood. Hours later, Henry's mother passed away and Henry went from being an ordinary citizen to a wanted fugitive. Henry attempted to flee to Michigan once again, but the police soon caught up with him and charged him with second degree murder. During the trial, Henry claimed that his mother had advanced towards him in a threatening manner, warranting the use of deadly force. The courts refused his claims of self-defense; however, Henry was sentenced to a minimum of twenty years with a maximum of forty years in prison.

The minimum 20 years in prison for Henry would not be met, and due to severe prison overcrowding in Michigan, Henry was released on June 17, 1970 only serving ten years of his prison sentence for killing his mother. Henry would not remain out of prison for long after police charged him with attempting to kidnap children one year later. This conviction held a five-year prison sentence that brought him in contact with a woman he would marry immediately upon his release from prison. However, the marriage lasted only two years when the woman's daughter alleged that Henry had sexually abused her. Henry fled and began living as a homeless man again in Virginia. In 1977, Henry moved to Jacksonville, Florida where he met Ottis Toole and moved in with him. Also living in the home were Toole's parents and Toole's niece Becky Powell who was considered autistic. For the next few years, Henry was employed as a roofer while also performing mild mechanical work on cars in the neighborhood, establishing himself as a friendly man who enjoyed being around people.

In 1982, Becky Powell's mother and grandmother died. The authorities attempted to place her in a mental institution, but Henry persuaded Becky to run away and live with him in his van. The two began making their way to California and soon were employed as the caretakers for Kate Rich, an 82-year-old widow in Ringgold, Texas. However, the family soon grew suspicious of the large volume of financial resources the couple was using on "emergency needs" for Rich and investigated. When the family found that Henry and Becky were failing to care for Rich and were instead writing checks in her name and purchasing whatever they needed for themselves, they immediately fired them and Henry and Becky began hitchhiking to Dallas, Texas. During one leg of the journey, they were picked up by a pastor who allowed them to stay in his shelter. During their stay, Henry and Becky got into a large argument that resulted in Henry murdering Becky and leaving the shelter to murder Rich, the woman whom they had recently been caring for. When police discovered that Rich had been murdered, they immediately made Henry the chief suspect, citing his financial needs as the necessary motive for murder. Three months later, Henry was arrested for illegally possessing a firearm. During his stay in prison, Henry complained that he was being severely bullied by other inmates and police officers alike. While he was being booked, Henry alleged that he was stripped naked in front of female officers, forced to bed on a concrete floor with no blankets or clothing, and restricted from being able to contact his attorney. Given his being a suspect in a high-profile murder case, the police did little to investigate these claims. Henry would maintain his living conditions until four days later when he confessed that he was the killer of Katie Rich and Becky Powell. However, Henry did not stop with just confessing to those 2 murders. Soon, police had confessions from Henry for over forty previously unsolved murders. The police were incredulous that a man would confess to such crimes unprompted. However, some police officers believed Henry simply made up the confessions to possibly sway the police officers into giving him better living conditions.

Four months after his arrest, Henry was sent to Williamson County, Texas where he would be held until his trial months later. Despite having better living conditions and friendly investigators, Henry continued his spree of confessing to crimes, resulting in 213 cases going from unsolved to solved. During these months, the police became very trusting of Henry, allowing him to wander about the police station without wearing handcuffs. Some police officers even allege that he knew various security codes for doors and could walk anywhere in the prison block that he wanted to. While some police officers continued to be dubious at Henry's apparent complying with the authorities, the allegations that he was falsifying these confessions was complicated by his supplement of specific details. In one case, Henry confessed that he lied about the confession but was able to produce a valid confession due to seeing the victim's glasses in one picture, therefore correctly asserting that his victim had glasses on when he killed her. The police were beginning to grow confident that they had corralled one of the most proficient killers in the history of the United States; a report from journalist Hugh Aynesworth revealed that Henry would have driven 11,000 miles in one month while using his antiquated station wagon in the process if he truly committed the crimes he confessed to. When this report surfaced, the media began to grow suspect of his validity and began to blame the police for believing such a falsehood without validating his story. After sorting through the various cases, the police narrowed the amount of confirmed homicides from 213 to eleven. Henry would be sentenced to death but would have this sentencing commuted to life in prison in 1998 by the governance of George W. Bush.

Following his death sentence being commuted to life in prison, Henry remained in prison for three more years. However, Henry was found dead in his cell on March 12, 2001. After performing an autopsy, police confirmed that the cause of death was heart failure and no foul play was suspected. For his role in confessing to crimes he had not committed, Henry was given the nickname "The Confession Killer," a nickname that remains his most famous to date.